THEORY AND INTERPRETATION OF NARRATIVE

James Phelan, Peter J. Rabinowitz, and Robyn Warhol, Series Editors

A drawing from Kafka's diaries

FRANZ KAFKA

NARRATION, RHETORIC, AND READING

EDITED BY

Jakob Lothe,

Beatrice Sandberg, AND

Ronald Speirs

THE OHIO STATE UNIVERSITY PRESS | COLUMBUS

Library of Congress Cataloging-in-Publication Data

Franz Kafka : narration, rhetoric, and reading / edited by Jakob Lothe, Beatrice Sandberg, and Ronald Speirs.
p. cm. — (Theory and interpretation of narrative)
Includes bibliographical references and index.
ISBN-13: 978-0-8142-5177-5 (pbk. : alk. paper)
ISBN-10: 0-8142-5177-3 (pbk. : alk. paper)
ISBN-13: 978-0-8142-1150-2 (cloth : alk. paper)
ISBN-10: 0-8142-1150-X (cloth : alk. paper)
1. Kafka, Franz, 1883–1924—Criticism and interpretation. I. Lothe, Jakob. II. Sandberg, Beatrice. III. Speirs, Ronald.
PT2621.A26Z71933 2011
833'.912—dc22

2010029746

This book is available in the following editions:
Cloth (ISBN 978-0-8142-1150-2)
Paper (ISBN 978-0-8142-5177-5)
CD-ROM (ISBN 978-0-8142-9249-5)

Cover design by James A. Baumann
Type set in Adobe Bembo, by Juliet Williams
Printed by Thomson-Shore, Inc.

∞ The paper used in this publication meets the minimum requirements of the American National Standard for Information Sciences—Permanence of Paper for Printed Library Materials. ANSI Z39.48-1991.

9 8 7 6 5 4 3 2 1

Contents

Acknowledgments

The editors and contributors owe their collaboration on this volume to the Centre for Advanced Study (CAS) in Oslo, Norway. Two of the editors—Jakob Lothe and Beatrice Sandberg—were members of the Narrative Theory and Analysis research project, which was proposed and led by Jakob and hosted and funded by CAS during the 2005–2006 academic year. CAS supported not just the project but also a symposium on Franz Kafka in May 2006 that served as the genesis of this book. We owe a profound debt to Professor Willy Østreng, who was director of the Centre at the time we were there, and the administrative staff of CAS, for their friendliness, encouragement, and assistance. Additionally, CAS generously contributed funding to offset the publication costs of this volume. We have also benefited from the collegial intellectual atmosphere fostered at CAS by the other members of the research team: Daphna Erdinast-Vulcan, Anniken Greve, Jeremy Hawthorn, J. Hillis Miller, James Phelan, Anette H. Storeide, Susan R. Suleiman, and Anne Thelle. Finally, two of the editors wish to give special thanks to the third—Ronald Speirs—for his invaluable input, not only generally but also with particular regard to his contribution to the writing of the introduction.

Abbreviations

Br	Franz Kafka. 1975. *Briefe 1902–1924.* In *Gesammelte Werke.* Ed. Max Brod. Frankfurt am Main: Fischer.
BrM	*Briefe an Milena.* 1986. Ed. Jürgen Born and Michael Müller. Frankfurt am Main: Fischer.
D1	Franz Kafka. 1948. *The diaries of Franz Kafka,* 1910–1913. Trans. Joseph Kresh. New York: Schocken Books.
DF	Franz Kafka. 1971. *Dearest Father.* Trans. Ernest Kaiser and Eithne Wilkins. New York: Schocken Books.
DW	Erich Heller and Joachim Beug. 1977. *Franz Kafka: Der Dichter über sein Werk.* Munich: Deutscher Taschenbuch Verlag.
F	Franz Kafka. 1967. *Briefe an Felice.* Ed. Erich Heller and Jürgen Born. Frankfurt am Main: Fischer.
KAF	Franz Kafka. 1994. *Gesammelte Werke in 12 Bänden.* Ed. Hans-Gerd Koch. Frankfurt am Main: Fischer Taschenbuch Verlag.
KD	Franz Kafka. 1964. *The diaries of Franz Kafka.* Ed. Max Brod. Trans. Joseph Kresh and Martin Greenberg. Harmondsworth: Penguin Books.
KKA	Franz Kafka. 1982. *Kritische Ausgabe der Schriften, Tagebücher, Briefe.* Ed. Jürgen Born, Gerhard Neumann, Malcolm Pasley, and Jost Schillemeit. Frankfurt am Main: Fischer.
KKAB1	Franz Kafka. 1999. *Briefe 1900–1912.* Ed. Hans-Gerd Koch. Frankfurt am Main: Fischer.
KKAB2	Franz Kafka. 1999. *Briefe 1913–März 1914.* Ed. Hans-Gerd Koch. Frankfurt am Main: Fischer.
KKAB3	Franz Kafka. 2005. *Briefe April 1914–1917.* Ed. Hans-Gerd Koch. Frankfurt am Main: Fischer.

KKAD	Franz Kafka. 1994. *Drucke zu Lebzeiten.* Ed. Hans-Gerd Koch, Wolf Kittler, and Gerhard Neumann. Frankfurt am Main: Fischer.
KKANI	Franz Kafka. 1993. *Nachgelassene Schriften und Fragmente I.* Ed. Malcolm Pasley. Frankfurt am Main: Fischer.
KKANII	Franz Kafka. 1992. *Nachgelassene Schriften und Fragmente II.* Ed. Jost Schillemeit. Frankfurt am Main: Fischer.
KKANIIA	Franz Kafka. 1993. *Nachgelassene Schriften und Fragmente.* Apparatband. Ed. Jost Schillemeit. Frankfurt am Main: Fischer.
KKAP	Franz Kafka. 1990. *Der Proceß.* Ed. Malcolm Pasley. Frankfurt am Main: Fischer.
KKAT	Franz Kafka. 1990. *Tagebücher.* Ed. Hans-Gerd Koch, Michael Müller, and Malcolm Pasley. Frankfurt am Main: Fischer.
KKAV	Franz Kafka. 1983. *Der Verschollene.* Ed. Jost Schillemeit. Frankfurt am Main: Fischer.
KKAVA	Franz Kafka. 1983. *Der Verschollene.* Ed. J. Schillemeit. Apparatband. Frankfurt am Main: Fischer.
KLF	Franz Kafka. 1974. *Letters to Felice.* Ed. Erich Heller and Jürgen Born. Trans. James Stern and Elizabeth Duckworth. London: Secker & Warburg.
KLM	Franz Kafka. 1953. *Letters to Milena.* Ed. Willi Haas. Trans. Tania Stern and James Stern. London: Secker & Warburg.
KSS	Franz Kafka. 2007. *Kafka's selected stories.* Ed. and trans. Stanley Corngold. New York: Norton.
L	*Letters to friends, family, and editors.* 1977. Trans. Richard and Clara Winston. New York: Schocken Books.
LF	Franz Kafka. *Letters to Felice.* 1977. Trans. James Stern and Elizabeth Duckworth. New York: Schocken Books.
LM	Franz Kafka. 1990. *Letters to Milena.* Trans. Philip Boehm. New York: Schocken Books.
MB	Pasley, Malcolm, ed. 1989. *Max Brod, Franz Kafka: Eine Freundschaft. Briefwechsel.* Frankfurt am Main: Fischer.

Introduction

NARRATION AND NARRATIVES IN KAFKA

Jakob Lothe, Beatrice Sandberg, and Ronald Speirs

The essays in this volume examine a number of questions presented by narration and narratives in Kafka's fiction. They originated as papers discussed at a symposium in May 2006 that formed part of the research project Narrative Theory and Analysis directed by Jakob Lothe at the Centre for Advanced Study in Oslo. The arguments (which have been revised in light of discussions then and since) relate both to the peculiarities of Kafka's story-telling and to general issues in narrative theory. The decision to select Kafka's work for discussion in the context of the research project was, if not inevitable, at least unsurprising, given that it has frequently attracted the attention of critics interested in the nature of narrative, arguably because of rather than despite the challenges his stories present to the general categories narrative theorists make it their business to develop. Since general narrative theory and Kafka's idiosyncratic fictions are both complex and contentious topics, some prefatory remarks are called for to outline the context in which the issues addressed in the individual contributions emerged.

Even to use the term "narrative theory" might be considered to invite misunderstanding, for there are not one but many competing accounts of what narration and narratives entail. For purely pragmatic reasons, we have decided to take as a starting point the basic understanding of narrative as rhetorical communication (a view offered by the theorist James Phelan, a member of the research project team) not because the contributors would all necessarily subscribe to this theoretical model but because it addresses a number of the key components of narrative that were much debated during the research project and that have for long played a role in Kafka criticism. The terms and concepts are not meant to provide "preset molds into which narratives will inevitably fit—or must be made to fit—but rather . . . available tools for opening up the workings of individual narratives" (see James Phelan's discussion in chapter 1). Phelan's general definition of narrative asserts that

> narrative can be fruitfully understood as a rhetorical act: somebody telling somebody else on some occasion and for some purpose(s) that something happened. In fictional narrative, the rhetorical situation is doubled: the narrator tells her story to her narratee for her purposes, while the author communicates to her audience for her own purposes both that story and the narrator's telling of it. (2007, 3–4)

While this definition is cast in the simplest of terms, each of the elements is susceptible to complex elaboration and to considerable variation in perception, as the contributions to the present volume demonstrate. The essays reflect the complexity of the issues surrounding the "somebody" doing the telling, the attitude of the narrator to what is told, the perceived purpose(s) of the telling, the implied or actual reader, the progression of events, and the progression of the telling. As these elements are interconnected to a high degree, an increased or decreased emphasis on any one of them will have an impact on the others. Where purpose is perceived to be important, for example, the narrator doing the telling is likely to assume a different profile in the mind of the reader than would be the case in narratives that do not convey a clear sense of authorial or narratorial purpose. Similarly, where historical "occasion" is considered to be important (as in Benno Wagner's chapter on "Building the Great Wall of China"), the critic's understanding of narration will differ markedly from that of critics who believe Kafka's understanding of life to have been categorically a-temporal.[1] As the range of emphases in these chapters makes clear, Kafka's mode of narration still appears as stubbornly enigmatic to today's readers as it did when he began to write, almost exactly a century ago. As the essays also demonstrate, Kafka's narratives still present a considerable challenge to, as well as a great resource for, narrative theory and analysis.

Of the various elements identified by Phelan, the questions surrounding the "somebody" who tells have long been of particular interest to

Kafka's commentators. In the development of Kafka criticism, the great editor and philologist Friedrich Beißner deserves credit for having been the first to focus attention effectively on the question of narration in Kafka's fiction in a trenchant public lecture given in 1952, subsequently published under the title *Der Erzähler Franz Kafka* ("The narrator Franz Kafka").[2] The lecture was prompted by Beißner's irritation at the practice, which had become widespread during the Kafka vogue of the early post-war years, of interpreting Kafka's fictions as encoded illustrations of various ideological positions (existential, religious, philosophical, psychoanalytic) dear to the hearts of the many interpreters who made the assumption that the stories were told by an authoritative narrator speaking from a position distinct from and superior to those of his characters. Beißner, by contrast, contended that Kafka always narrated from a single perspective ("Kafka erzählt . . . stets einsinnig" [1983, 37]), and that the narrative perspective, even when expressed in the third person, was always co-extensive with that of the protagonist: "There is no place for the narrator other than in the soul of his central figure: he narrates himself, he transforms himself into Josef K. and into the land-surveyor K." (1983, 38). According to Beißner, the narrator becomes one not simply with the protagonist but also with the events and circumstances of the story:

> The narrator is identical not only with the main figure (and this is the case even where Kafka narrates in the third person) but also with what is narrated. The distance between event and narration is cancelled ["aufgehoben"]. . . . Kafka allows the narrator no space beside or above the figures and no distance from events. . . . There is only the sequence of events that is narrating itself (paradoxically in the past tense). (1983, 41–42)[3]

A concomitant effect of this technique is to eliminate any distance between the reader and the protagonist: "If we understand things correctly, Kafka transforms not only himself but also the reader into the main figure" (Beißner 1983, 42).

A further consequence of the narrator's identification with the self-enclosed condition of the protagonist, in Beißner's view, is that narrative progression at the level of event effectively does not take place. Although the figure might believe that he is moving toward some goal, the unfolding of the narrative typically reveals the underlying and unchanging stasis of his situation. As Beißner put it with characteristic clarity in his next, equally influential lecture on Kafka, "Der Dichter Franz Kafka" ("Kafka the poet"), Kafka's enduring theme, was "the *failure to arrive* or the *failure to reach a goal*" (Beißner 1983, 63; emphasis in the original). As Beißner realized, this theme was also relevant to the question of narrative progression at the level of communication between author or narrator and reader. If the stories are told from within an isolated consciousness, the reader, although forced by the narrative techniques into an attitude of identification, can have no assurance of entering that consciousness effectively. Just as the stories told by figures within the stories usually do not achieve the intended effect on the other figures to whom the stories are told, the author's stories too may fail to reach their goal/reader.[4] Kafka himself recognized this danger when he wrote to Felice Bauer that *if* his "rather wild and senseless" story "Das Urteil" ("The Judgment") contained "innere Wahrheit" ("inner truth") this was something that could only be affirmed or denied by each individual reader (KLF, 87).

For Beißner this narrative constellation marked the end-point of a great historical arc that began with the Homeric epic, in which the poet-narrator derived his nigh-on omniscient authority from a unified world-view encompassing the actions of gods and mortals alike that he shared with his audience and his characters. In Kafka's fiction, by contrast, a radically different, modern view of the world had found its appropriate form of expression, an enclosed, "monadic" experience of isolated subjectivity in which no "windows" existed through which individuals might gain access either to the inner world of other subjects or to some Archimedean point of objectivity. Kafka's remark that he was concerned above all with the "Darstellung meines traumhaften inneren Lebens" (KAF, 10: 167) ("representation of my dreamlike inner life") was taken by Beißner to be the key to understanding the structure of Kafka's fiction, for within that "dreamlike inner life" no distinctions are tenable between the perspectives of the protagonist, the narrator, and even, ultimately, the author. If ever the narrator failed to abide strictly by the "principle" of identification with the protagonist, he committed what Beißner regarded as a compositional error or a breach of his own rule of narration. Beißner cited as evidence for this view the fact that Kafka left as one of the paralipomena of *Der Proceß* (*The Trial*) a draft chapter in which Josef K. is described from the perspective of an outside observer as the protagonist returns to waking consciousness after dreaming of a sequence of events in which he was a passive participant. Such a break between dreamt experience and a reflective consciousness that recognized the "unreal" nature of dream events could not possibly be acceptable, Beißner maintained, to an artist as concerned as Kafka was with artistic consistency and coherence, because "Das traumhafte innere Leben erscheint nicht einheitlich genug" (1983, 45) ("the dreamlike inner life does not appear sufficiently unified").

The isolation on which Beißner placed such stress was certainly an important element both in Kafka's experience of life and in his ideal conception of writing. In October 1921, for example, he characterized his situation thus:

> Alles ist Phantasie, die Familie, das Bureau, die Freunde, die Straße, alles Phantasie, fernere oder nähere, die Frau die nächste, Wahrheit aber ist nur daß Du den Kopf gegen die Wand einer fenster- und türlosen Zelle drückst. (KAF, 11:192)
>
> (All is imaginary, family, office, friends, the street, all imaginary, far away or close at hand, the woman the closest; the truth, however, is only this, that you are beating your head against the wall of a windowless and doorless cell.) (KD, 395; translation modified)

A week later, having taken part half-heartedly in a game of cards his parents were playing, Kafka observed that his whole life had been one of *almost* complete isolation:

> Dieses Grenzland zwischen Einsamkeit und Gemeinschaft habe ich nur äußerst selten überschritten, ich habe mich darin sogar mehr angesiedelt, als in der Einsamkeit selbst. Was für ein lebendiges schönes Land war im Vergleich hiezu Robinsons Insel. (KAF, 11:193)
>
> (I have seldom, very seldom, crossed this borderland between loneliness and community, I have even settled down there more than in loneliness itself. What a fine bustling place was Robinson Crusoe's island in comparison.) (KD, 396; translation modified)

The distinction Kafka drew here between living in this "borderland" and the elusive complete isolation he longed for as the pre-condition of total immersion in writing is helpful when it comes to understanding the position of the narrator or narrators in his fiction. Just as he was sufficiently involved in communal life at least to make a show of taking an interest in his parents' card game (a minor but telling example of a life lived in fact in the service of many other lives despite the subjective sense of alienation and the great cost to his own well-being), Kafka's narrative stance is not as solipsistic as Beißner claimed it was. As has often been pointed out, there are too many instances of what Beißner considered to be breaks in perspective for them to be mere artistic infelicities. Even if Beißner were correct in supposing that the fictions were the expression of a single personality, this would not necessarily entail the singularity of perspective (*Einsinnigkeit*) he insisted on, for being "of two minds" is not only a familiar enough experience,[5] but Kafka had a particularly strong sense of the multi-occupancy of the self:

> Jeder Mensch trägt ein Zimmer in sich. Diese Tatsache kann man sogar durch das Gehör nachprüfen. Wenn einer schnell geht und man hinhorcht, etwa in der Nacht wenn alles ringsherum still ist, so hört man z.B. das Scheppern eines nicht genug befestigten Wandspiegels oder der Schirm. (KAF, 6:44)
>
> (Every human being carries a room within himself. One can even test this fact with the ear. If someone walks quickly and one listens attentively, at night, say, when everything around is quiet, one hears for example the rattle of a mirror that is not properly fixed to the wall or the screen.)

Although Beißner's argument that Kafka's narrator always identifies unreservedly with the protagonist was crucial in directing attention to the issue of narrative perspective and modes in Kafka, many subsequent critics, including the contributors to this volume, stress the element of irony in his presentation of events, and argue that the repeated and contrasting patterns created by the narrated images show a shaping consciousness at work that invites us to look at things from a perspective (or perspectives) distinct from the protagonist's.[6] There is also external evidence that the author Kafka at times far exceeded the quietly ironic distance detectable in his narrators. When reading aloud the first chapter of *The Trial,* for example, it is reported by Max Brod that Kafka was so convulsed with laughter that he could scarcely finish the reading (1996, 156). Reading "Die Verwandlung" ("The Metamorphosis") to friends, by contrast, had two quite different effects on Kafka, with laughter following hard on the heels of a "frenzied" recitation, possibly to release the tensions generated by the oral delivery: "Ein schöner Abend bei Max. Ich las mich an meiner Geschichte in Raserei. Wir haben es uns dann wohl sein lassen und viel gelacht" (F, 320) ("A pleasant evening at Max's. I read myself into a frenzy with my story. But then we did let ourselves go, and laughed a lot" [KLF, 209]).

On another occasion Kafka contrasted his own detached view of the death of a character with the sympathetic response he expected his manner of narrating to elicit from the reader:

> Auf dem Nachhauseweg sagte ich Max, daß ich auf dem Sterbebett vorausgesetzt daß die Schmerzen nicht zu groß sind, sehr zufrieden sein werde. Ich vergaß hinzuzufügen und habe es später mit Absicht unterlassen, daß das Beste was ich geschrieben habe, in dieser Fähigkeit zufrieden sterben zu können, seinen Grund hat. An allen diesen guten und stark überzeugenden Stellen handelt es sich immer darum, daß jemand stirbt, daß es ihm sehr schwer wird, daß darin für ihn ein Unrecht und wenigstens eine Härte liegt und daß das für den Leser wenigstens meiner Meinung nach rührend wird. Für mich aber, der ich glaube auf dem Sterbebett zufrieden sein zu können, sind solche Schilderungen im geheimen ein Spiel, ich freue mich ja in dem Sterbenden zu sterben, nütze daher mit Berechnung die auf den Tod gesammelte Aufmerksamkeit des Lesers aus, bin bei viel klarerem Verstande als er, von dem ich annehme, daß er auf dem Sterbebett klagen wird, und meine Klage ist daher möglichst vollkommen, bricht auch nicht etwa plötzlich ab wie wirkliche Klage, sondern verläuft schön und rein. (KAF, 11:63–64)

> (On the way home told Max that I shall lie very contentedly on my deathbed, provided the pain isn't too great. I forgot, and later purposely omitted, to add that the best things I have written have their basis in this capacity of mine to meet death with contentment. All these fine and very convincing passages always deal with the fact that someone is dying, that it is hard for him to do, that it seems unjust to him, or at least harsh, and the reader is moved by this, or at least he should be. But for me, who believe that I shall be able to lie contentedly on my deathbed, such scenes are secretly a game, indeed in the death enacted I rejoice in my own death, hence calculatingly exploit the attention that the reader concentrates on death, have a much clearer understanding of it than he, of whom I suppose he will loudly lament on his deathbed, and for these reasons my lament is as perfect as can be, nor does it suddenly break off, as is likely to be the case with a real lament, but dies beautifully and purely away.) (KD, 321)

Yet this is not in fact how Kafka always responded to his own descriptions of painful subjects. When, late one night, he re-read to himself a passage from *Der Verschollene* (*The Man Who Disappeared*), for example, Kafka confessed to being so moved that he feared his sobbing might wake his parents in the next room (KLF, 72).

The views Kafka expressed at different times about the point or purpose of his writing were equally contradictory. In one particularly black moment, he described writing as a sweet reward for "service to the devil," devilish both because it unleashed powers that nature otherwise held in check and because it led to a narcissistic withdrawal from normal life:

> Und das Teuflische daran scheint mir sehr klar. Es ist die Eitelkeit und Genußsucht, die immerfort um die eigene oder auch um eine fremde Gestalt—die Bewegung vervielfältigt sich dann, es wird ein Sonnensystem der Eitelkeit—schwirrt und sie genießt. (Br, 385)
>
> (And what is devilish about it seems very clear to me. It is the vanity and addiction to pleasure which constantly flutters around its own figure and enjoys it—or around some other figure, the movement then multiplies, it becomes a solar system of vanity.)

Yet there were other times when he felt writing to be a form of *Erhebung* ("elevation") that permitted things to be seen from a new, freer point of view:

> Merkwürdiger, geheimnisvoller, vielleicht gefährlicher, vielleicht erlösender Trost des Schreibens: das Hinausspringen aus der Totschlägerreihe Tat—Beobachtung, Tat—Beobachtung, indem eine höhere Art der Beobachtung geschaffen wird, eine höhere, keine schärfere, und je höher sie ist, je unerreichbarer von der "Reihe" aus, desto unabhängiger wird sie, desto mehr eigenen Gesetzen der Bewegung folgend, desto unberechenbarer, freudiger, steigender ihr Weg. (KAF, 11:210)
>
> (The strange, mysterious, perhaps dangerous, perhaps saving comfort that there is in writing: it is a leap out of the murderers' row, action-observation, action-observation, that is made possible by the creation of a higher type of observation, a higher, not a keener type, and the higher it is and the more out of reach of the "row," the more independent it becomes, the more obedient to its own laws of motion, the more incalculable, the more joyful, the more ascendant its course.) (KD, 406–7)

At such moments, Kafka felt confirmed in the belief that writing was the purpose or even the mission that it had been given to him to fulfill, whatever it might cost him:

> Die ungeheuere Welt, die ich im Kopfe habe. Aber wie mich befreien und sie befreien ohne zu zerreißen. Und tausendmal lieber zerreißen, als sie in mir zurückhalten oder begraben. Dazu bin ich ja hier, das ist mir ganz klar. (KAF, 10:179)

> (The tremendous world I have in my head. But how to free myself and free it, without being torn to pieces. And a thousand times rather be torn to pieces than retain it in me or bury it. That, indeed, is why I am here, that is quite clear to me.) (KD, 222)

Yet such affirmations of his purpose or calling as a writer exist alongside a sense of the self as a non-identical, multiple and even dispersed being from whom singleness of purpose or viewpoint is hardly to be expected:

> Er lebt in der Diaspora. Seine Elemente, eine frei lebende Horde, umschweifen die Welt. Und nur, weil auch sein Zimmer zur Welt gehört, sieht er sie manchmal in der Ferne. Wie soll er für sie die Verantwortung tragen? Heißt das noch Verantwortung? (KAF, 11:176)

> (He lives in dispersal, in diaspora. His elements, a horde that lives freely, fly around the world. And only because his room also belongs to the world does he sometimes see them in the distance. How is he to bear the responsibility for them? Can that still be called responsibility?)[7]

Seen in relation to Phelan's definition of narration as a purposive communicative act, the extra-textual evidence Kafka provided about his writing is too contradictory to support any simple view. For Kafka, writing stories involved, on the one hand, cutting himself off utterly from others, ideally in some deep dungeon where he was provided only with the means to write (KLF, 156), and in consequence feeling guilt that writing might merely be an act of vain self-reflection and self-indulgence.[8] On the other hand, despite this view of his writing as non-communicative behavior, Kafka did actually publish a number of stories during his lifetime (and was punctilious in demanding that the printer should adhere precisely to his at times idiosyncratic punctuation, which had both a rhythmic and psychological purpose), dedicated stories occasionally to real people, read some stories aloud, and believed, at good moments, that it was the purpose of his being "here" to get the "tremendous world in his head" down on paper and thus make it accessible to others. In a late letter to Max Brod in which he apologized for writing so few letters recently, explaining that he had done so out of "strategic" consideration for his friend's feelings, Kafka even insisted that art alone, because it is free of such personal constraints, could enable truthful communication to take place: "Manchmal scheint mir überhaupt das Wesen der Kunst, das Dasein der Kunst allein aus solchen 'strategischen Rücksichten' erklärbar, die Ermöglichung eines wahren Wortes von Mensch zu Mensch" (Br, 172), ("Sometimes it even seems to me that such 'strategic considerations' alone explain the essence of art, the existence of art, the making possible of a true word from one human being to another").[9] Circumstantial evidence suggests, then, that the author Kafka at least *wanted* to communicate through his writing, even if the narratives themselves are profoundly enigmatic and frequently raise severe doubts about the very possibility of communication. Whatever the external evidence of authorial intention or self-understanding, however, what matters to the textual critic is the actual practice of narration found in the stories themselves. Accordingly, the evidence considered in the essays in the present volume is for the most part intra- or inter-textual, assuming "a recursive relationship (or feedback loop) among authorial agency, textual phenomena (including intertextual relations), and reader response" (Phelan 2007, 4).

Of the various elements cited in James Phelan's rhetorical definition of narrative, the question of authorial purpose receives particular attention in three contributions to this volume, those by James Phelan, Anniken Greve, and Benno Wagner. Phelan's analysis of the rhetorical strategy in "The Judgment" aims to advance both our practical understanding of the dynamics of the story and our theoretical understanding of narrative progression, narrative judgment, and narrative speed. Phelan views progression as the "interaction of two kinds of change over time: that experienced by the characters and that experienced by the audience in its developing responses to the characters' changes," and he views those readerly responses as the result of three kinds of judgment: interpretive, ethical, and aesthetic (see James Phelan's discussion in chapter 1). According to Phelan, the interaction of the two kinds of change arouses three kinds of readerly interest, which develop and interact across the span of the narrative: the mimetic (interest in characters as possible people and the events as occurring in a recognizable possible world); the thematic (interest in the characters and situations as representative of ideas, attitudes, ethical values, political positions, and so on); and the synthetic (interest in the characters, situations, and arrangement of events as artificial constructs). Tracking these interests, Phelan suggests, is a good way to discover a narrative's purposes. As Phelan notes, this model displaces thematic interpretation from its usual position at the center of critical commentary and directs critical attention instead to the ethical, affective, and aesthetic dimensions of reading. Phelan uses this model to explain why a story like "The Judgment," which changes its speed and which has an unbridgeable "hermeneutic gap" at the very point where the action reaches its climax, is not only amenable to so many, often widely divergent, thematic interpretations, but actually has its narrative and ethical force enhanced rather than diminished by the deliberate, stubborn inscrutability of its final turning point. Just as important, Phelan uses "The Judgment" as the basis for some theoretical generalizations about the interaction of narrative speed and readerly judgments and for revisions of some of his previous generalizations about surprise endings.

In her analysis of "The Metamorphosis," Anniken Greve argues, along similar lines, that Kafka's narrative techniques create both the difficulty and the necessity of confronting the issue of authorial purpose. From the first paragraph of the story onward, the reader is faced with a perplexingly contradictory text that resists assimilation to any of the familiar codes we are tempted to apply in an effort to make some sense of its strangeness. On the one hand, some features of the story point toward the genre of a realist family drama in which one member finds himself in unexpected conflict with the rest of the family. Yet the fictive event that precipitates the conflict is incompatible with our entire experience of the kinds of things that *can* happen in the world where family dramas take place. The author articulates the reader's resistant, habitual assumptions about the world through the reaction of the protagonist ("What has happened to me?"), only to cut off the obvious escape route out of the dilemma by the very same means ("It was no dream"). Equally, the pull of the extraordinary event toward the story's generic assimilation (and hence naturalization) as fairy tale, legend or myth is frustrated by the absence of any supernatural power whose intervention might otherwise have caused the laws of the natural world to be suspended. The result is an effect defined by Greve as "ontological fuzziness" (see Anniken Greve's discussion in chapter 2). The rhetorical design appears calculated to induce conflict and confusion in the mind of the reader; Greve concludes that it compels us to search for some implied philosophical and ethical purpose to account for the story's pulling-apart and re-assembly of the world as we thought we knew it.

According to the analysis offered by Benno Wagner, the underlying purpose guiding Kafka's choice of narrative technique in "Building the Great Wall of China," a later, fragmentary story with an intra-diegetic narrator, was a political one. In opposition to Karl Heinz Bohrer's insistence (2005) on the strict separation of literary art from culture (understood as the expression of social consensus), Wagner argues that Kafka's story needs to be examined in its historical context, as a literary response to the mobilization of culture undertaken in support of the German and Austrian national cause during the First World War. Wagner describes Kafka's narrative method as the construction of a kind of echo-chamber in which multiple allusions to the stereotypes used in war-time discourse reveal the enterprise of defending German culture from the encircling "barbarians" to be as fragmentary, as contradictory, and hence as ineffectual as the conception and execution of the Great Wall of China (as re-invented within this fiction). Kafka's aim, Wagner argues, was to free the reader from the manipulative rhetorical designs of the war's cultural advocates by exposing the fragmentary and groundless nature of all "grand narratives" purporting to link the attainment of national unity to the destruction of other nations.

If the essays by Phelan, Greve, and Wagner all argue that Kafka achieves his authorial purpose by engaging in a form of deliberately difficult, even obstructive, communication designed to provoke disturbed reflection in the reader, the next three chapters, by Gerhard Neumann, Gerhard Kurz, and J. Hillis Miller, focus on communication as a problem in itself, a problem of which Kafka was acutely aware:

> Ich suche immerfort etwas Nicht-Mitteilbares mitzuteilen, etwas Unerklärbares zu erklären, von etwas zu erzählen, was ich in den Knochen habe und was nur in diesen Knochen erlebt werden kann. (M, 249)
>
> (All the time I am trying to convey something unconveyable, to explain something inexplicable, to tell about something I have in my bones and which can only be experienced in these bones.) (KLM, 220)

In all three essays, the emphasis is on the deficiency of communication apparent in the internal acts of narration performed by various characters in Kafka's first and last novels, *The Man Who Disappeared* (discussed by Neumann and Kurz) and *Das Schloß* (*The Castle*) (discussed by Miller).

In his analysis of "The Stoker" (originally intended to be the opening chapter of *The Man Who Disappeared* but published separately when

Kafka realized he would not complete the novel), Gerhard Neumann elaborates on the significance of a detail noticed only in passing by the protagonist Karl Roßmann, namely an unoccupied writing desk in an empty cabin in the bowels of the ship on which he has sailed to New York. Neumann reads this detail as a hint by the author that "The Stoker" is a story lacking the kind of narrator who might act as a single source of narrative coherence and authority and thus help the reader to grasp the hidden originating event of the action that lies beyond the reach of the characters' verbal recall.[10] Neumann's suggestion that we are dealing with an *auctor absconditus* in Kafka's work recalls Beißner's early observation that "the action (*Vorgang*) narrates itself" (1983, 42), but with the difference that the narrator now appears far more detached from events than in Beißner's conception of the narrator as the co-sufferer along with the protagonist (and the reader) of the unfolding action. Neumann sees Kafka rather as allowing the narrator to shed responsibility almost entirely for relating events by having him act simply as the unseen recorder of a whole series of stories being told and retold, either to themselves or to one another, by the figures of his narrative. Although the narrator may have vacated his seat at the writing desk in the cabin below deck, his hovering presence can still be detected in the ironies built into this sequence of retellings, as, for example, when Karl is obliged to listen to what he regards as a distorted account of his life just after he in turn has assumed that he can narrate the experiences of the ship's stoker more effectively than the man himself.

The aspect of communication dealt with by Gerhard Kurz is not so much the problem of an un-tellable experience at the heart of personal narrative (though this does play a part) as the problem of a story's arrival, or rather failure to arrive, at its intended destination. Kurz examines in some detail the scene in which a young serving girl, Therese, who is as much a refugee in the Hotel Occidental as Karl Roßmann, tells him about her own experiences of abandonment, wandering, and exclusion in America. Although Therese's story about her mother's death has greater poignancy than most narratives within the novel, it is embedded in a context of irony, which reveals the failure of even this story to capture the interest of Karl, in whom Therese believes she has found a sympathetic listener. Even similarity of fate, it appears, is no guarantee that the telling and hearing of life-stories will facilitate genuine communication.

That non-communication is the rule rather than the exception in human interaction, both in Kafka's fictional universe and arguably elsewhere, is a view strongly supported by J. Hillis Miller's analysis of the irremediably isolated condition of K. and of all the other characters he encounters in his fruitless efforts to enter the Castle. The darkness enveloping the mysterious Castle on the hill at the moment when K. first pauses at the bridge before crossing over to the village has its human counterpart in the impenetrability of every individual in the novel. The many lengthy stories they tell to and about one another or about the Castle do little or nothing to lighten that darkness, for they all offer interpretations that are contradictory and unverifiable. If the disappearance of narratorial authority was signaled in "The Stoker" by the unoccupied writing desk, the "strange, disembodied power of narration" that "stages"[11] events in *The Castle* appears to have only marginally less restricted access to what is going on inside K. (the only character to whom it has any such access) than the characters have to one another or to the facts of many situations. According to Miller, the incompleteness of the novel (the manuscript breaks off mid-sentence) is of a piece with its lack of overall narrative progression, "as it wanders this way and that, always starting over again from the beginning and never getting any closer to the Castle." The overall effect is an illusion of movement centered on stasis. Thus, Miller's reading of the novel suggests that, provided the notion of "purpose" is kept flexible enough to encompass the expression of a particular experience of the world, Phelan's definition of the constitutive elements of narrative is helpful in understanding the features of even such strangely inconclusive tales as *The Castle.*

As the fragments of *The Man Who Disappeared* and *The Castle* confirm, narrative progression, in the basic sense of writing stories with a beginning, middle, and end, was a lifelong problem for Kafka. Many diary entries show that he was unusually dependent on inspiration or the occurrence of a narrative idea or *Einfall*, a term which in his case remained close to its root sense of a "falling into" his imagination of a figure, situation, or image capable of initiating a narrative, which means of course that "purpose" could, at best, only enter the process of writing once the writing had begun. As Malcolm Pasley, one of the main editors of Kafka's complete works, demonstrated from the evidence of the manuscripts, Kafka normally did not compose his stories on the basis of a pre-existing plan.[12] The physical organization of the manuscripts, such as the closely spaced lines, which militated against inter-linear corrections, confirms Max Brod's report that Kafka's chosen method of composition was to write as if going through a tunnel, following the figures wherever they led, without any prior knowledge of where this might end (1966, 114). As a result, many of Kafka's stories were abandoned in a fragmentary state because he simply did not know where they were meant to go next.

On one occasion Kafka did try to ensure that he was not left with yet another fragment by writing the last chapter of his second novel, *The Trial,* immediately after he had ended the first chapter, but the novel remained a fragment nevertheless, because Kafka's linear method of writing within each chapter did not produce the sense of narrative progression and *Zusammenhang* ("connectedness" or "coherence") that would carry him in a compelling way from the beginning to the pre-conceived yet ambiguously open ending.

What went into a story by Kafka came into being, then, not beforehand but at the very moment he wrote it down, and what he wrote down he seldom corrected, so important was it to him that each word should generate the next in an unbroken stream of connectedness. He once characterized the immediacy of the relation between inspiration and writing thus:

> Die besondere Art meiner Inspiration in der ich Glücklichster und Unglücklichster jetzt um 2 Uhr nachts schlafen gehe . . . ist die, daß ich alles kann, nicht nur auf eine bestimmte Arbeit hin. Wenn ich wahllos einen Satz hinschreibe z. B. Er schaute aus dem Fenster so ist er schon vollkommen. (KAF, 9:27)

> (The special nature of my inspiration, in which I, the most fortunate and unfortunate of men now go to sleep at 2am . . . is such that I can do everything, and not only what is directed to a definite piece of work. When I arbitrarily write a single sentence, for instance, "He looked out of the window," it already has perfection.) (KD, 38)

This gift was a double-edged sword, however, for the inspiration that could yield such "perfect" sentences was also the source of much misery, abandoning Kafka to long periods of utter barrenness because it was quite simply not in his power to summon up inspiration or even determine its duration by an act of will. Thus, stories that began promisingly enough would often come to a sudden halt. When this happened to Kafka during the writing of *The Man Who Disappeared,* he simply landed Karl Roßmann with the unsolved problem of progression by abandoning him in the dark at the unprotected edge of an unfinished building and breaking off the manuscript at that point; fortunately for Karl, it occurred to Kafka later how he might have him called away from the abyss and taken back along the unlit corridor that had led him to its edge (Schillemeit 2007, 145).

As the chapter by Beatrice Sandberg demonstrates, Kafka's writing impulse could be frustrated not only by stories suddenly stopping in their tracks, but also by the "special nature of his inspiration," which created problems with beginnings. He once complained that things which "fell into" his imagination did so not from the "root" but "somewhere about the middle" (KD, 12); later, he wrote of having to struggle with beginnings and endings like a fisherman who gets hold of a long, heavy, and unwieldy "sea-snake" around the middle. Sandberg considers the range of strategies Kafka developed to deal with this particular quirk of his imagination, the most important of which was intertextual allusion to some well-known, often mythical, "well made" story with a familiar shape that gave him the freedom to create the sudden reversals, deviations, or inconsistencies that conveyed the resistance of the stories he pulled up from his unfathomable inner self to any attempt to accommodate them within traditional narrative patterns.

In his chapter on "In der Strafkolonie" ("In the Penal Colony"), Jakob Lothe argues that, whether formally completed or not, there is a sense in which every story Kafka wrote begins "somewhere in the middle," for this is the existential situation in which all of Kafka's characters find themselves, without full or possibly even any access to the point at which "their" story could be said to originate and without knowledge of what might evolve out of any situation in which they find themselves. Beginnings that pitch the characters *in medias res* favor a form of narration that consists in the unfolding and elaboration of a dilemma. Regardless of the (generally only implied, not narrated) preceding chain of events that placed them in the given situation, what each character is faced with is the question of justification (*Rechtfertigung*), a haunting question for Kafka himself, as a much quoted diary entry attests: "Kämest du, unsichtbares Gericht!" (KAF, 9:106) ("Were you to come, invisible judgment!") (KD, 31).[13] Here as elsewhere, Kafka's narrative techniques ensured that neither his characters nor his readers could evade the dilemmas he placed them in by withdrawing to a position of observational neutrality, while at the same time denying them any firm ground on which to make the ethical choices the fictional events demand of them.

The issue of narrative progression provides the central focus for the last two contributions to this volume. Stanley Corngold examines the unfolding of the narrative and the mental movements of the first-person narrator in one of Kafka's later stories, "Forschungen eines Hundes" ("Investigations of a Dog"), while Ronald Speirs considers narrative progression in connection with both physical and mental movement, a persistent and unusually prominent feature of Kafka's narratives from

Betrachtung (*Contemplation*), his first published collection of prose, onward. The feature of "Investigations of a Dog" that particularly interests Corngold is the peculiar "looping" movement by which the story proceeds, a pattern that reflects competing tendencies in the mind of the dog-narrator as he feels compelled both to confront and to avoid facing an early, overwhelming experience of music, something he first encountered when he came across a group of dancing, hovering dogs. For Corngold, the obsessively circling movements of this story, going off in one direction only to be pulled back reluctantly in another, illustrate the characteristic self-referentiality of narration in Kafka as it seeks a lost, haunting point of origin.[14]

The subject of the chapter by Ronald Speirs is the role played by movement in three areas: the "something that happened"; the source of narration for Kafka; and the feature relating the sequence of words, sentences, and paragraphs to the succession of mental and physical events being described. The conflict noted by Corngold between forward-moving and retarding or deviating impulses is already to be found in *Betrachtung,* a collection of very short narratives in which it is possible for the protagonists neither to realize, at one extreme, the impulse for pure movement that is articulated in "Wish to Become a Red Indian" nor, at the other extreme, to withdraw completely from the hectic motion of the surrounding world into a condition of isolated stasis. Although Kafka's stories are frequently marked by narrative irony, it is problematic, Speirs argues, to characterize Kafka as a writer who sets out to narrate with a "purpose," since, by his own evidence, the dynamic force that found a shape in his stories lay largely beyond his control, much as the fictional figures often find themselves having to submit to an irresistible restlessness that will carry them to their destruction (as in the case of Georg Bendemann), forcing the reader to leap across unbridgeable "hermeneutic gaps." If, on the one hand, Kafka can at times be seen as using movement and stasis to narrate the conflicts in his "dreamlike inner life" in an ironically reflective manner, it is equally possible to see the narrative dynamism at work in his writing (as he himself did repeatedly, despite his metaphysical reflections on the inherent stasis of the human condition), as an irresistible creative force that used *him* as the vehicle for its own expression.

What emerges from the essays in this volume is that Kafka's narrative practice(s) cannot be captured by a single theoretical approach. As the implied author of his stories and novels adopts the lowest of profiles, whether hidden behind an intra-diegetic, first-person narrator or employing a variant of free indirect discourse to describe events largely from the perspective of a protagonist, or simply "staging" the events dispassionately, discerning the meaning or purpose of the "something [that] happened" depends to an unusual, perhaps unique degree on the perceptions and preconceptions of the reader.[15] The limited, often erroneous efforts of Kafka's characters to grasp their own predicament offer little assurance to his readers, professional or otherwise, that they will fare any better. The "system of partial construction" employed by the builders of his Great Wall of China seems, so far, to be the best we can hope for.

Notes

1. See, for example, the influential essay by Beda Allemann, "Stehender Sturmlauf: Zeit und Geschichte im Werk Kafkas" (first published in 1962), which puts at the center of attention Kafka's aphoristic observations on the relation between the time before time in the Garden of Eden and the mortal existence of human beings trapped forever at the threshold of expulsion, where they must live separated from the unchanging peace originally enjoyed by Adam and Eve, never to be released to live wholly within a temporal world. Allemann's emphasis on the notion of "stehender Sturmlauf" ("charging on the spot") has been taken up, elaborated on, and interpreted in contrasting ways by numerous critics interested in narrative progression in Kafka, notably Klaus Ramm (1979), Gerhard Neumann (1968), and Stanley Corngold (1986).

2. Beicken (1979, 36), for example, follows Beißner's account of the situation of the modern narrator. Even in the most recent *Kafka-Handbuch,* edited by Jagow and Jahraus (2008), Beißner's fundamental importance for the development of a "philological" reading of Kafka is still acknowledged (343), whether in the form of elaborations on his central concept of *Einsinnigkeit* (e.g., by Beißner's pupil Martin Walser, with his emphasis on artistic autonomy rather than psychological expression [1961]) or in disagreement with him, as when Klaus Ramm argues that Kafka "neither narrates from the perspective of the protagonist nor presents his standpoint as the standpoint of the protagonist" (1979, 102).

3. Unless otherwise indicated, all translations in this introduction have been supplied by the editors.

4. For examples of such failures of communication within the narratives, see the chapters by Kurz, Miller, and Neumann in the present volume.

5. Thus the central argument in Walter Sokel's major study, *Franz Kafka: Tragik und Ironie* (1964), is that Kafka's entire narrative world is structured not by a singular perspective but by conflict between two aspects or dimensions of the self. See also his essay of 1984 on "Narzißmus, Magie und die Funktion des Erzählens," where narration as a communicative act is expressly set against the "magic" of withdrawal into a solipsistic world of self-indulgent *Belustigungen* ("amusements").

6. See, for example, Richard Sheppard's study of *The Castle* (1973) in which the patterns of repetition, parallelism and inversion are likened to Brecht's technique of

distancing. The narrator's critical posture toward the protagonist is also central to the studies by Henel (1967), Kobs (1970), and Pascal (1982).

7. The shifting narrative perspectives analyzed in Gerhard Neumann's chapter on "The Stoker" may be rooted in this "dispersed" sense of identity. See also the comments by Ronald Speirs on the very early story about a shopkeeper's return from work. The metaphor of the "rhizome" in the study by Deleuze and Guattari (1986) elaborates this idea in the context of an "anti Oedipal" reading.

8. Kafka repeatedly referred in his letters to Felice to an incident in which Flaubert, observing a family out for a walk, commented "ils sont dans le vrai." The conflicts in Kafka between the compulsion to write and his guilt about writing, and the imprint of these conflicts on his method of narration, are a central concern of Stanley Corngold's *Lambent Traces* (2004).

9. By "strategic considerations" Kafka was referring to his having become increasingly reluctant to write letters because correspondence brought with it not only the danger of being less than entirely honest (out of tact) but also the risk of having one's feelings distorted by the "ghosts" that play with words during their epistolary transmission.

10. For an analysis of the elusiveness or instability of meaning generated by Kafka's narrative techniques, see Neumann's influential essay of 1968, "Umkehrung und Ablenkung: Franz Kafkas 'Gleitendes Paradox.'" Neumann's close reading of short texts gives a more detailed account of paradox as a linguistic effect than that provided by Politzer (1961).

11. For a study that puts the metaphor of the "staging" of behavior and events at the center of the analysis of narration, see James Rolleston's study *Kafka's Narrative Theater* (1974).

12. See Malcolm Pasley, "Der Schreibakt und das Geschriebene: Zur Frage der Entstehung von Kafkas Texten" (1978). The essays by Pasley (1978) and Schillemeit (2007), which are based on their work on Kafka's manuscripts as editors of the critical edition, have demonstrated convincingly the intimate connections between the processes of writing and the progress of narration in Kafka's texts.

13. For an exploration of this topic from a variety of perspectives, see Sandberg and Lothe (2002).

14. Arguably, the most radical version of the view that Kafka's narratives are concerned entirely with the act of narration itself, which struggles incessantly with the impossibility of knowing how to begin or how to proceed beyond the arbitrarily set beginning marked by the first words on the page, is that developed by Klaus Ramm both in his monograph, *Reduktion als Erzählprinzip bei Kafka* (2006) and in his contribution to the *Kafka-Handbuch* edited by Hartmut Binder (1979). Here "Reduktion" refers to the reduction of writing to concern with its own processes. The studies by Corngold (2004) and Koelb (1989) also concentrate on the self-reflexivity of Kafka's "linguistic imagination."

15. See, for example, David Constantine's chapter "Kafka's Writing and Our Reading" (2002, 9–24), the chapter "Reading Kafka" in Speirs and Sandberg (1997, 17–28), and Schmidt's survey of approaches to the "Türhüterlegende" (2007).

Works Cited

Allemann, Beda. 1998. Stehender Sturmlauf: Zeit und Geschichte im Werk Kafkas. (First published 1962.) In *Zeit und Geschichte im Werk Kafkas,* 15–36. Göttingen: Wallstein Verlag.

Beicken, Peter U. 1979. Erzählweise. In *Kafka-Handbuch,* ed. Hartmut Binder. Vol. 2, *Das Werk und seine Wirkung,* 36–48. Stuttgart: Alfred Kröner Verlag.

Beißner, Friedrich. 1983. *Der Erzähler Franz Kafka und andere Vorträge.* Frankfurt am Main: Suhrkamp Verlag. The first of these collected lectures was published as a brochure in 1952. *Der Erzähler Franz Kafka.* Stuttgart: Kohlhammer.

Binder, Hartmut. 1979. Bauformen. In *Kafka-Handbuch,* ed. Hartmut Binder. Vol. 2, *Das Werk und seine Wirkung,* 48–93. Stuttgart: Alfred Kröner Verlag.

Bohrer, Karl Heinz. 2005. Literatur ist nicht Kultur: Zur Verteidigung einer Disziplin. *Süddeutsche Zeitung* 251 (October 31–November 1): 20.

Brod, Max. 1966. *Über Franz Kafka.* Frankfurt am Main: Fischer.

Constantine, David. 2002. Kafka's writing and our reading. In *The Cambridge companion to Kafka,* ed. Julian Preece, 9–24. Cambridge: Cambridge Univ. Press.

Corngold, Stanley. 1986. *The fate of the self: German writers and French theory.* New York: Columbia Univ. Press.

———. 2004. *Lambent traces: Franz Kafka.* Princeton, NJ: Princeton Univ. Press.

Deleuze, Gilles, and Félix Guattari. 1986. *Kafka: Toward a minor literature.* Minneapolis: Univ. of Minnesota Press.

Henel, Ingeborg. 1967. Die Deutbarkeit von Kafkas Werken. *Zeitschrift für deutsche Philologie* 86 (2): 250–66.

Jagow, Bettina von, and Oliver Jahraus, eds. 2008. *Kafka-Handbuch: Leben—Werk—Wirkung.* Göttingen: Vandenhoeck & Ruprecht.

Kobs, Jörgen. 1970. *Kafka: Untersuchungen zu Bewußtsein und Sprache seiner Gestalten.* Ed. Ursula Brech. Bad Homburg: Athenäum Verlag.

Koelb, Clayton. 1989. *Kafka's rhetoric: The passion of reading.* Ithaca, NY: Cornell Univ. Press.

Neumann, Gerhard. 1968. Umkehrung und Ablenkung: Franz Kafkas "Gleitendes Paradox." *Deutsche Vierteljahresschrift für Literaturwissenschaft und Geistesgeschichte. Sonderheft, Literatur des 20. Jahrhunderts* 42: 702–44.

Pascal, Roy. 1982. *Kafka's narrators: A study of his stories and sketches.* Cambridge: Cambridge Univ. Press.

Pasley, Malcolm. 1978. Der Schreibakt und das Geschriebene: Zur Frage der Entstehung von Kafkas Texten. In *Franz Kafka: Themen und Probleme,* ed. Claude David, 9–25. Göttingen: Vandenhoeck & Ruprecht.

Phelan, James. 2007. *Experiencing fiction: Judgments, progressions, and the rhetorical theory of narrative.* Columbus: Ohio State Univ. Press.

Politzer, Heinrich. 1961. *Franz Kafka: Parable and paradox.* Ithaca, NY: Cornell Univ. Press.

Ramm, Klaus. 1979. Handlungsführung und Gedankenführung. In *Kafka-Handbuch,* ed. Hartmut Binder. Vol. 2, *Das Werk und seine Wirkung,* 93–107. Stuttgart: Alfred Kröner Verlag.

———. 2006. *Reduktion als Erzählprinzip bei Kafka.* Frankfurt am Main: Athenäum.

Rolleston, James. 1974. *Kafka's narrative theater.* University Park: Pennsylvania State Univ. Press.

Sandberg, Beatrice, and Jakob Lothe, eds. 2002. *Franz Kafka: Zur ethischen und ästhetischen Rechtfertigung.* Freiburg: Rombach Verlag.

Schillemeit, Jost. 2007. Das unterbrochene Schreiben: Zur Entstehung von Kafkas Roman *Der Verschollene.* In *Kafka-Studien,* ed. Barbara Elling, 137–52. New York: Lang.

Schmidt, Friedrich. 2007. *Text und Interpretation: Zur Deutungsproblematik bei Franz Kafka.* Würzburg: Königshausen & Neumann.

Sheppard, Richard. 1973. *On Kafka's castle: A study.* London: Croom Helm.

Sokel, Walter. 1964. *Franz Kafka: Tragik und Ironie: Zur Struktur seiner Kunst.* Munich: Langen Müller.

———. 1984. Narzißmus, Magie und die Funktion des Erzählens in Kafkas *Beschreibung eines Kampfes:* Zur Figurenkonzeption, Geschehensstruktur und Poetologie in Kafkas Erstlingswerk. In *Der junge Kafka,* ed. Gerhard Kurz, 102–32. Frankfurt am Main: Suhrkamp.

Speirs, Ronald, and Beatrice Sandberg. 1997. *Franz Kafka.* Basingstoke: Macmillan.

Walser, Martin. 1961. *Beschreibung einer Form: Versuch über Franz Kafka.* Munich: Carl Hanser.

1

PROGRESSION, SPEED, AND JUDGMENT IN "DAS URTEIL"

James Phelan

This chapter seeks to open up some two-way traffic between Kafka the narrative artist and the rhetorical theory of narrative. More specifically, I seek to identify the narrative logic underlying what I take to be the irreducible strangeness of Kafka's "Das Urteil" ("The Judgment") and then to use the results to expand the explanatory power of rhetorical theory. I choose "Das Urteil" as my case study for three reasons. First, although I do not view the story as representing the quintessence of Kafka's narrative practice, it was a significant milestone in his career. "Das Urteil" is widely acknowledged to be, in Frederick Karl's words, "the first of [Kafka's] mature works" (1991, 434), and Kafka himself regarded the eight-hour writing session on the night of September 22–23, 1912, which ended with his completion of the story, as one of the formative experiences in his development as a writer. Second, the story has received extensive, insightful comments from critics, thus relieving me of the burden of producing an original reading of the story and allowing me to focus on explaining the underlying sources of its strangeness, which I also take to be a source of its power. In other words, like many other critics, I want to respect and hold onto the story's strangeness rather than trying to master it—even as I offer an account of its underlying logic. Third, in some recent work, I have been examining the interconnections between the concepts of progression and judgment, and Kafka's story provides an especially good location from which to extend and test that work.

With respect to progression, "Das Urteil" opens up issues about how we determine narrative speed and about the nature of surprise endings. With respect to judgment, "Das Urteil" invites a consideration of the connection between the complexities of interpretive and ethical judgments of the characters and their actions, on the one hand, and the ethics of Kafka's storytelling itself, on the other. Let me, then, start down my two-way highway—or winding country road—by saying more about my version of the rhetorical approach to narrative.

This approach conceives of narrative as a purposeful communicative act. In this view, narrative is not just a representation of events, a fusion of story and discourse, but is also itself an event—one in which someone is doing something with a representation of events, and that doing something involves a design on an audience. In this way, the approach attends to both the consciousness designing the communicative act, the implied author, and his or her intended or authorial audience. As the reference to the implied author suggests, my version of the approach has its roots in Wayne C. Booth's work. In *The Rhetoric of Fiction* (1961/1983), Booth argues that prevailing modernist dogmas about novelistic practices such as "showing is better than telling" are inadequate by demonstrating that the effectiveness of any technique depends on how well it helps authors accomplish their purposes—or to put it another way, narrative technique is always a means to an end, and it needs to be assessed not according to an abstract rule but according to how well it serves its specific purpose. In developing this argument about overt commentary by authorial narrators, Booth also realized that the author's use of any technique (showing, telling, reliable narration, unreliable narration, etc.) has rhetorical consequences; that is, it influences the implied author's relation to his audience. My version of the rhetorical approach follows Booth's lead in seeing that relationship between the implied author and the authorial audience as lying at the center of the experience of narrative, but my version expands upon Booth's work by developing some new concepts, which are designed to analyze the multiple dimensions of that relationship.

The approach also recognizes that the concept of an authorial audience (proposed and developed by Peter J. Rabinowitz [1976, 1987/1998]) is a valuable heuristic, a hypothetical ideal reader who is able to be the implied author's perfect audience. This concept has some similarities with Iser's concept of the implied reader, but the two approaches are far from interchangeable, and that disparity points to a larger difference between the rhetorical approach and Iser's phenomenological approach. The concepts are similar because they both refer to hypothetical audiences that are implied by the text. But the concepts are ultimately distinct because they are connected to different accounts of the activity of reading. For Iser, the main activity of reading consists in filling in the gaps that literary texts inevitably contain, with actual readers filling in those gaps in different ways. For the rhetorical theorist, the main activity of reading is responding to the text as it has been designed by its implied author. From the rhetorical perspective, Iser is describing only one kind of textual design (namely, one with gaps that are designed to be filled in different ways). Rhetorical theory posits that some gaps are designed to be closed in a determinate way, that some are designed to be closed in a variety of ways, and that still others are designed to resist our capacity to fill them. Indeed, I shall argue that "Das Urteil" has a central gap of this last kind. Like Rabinowitz, I am interested in how actual readers can become members of the authorial audience. To put this point another way, the heuristic construct of the authorial audience identifies a role the actual reader seeks to take on. Thus, when I use the first-person plural pronoun here to describe how Kafka's audience responds to the story, I am referring to Kafka's authorial audience.

More formally, the rhetorical theorist defines narrative as somebody telling somebody else on some occasion and for some purpose(s) that something happened. The concept of narrative progression attends to the two main participants in the rhetorical action—the somebody who tells and the somebody else who is told—and to the means by which they communicate. Focusing on the dynamics of progression is a particularly effective way of getting at the trajectory of the implied author-authorial audience relationship over the course of the narrative.

This definition of narrative helps us see that the rhetorical situation in fictional narrative is doubled: an implied author communicates to the authorial audience by means of a narrator's communication to a (characterized or uncharacterized) narratee. In addition, narrative, whether fictional or nonfictional, is a double-layered phenomenon in another sense: it involves both a dynamics of character, event, and telling and a dynamics of audience response. The phrase "somebody telling . . . that something happened" gets at the first layer: narrative involves the report of a sequence of related events during which the characters and/or their situations undergo some *change.* As I have discussed elsewhere,[1] the report of that change typically proceeds through the introduction, complication, and resolution (in whole or in part) of unstable situations within, between, or among the characters. These dynamics of instability may be accompanied by a dynamics of tension in the telling—unstable relations among authors, narrators, and audiences—and the interaction of the two sets of dynamics (as in narratives that employ unreliable narration) may have significant consequences for our understanding of the "something that happened."

Narrative judgments are crucial components of the second layer of progression. The dynamics of audience response depend on two main readerly activities: observing and judging. (In this respect, narrative is different from lyric, which invites us to participate in rather than judge a speaker's emotions or attitudes.) As observers, we perceive the characters of the narrative both as external to ourselves and as distinct from their implied authors. Consequently, we make interpretive and ethical judgments about them, their situations, and their choices. Furthermore, our interpretive and ethical judgments are integral to our emotional responses as well as to our desires concerning future events. In addition, this trajectory of judgment and response is intertwined with another kind of judgment—an aesthetic judgment about the overall quality of our experience, both as it is happening and once it is complete. Finally, because readerly dynamics involve interpretive, ethical, and aesthetic judgments that develop over time and that thus can themselves be revised, the readerly side of progression often involves a process of configuration and reconfiguration—that is, a process of forming a hypothesis about the trajectory of the narrative and about how its parts contribute to that trajectory and then revising that hypothesis in light of new judgments.

In sum, from the rhetorical perspective, narrative involves the interaction of two kinds of change over time: that experienced by the characters and that experienced by the audience in its developing responses to the characters' changes. Moreover, these two layers of progression, the textual dynamics rooted in instabilities and tensions, and the readerly dynamics rooted in observation and judgment, are reciprocally influential. Even as the audience's trajectory through the progression depends on textual dynamics, the author constructs those dynamics with one eye on how they will affect the reader—as a moment's reflecton on narratives with surprise endings such as "Das Urteil" indicates. Analyzing the interactions between progression and judgments allows one to develop an understanding of a narrative's underlying logic and of a narrative's rhetorical purposes. Such analysis reveals (1) the principles upon which the author constructs the narrative's unfolding in time and (2) the interpretive, ethical, and aesthetic underpinnings of its audience's responses.[2]

Before I turn to Kafka's story, I want to touch on three other consequences of this rhetorical conception of narrative. (1) Since judgment is itself such a necessary part of human life, narratives often represent characters making judgments. Consequently, the readerly dynamics of progression often lead us to judge characters' judgments. "Das Urteil" often puts us in this position. (2) Just as there is an ethics of the told (that is, an ethics that applies to the characters and their interactions), there is also an ethics of the telling (that is, an ethical dimension to the interactions among authors, narrators, and audiences). (3) The system of instabilities and tensions in combination with characterization and narrative technique helps define the relation among three broad components of readerly interest that I call the mimetic, the thematic, and the synthetic. The mimetic component, what Aristotle called "imitation," involves our interest in the characters and events; the thematic involves our interest in the characters and events as a means to explore ideas or beliefs about the world; and the synthetic involves our interest in characters and events as artificial constructions of an authorial design. Different narratives will establish different relations among these three components as they pursue their different purposes. The larger point here is that the rhetorical approach does not assume, as much other criticism does, that the goal of interpretation is to establish thematic meaning. Instead, it is interested in the thematic as one of the components of readerly interest and one of the possible purposes of narrative as a rhetorical action. In addition, by displacing thematic interpretation from the center of the critical enterprise and focusing on progression, judgment, and the underlying logic of narrative, the rhetorical approach can, in a case such as "Das Urteil," help explain why the narrative is amenable to so many thematic interpretations.[3]

Progression, Speed, and Judgment in "Das Urteil"

Since there has been so much good commentary on the story, I will work from a helpful summary by Henry Sussman of what that commentary has established and then suggest how a rhetorical approach can extend and refine this baseline understanding. In a section titled "The Aesthetics of Confusion" within a broader essay on Kafka's aesthetics, Sussman writes that "onto Georg Bendemann's best-case scenario of his role in his family, his forthcoming marriage, his business success, and his empathy for his friend, Kafka seamlessly splices, within the continuity of the narrative, his father's very different account of the events and arenas in Georg's life. The 'hinge' or 'graft' between the counternarratives is a fulcrum for confusion existing at least *in potentia* for the duration of Kafka's fiction" (2002, 135). From the perspective of rhetorical theory, Sussman's overview of the story is fine as far as it goes, but it does not go far enough. Indeed, because it posits a standoff between Georg's best-case scenario and Herr Bendemann's counternarrative, it ends up flattening the story, sacrificing its strangeness to an account of confusion as unresolvable ambiguity. Focusing on progression and judgment leads to a revision of Sussman's account, a revision that seeks to preserve strangeness in three main ways: (1) by giving the speed of the narrative its due; (2) by distinguishing more clearly between what is determinate in the story and what remains in an interpretive gap; and (3) by accounting for the consequences of that gap for our overall experience of the story. The results of this analysis will lead me in turn, first, to consider first, the traffic going the other way—that is, how Kafka's story complicates some ideas of rhetorical theory—and second, to assess the ethics of Kafka's telling.

Looking globally at the progression of "Das Urteil," we can discern three recognizably distinct stages. Stage one consists of Georg Bendemann sitting at his writing desk and reflecting on his relationship with the friend to whom he has just written a letter. Stage two consists of Georg's conflictual conversation with his father, a conversation that culminates in his father's condemning him to death by drowning. Stage three consists of Georg's acceptance of and immediate capitulation to his father's judgment. Thus, we move from a stage where Georg is alone, to one where he interacts with his father, and then back to one where he is alone. In addition to highlighting this movement, identifying the three stages also helps us recognize the relation between the story's strangeness and its narrative speed, and indeed looking at that relation can help lead us to a richer understanding of narrative speed from a rhetorical perspective. Identifying the three stages of "Das Urteil" helps us see that it begins at a leisurely pace in stage one, rapidly accelerates in stages two and three, and then slows down again in the final sentences. It will be helpful to sketch this movement, first in broad terms so that we can grasp the overall pattern, and then to move to a closer analysis of its details. That closer analysis will benefit from an engagement with Jan Baetens and Katherine Hume's recent theoretical discussion of narrative speed, a discussion that itself arises from Hume's initial proposals (2006, 2005).

My initial description of the story's speed is more than impressionistic because it is based on the interaction of textual and readerly dynamics in each of the stages. The first stage is leisurely in spite of its revealing two instabilities, because the initial one, about Georg's relation to his friend, appears to get resolved within this first stage, and because the next, more substantial, instability, involving dissonance between Georg's ethical character and his own understanding of that ethical character, does not get complicated until stage two.

Furthermore, the interpretive and ethical judgments evolve slowly, in part as a result of Kafka's handling of temporality in the first stage. We meet Georg after he has just finished his letter, and, after reading about a third of the story, we learn, through the narrator's statement, that he has been sitting at the desk for a long time. In the space between the two statements describing Georg at his desk, Kafka's narrator does not call attention to time passing in the narrative present but rather engages in a narration about the past, reviewing Georg's perceptions of his friend, Georg's self-flattering comparisons between their respective situations, and the contents of the letter itself. While this material introduces the dissonance between Georg's judgment of himself and our judgment of him, the movement into the past works as a brake on the story's pace. Kafka's strategy allows for the gradual evolution of our judgments about Georg even as it defers any complication of the instability until the review of the past is complete.

Once Georg goes to talk with his father, however, the pace of the narrative accelerates rapidly because (1) the instabilities get complicated with each line of dialogue and (2) each new complication requires new interpretive and ethical judgments. As a result, Kafka's authorial audience is likely to have difficulty handling the accelerated pace. At the end of the second stage, the speed shifts into yet a higher gear as the progression takes a sharp and sudden turn to its climax in Herr Bendemann's judgment of Georg. The breakneck pace continues as the story hurtles on to the third stage, which begins with Georg's surprising acceptance of the judgment. Just as important, when Herr Bendemann delivers his judgment at the end of stage two, the authorial audience's struggle to keep up with the necessary interpretive and ethical judgments can meet with only partial success because Kafka builds into that moment a major interpretive gap. Consequently, we follow Georg in his headlong rush to the river with only partial comprehension of the reasons for his behavior, something that further contributes to the story's speed: events are happening faster than we can comprehend them.

Once Georg is on the verge of drowning himself, Kafka slows the pace again by focusing on his last actions and last words, allowing the audience to take in the deliberateness of Georg's act. This slowing down does not allow us to close the interpretive gap but instead emphasizes both the radical change the story has represented and the strangeness associated with that change. Among other things, the final sentence of the story, "In diesem Augenblick ging über die Brücke ein geradezu unendlicher Verkehr" (KAF, 1:52) ("At that moment the traffic going over the bridge was nothing short of infinite" [KSS, 12]), in introducing for the first time a narrative perspective other than Georg's, underlines that strangeness by way of contrast between what has just happened and the everyday quality of what it describes.

In light of this general sketch of the story's progression, I identify much of the story's power and strangeness as stemming from its combining shifts in speed with the unfillable gap between the end of stage two and the beginning of stage three. If the claim holds up, then Kafka has discovered something remarkable: a way to make a significant interpretive gap surrounding the climax of a narrative enhance rather than detract from an audience's interpretive, ethical, and aesthetic experience. In other words, though the climactic events do not finally yield to our efforts to comprehend them, their recalcitrance enhances the story's power. I call this kind of recalcitrance "textual stubbornness," and I will have more to say about it as the analysis proceeds. Let us turn now to a longer—and slower—look at the story's progression.

Because Kafka uses analepsis so extensively in stage one, a major function of Georg's eight paragraphs of reflections is exposition, and that exposition reveals that, according to his own judgments, he has made his way in the world very well indeed. Although his mother died two years previously, he has become the dominant force in the increasingly successful family business, and he has recently become engaged to Frieda Brandenfeld, "einem Mädchen aus wohlhabender Familie" (KAF, 1:42) ("a young woman from a well-to-do family" [KSS, 5]). Indeed, the only apparent problem in Georg's life that emerges from these reflections is his inability to speak openly and honestly to his childhood friend. But Georg himself, in order to please Frieda, decides to write to the friend, and thus, as noted above, that instability appears to get resolved.

Nevertheless, Kafka's handling of the narration brilliantly reveals that underneath this superficial instability is a more substantial one, involving Georg's relation to himself. As many critics have pointed out, Kafka uses Georg's perspective to show that while Georg appears to make reasonable judgments about the difference between his situation and that of his friend, those judgments are ultimately self-serving. John M. Ellis offers a perceptive summary of this effect: "The superficial impression of the breadth of [Georg's] human sympathy for his friend is overshadowed by a contrary impression of narrowness in Georg's judgments of value, for judgments of his friend's life are made rigidly on the basis of Georg's values" (1977, 78). Ellis's subsequent general summary is over the top, but it effectively captures both the instability within Georg and the discrepancy between his self-judgments and those that Kafka guides his audience to make. "There is, after all, something destructive in Georg's 'considerateness' toward his friend; it seems to provide the opportunity for an orgy of denigration of him, a very full series of imaginings of his helplessness, wretchedness and even disgrace which are very flattering to Georg" (Ellis 1977, 79).[4]

This dimension of the first stage of the progression becomes more prominent when we reflect on what it reveals about Georg's investment in this correspondence. He speaks to Frieda about their "besondere Korrespondenzverhältnis" (KAF, 1:42) (the "special relationship of correspondence between them"), when all the evidence is that their correspondence in recent years has been anything but special. Georg writes only about "bedeutungslose Vorfälle" (KAF, 1:42) ("insignificant events") while his friend expresses his sympathy about the death of Georg's mother "mit Trockenheit" (KAF, 1:41) ("with dryness"). More significantly, after finishing the letter, Georg sits at his desk lost in thought for a long time. We infer that the correspondence is fulfilling some purpose for Georg beyond the maintenance of the friendship itself, namely, the shoring up of his own self-esteem as he is poised to take his next step into adulthood with his marriage to Frieda. Thus, as we come to the end of the first stage of the progression, Kafka opens up a substantial distance between Georg's interpretive and ethical judgments and those of his authorial audience.

As the progression moves into the second stage and picks up speed, Kafka guides us to see that Georg's approach to his father is similar to his way of thinking about his friend. That is, Kafka shows Georg to be acting in a way that he regards as showing legitimate concern for his father, but Kafka also allows us to see that Georg is ultimately self-serving and condescending. Here, too, Georg's approach initially appears to serve him well, as he blunts his father's skepticism about the existence of his friend by saying that his father is much more important and by helping him get undressed and then carrying him to the bed and covering him up. However, once Herr Bendemann rises from the bed and escalates his verbal assault on Georg, a new element enters the progression. Georg loses not only the upper hand in the conflict but also full control over his own mind. After his father makes his strongest accusations, namely, that because Frieda lifted her skirts, Georg decided to betray his friend, profane his mother's memory, and put his father in bed, the narrator reports: "Vor einer langen Weile hatte er sich fest entschlossen, alles vollkommen genau zu beobachten, damit er nicht irgendwie auf Umwegen, von hinten her, von oben herab überrascht werden könne. Jetzt erinnerte er sich wieder an den längst vergessenen Entschluß und vergaß ihn" (KAF, 1:50) ("A long time ago he had firmly decided to observe everything very exactly so as to avoid being taken by surprise in some devious way, from behind or from above. Now he remembered that long forgotten decision once again and forgot it" [KSS, 10]). This pattern of a disparity between Georg's intentions and his actual agency continues, as he blurts an insult at his father—"Komödiant!" (KAF, 1:50) ("Play actor!" [KSS, 10])—and as his efforts to mock his father ironically turn into a confirmation of his father's accusations.

In the authorial audience, we are able to make two related interpretive judgments. First, as Herr Bendemann attacks Georg's conception of his relationship with his friend, Georg begins to lose the sense of self shored up by that conception. Second, as this sense of self breaks down, Georg begins to feel guilty, though the exact nature and extent of that guilt is not yet clear. Significantly, just before Herr Bendemann's judgment, Georg accuses his father of lying in wait for him, "Du hast mir also aufgelauert!" (KAF, 1:52) ("And so you've been lying in ambush for me!" [KSS, 12]), but the accusation implicitly reveals both his powerlessness and his guilt. Before I consider our ethical judgments of Georg here, it will be helpful to consider our interpretive and ethical judgments of Herr Bendemann—and of his judgments.

Kafka claimed that he was thinking of Freud in writing the story, and indeed much of the father-son dynamic can be explained as an Oedipal struggle (see, for example, Hughes [1995]). But from the rhetorical perspective what is more significant is that, even as Kafka gradually increases our distance from Georg's interpretive and ethical judgments, he keeps us even more distant from most of Herr Bendemann's judgments. Once Herr Bendemann stands on the bed and goes on the attack, he reveals himself to be not a loving but a jealous and vengeful father. In addition, as Russell Berman perceptively points out (2002), Herr Bendemann contradicts himself. He contends, first, that Georg has no friend in St. Petersburg and, later, that Georg and the friend have been in constant correspondence. Herr Bendemann attacks Georg both for wanting to marry and for delaying the marriage. Finally, he berates Georg for both his childishness and his ambitions with the business and with his marriage. The resulting interpretive and ethical distance between Herr Bendemann and Kafka's audience is compounded by Kafka's restricting the focalization to Georg, so that we never see Herr Bendemann from the inside. At the same time, Kafka effectively uses the dialogue (1) to show that Herr Bendemann does have what Sussman calls a counternarrative to Georg's account of his life and (2) to suggest that two of Herr Bendemann's motives are to rebel against Georg's neglect of him and to shake Georg out of his complacent self-satisfaction.

When we get to Herr Bendemann's ultimate judgment of Georg, Kafka does not give us enough guidance to make a clear interpretive judgment of Herr Bendemann's motives or of its basis in Georg's behavior. Why should this father, who claims to love his son, condemn that son to death? Not even the accusations the father makes warrant such a harsh judgment. The psychoanalytic explanation, namely that Herr Bendemann is a version of Laius striking back against Oedipus, strikes me as insufficiently responsive not only to the strangeness of the story but also to the particular form that the striking back takes, since Georg/Oedipus could easily sidestep or repel this verbal strike by rejecting the judgment. Is there some other knowledge that either Herr Bendemann or Georg has that we don't that makes the judgment appropriate? Why the judgment, and then why the acceptance of it? These questions hover over this moment in the progression, and because they remain unanswerable, Kafka introduces a permanent gap in the progression.

Let me clarify the claim I am making about the nature of this interpretive gap and thus clarify what I mean by textual stubbornness. This gap is significantly different, for example, from the one that exists regarding Herr Bendemann's fate after he delivers the judgment. That gap—specifically, whether Georg's hearing him crash onto the bed is a sign of temporary collapse or of death—is an issue about whether one event or another occurs in the fabula, and it is a gap that underlines the compulsion Georg feels to act on his father's judgment. Georg hears the crash but is too intent on taking his own life even to wonder what the crash signifies. In other words, Kafka's decision to leave this gap in the textual dynamics contributes to the effectiveness of our interpretive and ethical judgments of Georg and thus to the story's progression as a whole. The gap is not an instance of stubbornness but of determinate ambiguity. That is, we can adequately fill in the gap: there are only two possibilities, and though they are substantially different, their consequences for our understanding of the protagonist's action are not. By contrast, the gap surrounding Herr Bendemann's judgment is not a gap in the fabula—the event occurs—but a gap in readerly dynamics that leaves us in a position of being unable to fully interpret the judgment, meaning, in turn, that we cannot make a clear ethical judgment of it, of Herr Bendemann, or of Georg in his acceptance of it. This gap is an instance of stubbornness because we cannot comprehend the event within the logic of the narrative to this point, and yet the event remains crucial to the overall progression.

One way in which Kafka maintains stubbornness is to block a conventional judgment that Georg is overreacting to his father's condemnation by showing Georg regaining his agency, even as the pace of the progression slows. Although, as Ronald Speirs has noted (1987), Georg is initially driven out of the house by an impersonal force referred to only by *es* (it), once he is hanging from the bridge, his agency returns. Georg thinks about when he should let go, and he utters his declaration of love for both of his parents. The slower pace, the return of Georg's agency, the affirmation of his love for his parents—all these elements underline the point that he accepts the judgment, and that conscious acceptance unsettles our ethical judgment of Georg. We can conclude neither that he should nor that he should not have accepted his father's judgment, even as the story puts pressure on us to judge Georg's decision.

At the same time, the interpretive gap and Georg's acceptance of his father's judgment have another significant effect on the progression, specifically on the relation between its mimetic component, on the one hand, and its thematic and synthetic components, on the other. Although John Ellis rightly points out that even the first paragraph of the story does not fully conform to the tenets of straightforward realism, the dominant signals of the first stage of the progression are those that activate our interest in its mimetic component, and the story rewards our efforts to read such things as the psychology of the characters. But one consequence of the textual stubbornness is to move the story from a straight mimetic account to one in which the thematic and the synthetic become more prominent. The gap encourages us to read the story as a parable rather than as a psychological study. In such readings, Georg and Herr Bendemann function as types whose interactions we can explain less by reference to plausible psychological behavior of autonomous individuals than by reference to Kafka's working out of the relations among certain ideas. But it is important to see that while the move to a greater emphasis on the thematic and the synthetic encourages such readings, it does not resolve the story's textual stubbornness. Instead, it is the textual stubbornness itself that allows for the proliferation of such readings. "Das Urteil" is a parable of guilt that includes elements of father-son struggles going back to Oedipus. It is a story about the power of patriarchy, about both the necessity and the inevitable imperfections of judgment. And it is many other things as well. These thematic readings can be very insightful, and, indeed, I have learned from many of them. But to the extent that they claim to close the interpretive gap at the climax of the story, they overreach. Even if we say that "Das Urteil" belongs to the genre of the parable and that parables are often enigmatic, we cannot convert the stubbornness of Kafka's story into a more conventional textual difficulty, because the location of the unbridgeable gap at the climax of the story moves it beyond the enigmatic to the inscrutable. All of these considerations have consequences for our aesthetic judgments of the story, but I will defer that discussion until after I look at the traffic going in the other direction—that is, between "Das Urteil" and the rhetorical theory of narrative.

What Kafka Can Do for Rhetorical Theory

Traffic in this direction stops at four stations: at the first, a principle of rhetorical theory gets reinforced; at the second, rhetorical theory offers some new generalizations about narrative speed; at the third, rhetorical theory learns something new about progressions with surprise endings; and at the fourth, rhetorical theory adds to its understanding of textual stubbornness. The principle at the first station is that rhetorical theory wants to work in an *a posteriori* fashion. Although the theory has constructed a large warehouse of terms and concepts (and I have given you just a small sample in this chapter), it regards them not as forming preset molds into which narratives will inevitably fit—or must be made to fit—but rather as providing tools for opening up the workings of individual narratives. "Das Urteil" reinforces this lesson because it does not fit any predetermined rhetorical mode, and, indeed, the challenge it presents to the rhetorical critic is to uncover its logic while also preserving its strangeness.

At the same time, rhetorical theory is not averse to offering generalizations after it has done its *a posteriori* work on a number of narratives. To eschew generalization altogether is, in effect, to be anti-theory. It is also to suggest that what one learns from the analysis of one narrative cannot apply to the analysis of another. The delicate matter of course is to engage in appropriate generalization, to develop theoretical conclusions that help us work on new narratives without leading us to take the High Priori Road. I shall keep this point in mind as I move on to the next three stations on this side of the road.

Station two. Attending to speed in "Das Urteil" helps rhetorical theory extend the recent work of Jan Baetens and Katherine Hume (2006), who have offered a helpful overview of narrative speed as involving both textual and readerly components. This dual concern with text and audience means that their findings are of special interest to rhetorical theory. On the textual side, Baetens and Hume identify speed effects as occurring at the story level (where there are references to and descriptions of speed), at the discourse level (where effects fall along a spectrum that has elliptical syntax at one end and pauses in the narration of events in favor of description at the other),[5] and at the narration level (where the typography or the oral delivery of the text affects the speed). On the readerly side, Baetens and Hume work with the distinctions among the implied reader (the authorial audience in rhetorical theory), the narratee, and the empirical reader (the flesh-and-blood reader in rhetorical theory). Baetens and Hume note that the first two audiences are encoded in the text while the third operates independently of textual encoding. They also make the astute observation that encoded speed is "never just determined by what is being read here and now, but also by what has just been read and by what one has been expecting to read immediately afterwards" (2006, 352). In this sense, as Baetens and Hume point out, speed is connected to the larger concept of textual rhythm.

My version of rhetorical theory is primarily interested in encoded speed, and I endorse Baetens and Hume's point about the relation between speed and rhythm (2006). But as my analysis of "Das Urteil" suggests, rhetorical theory can offer greater precision about the interaction between textual and readerly components of speed through its attention to the dynamics of progression and especially through its attention to the role of interpretive and ethical judgments—and to the strategic placement of an interpretive gap. In other words, what Kafka's story teaches us is that a narrative can accelerate its pace, not simply by increasing the pace of the complication of instabilities but also by accompanying that acceleration with an increasing number of interpretive and ethical judgments—and by requiring that the audience jump over a space in which one would normally expect to make such judgments. Indeed, as I have indicated above, this combination of accelerated judgments with the strategic gap seems central to both the story's power and its strangeness.

Station three. In my discussion of Edith Wharton's "Roman Fever" (1934/1997) in chapter four of *Experiencing Fiction,* I have made what I regarded as an appropriate generalization by proposing that effective surprise endings meet three conditions. The surprise must (1) lead to a plausible reconfiguration of the narrative, (2) be prepared for (that is, in retrospect, it must be part of a recognizable pattern), and (3) enhance in some way the overall effect of the narrative. Narratives in which the surprise depends on characters acting in accord with traits that they have not previously exhibited, narratives that include absolutely no clues to the surprise (for example, many versions of the "it was only a dream" ending), and narratives in which the surprise, though congruent and prepared for, is an elaborate contrivance rather than a necessary part of a larger purpose—all either fall flat or come across as ethical or aesthetic cheats.

With consummate skill, Wharton constructs "Roman Fever" so that it meets all of the conditions for a successful surprise ending. The story ends with Grace Ansley's surprising revelation to her rival Alida Slade that the father of Grace's admirable daughter Barbara is not Grace's husband, but Alida's. Grace's revelation causes both Alida and the authorial audience to reconfigure their understanding of what happened in Rome twenty-five years previously, when Alida developed a scheme to have Grace contract tuberculosis and so be unavailable as a possible love interest for her future husband, Delphin. Alida's scheme was to forge Delphin's signature to a note asking Grace to meet him after dark in the Colosseum. Thus, it is only with this final revelation that Alida realizes how her scheme brought about the tryst that led to Grace's conception of Barbara. The surprise fits with the previous progression because it does not contradict but rather rounds out our understanding of Grace's character, and it effectively concludes the women's conversation that has in some way been a re-enactment of the rivalry that they engaged in twenty-five years previously. The surprise has been prepared for in numerous ways, including the narrator's disclosure of seemingly incidental information about Barbara and the narrator's calling attention to odd emphases or silences in Grace's half of the conversation. And the surprise enhances the story by showing how its present-tense conversation not only re-enacts the rivalry but also concludes it in a similar way: Alida has been trying to establish her superiority over Grace only to discover once again that Grace has gotten the better of her.

Kafka's "Das Urteil" teaches rhetorical theory something new because its surprise ending works in a remarkably different way, but no less effectively. The stubbornness associated with the moment of judgment means both that the surprise is not fully congruent with the rest of the progression and that it is not prepared for in the way that the surprise of "Roman Fever" is. Nevertheless, as we have seen, the surprise significantly enhances the story's strange power and appeal. What "Das Urteil" teaches, then, is that the neat reversals and coherent reconfigurations that characterize "Roman Fever," Ambrose Bierce's "An Occurrence at Owl Creek Bridge" (1890), Ian McEwan's *Atonement* (2001), and other effective stories with surprising endings are not an absolute necessity for all narratives built on the principle of surprise. To put the lesson in more positive terms, "Das Urteil" shows that a limited stubbornness—even, or especially, when associated with a climactic moment in the progression—can significantly enhance the power of the story, even as it points to a purpose different from the kind we find in the stories that meet my three conditions. Rather than getting its power from a tighter and deeper understanding of the characters' actions, Kafka's story gets its power by keeping things open and broadening our explorations into the ethical and psychological dynamics—and thematic meanings—of the events we have just read about. In other words, the value added by the surprise is not that it takes us deeper into the mimetic situation but rather that it invites us to relate the story to an ever-widening range of issues and contexts.

Station four. The lesson here is about stubbornness itself. In my previous explorations of this phenomenon, I have focused on the recalcitrance we encounter in our efforts to interpret adequately characters such as Toni Morrison's Beloved in *Beloved* (1987), John Fowles's Sarah Woodruff in *The French Lieutenant's Woman* (1969), and Jim in Conrad's *Lord Jim* (1900). In an analysis of Robert Frost's "Home Burial" (1916) in *Experiencing Fiction* (2007), I have also considered the textual stubbornness that results when an author does not take sides in an argument between two sympathetic characters who embrace opposed ethical principles. The case of Kafka's practice in "Das Urteil" encourages me to propose the broad generalization that any element of a narrative is potentially available for the productive functions of the stubborn.[6]

Aesthetics and Ethics

As I turn toward my conclusion, the traffic of my discussion is ready to move back in the other direction and consider what the consequences of these conclusions are for our aesthetic judgments of "Das Urteil." Given what I've said so far, I realize that I have spoiled any possible surprise. The story is a remarkable aesthetic achievement, one whose speed, limited stubbornness, and consequent openness offer a strange and unsettling experience whose value is indisputable, even if—or because—it is not easy to pin down. To put this point another way, "Das Urteil" is a formally innovative story that suggests new possibilities for storytelling itself. It is no wonder that Kafka regarded his composition of the story as marking a significant phase in his development as a writer. In addition, the story's formal innovation is productive precisely because it brings us face-to-face with, among other things, the uncanny elements of father-son relationships and the unsettling nature of guilt, love, and individual agency.

Finally, I turn to consider the ethics of Kafka's telling as revealed in the trajectory of the implied author-authorial relationship across the progression. The implied Kafka is at once a subtle guide and a formidable figure who keeps his distance. Furthermore, at a key point in the trajectory, he leaves a major gap. Consequently, he is as interested in unsettling us as in guiding us—indeed, perhaps he guides us to the point at which he can unsettle us most profoundly. But it is also clear that he wants to unsettle us because he believes it will be for our own good. I, for one, am willing to conclude that he's right.

Notes

1. See *Experiencing Fiction* (Phelan 2007, 15–22, 151–54). For additional background, see *Reading People* (Phelan 1989), especially the introduction and chapter 4.

2. For a fuller discussion and demonstration of these points, see *Experiencing Fiction* (Phelan 2007).

3. For a fuller discussion of the rhetorical approach, see *Reading People* (Phelan 1989), *Narrative as Rhetoric* (Phelan 1996), *Living to Tell about It* (Phelan 2005), and *Experiencing Fiction* (Phelan 2007).

4. For additional—and very insightful—commentary on Ellis's reading, see Pascal (1982, 27–31). More generally, Pascal is a very fine reader of Kafka, and his larger conclusion about "Das Urteil," though arrived at via a different route, is similar to mine: the story leaves us with "a baffling and painful puzzle" (Pascal 1982, 30).

5. Baetens and Hume (2006) actually locate pauses for description at the story level, but that seems counterintuitive to me.

6. As these examples indicate, textual stubbornness is a feature available across genres and across works of different lengths. Although I believe, as my attention to narrative speed indicates, that the brevity of the short story form aids and abets the effectiveness of the stubbornness of "Das Urteil," I do not see any necessary general connection between brevity and stubbornness. Indeed, since stubbornness is textual recalcitrance that will not yield to our interpretive efforts and since reading always involves interpretation, stubbornness is potentially a feature of any text. But from an authorial perspective, the difference between constructing a textual recalcitrance that won't yield to interpretation and having that recalcitrance function to contribute to the power of one's design is huge.

Works Cited

Baetens, Jan, and Katherine Hume. 2006. Speed, rhythm, movement: A dialogue on K. Hume's article "Narrative speed." *Narrative* 14 (3): 349–55.

Berman, Russell A. 2002. Tradition and betrayal in "Das Urteil." In *A companion to the works of Franz Kafka,* ed. James Rolleston, 85–100. Rochester, NY: Camden House.

Booth, Wayne C. 1961/1983. *The rhetoric of fiction.* 2nd ed., Chicago: Univ. of Chicago Press.

Ellis, John M. 1977. The bizarre texture of "The judgment." In *The problem of "The judgment": Eleven approaches to Kafka's story,* ed. Angel Flores, 73–96. New York: Gordian.

Hughes, Kenneth. 1995. A psychoanalytic approach to "The judgment." In *Approaches to teaching Kafka's short fiction,* ed. Richard T. Gray, 84–93. New York: MLA Publications.

Hume, Katherine. 2005. Narrative speed in contemporary fiction. *Narrative* 13 (2): 105–24.

Iser, Wolfgang. *The implied reader: Patterns of communication in fiction from Bunyan to Beckett.* Baltimore: Johns Hopkins Univ. Press, 1974.

Karl, Frederick. 1991. *Franz Kafka: Representative man.* New York: Ticknor & Fields.

Pascal, Roy. 1982. *Kafka's narrators: A study of his stories and sketches.* Cambridge: Cambridge Univ. Press.

Phelan, James. 1989. *Reading people, reading plots: Character, progression, and the interpretation of narrative.* Chicago: Univ. of Chicago Press.

———. 1996. *Narrative as rhetoric: Technique, audiences, ethics, ideology.* Columbus: Ohio State Univ. Press.

———. 2005. *Living to tell about it: A rhetoric and ethics of character narration.* Ithaca, NY: Cornell Univ. Press.

———. 2007. *Experiencing fiction: Judgments, progressions, and the rhetorical theory of narrative.* Columbus: Ohio State Univ. Press.

Rabinowitz, Peter J. 1976. Truth in fiction: A reexamination of audiences. *Critical Inquiry* 4 (1): 121–41.

———. 1987/1998. *Before reading: Narrative conventions and the politics of interpretation.* Columbus: Ohio State Univ. Press.

Speirs, Ronald. 1987. Movement, time, language: Forms of instability in Kafka's "Das Urteil." *Forum for Modern Language Studies* 23 (3): 253–64.

Sussman, Henry. 2002. Kafka's aesthetics: A primer; From the fragments to the novels. In *A companion to the works of Franz Kafka,* ed. James Rolleston, 123–48. Rochester, NY: Camden House.

Wharton, Edith. 1934/1997. Roman fever. In *Roman fever and other stories,* 3–20. New York: Scribner.

2

THE HUMAN BODY AND THE HUMAN BEING IN "DIE VERWANDLUNG"

Anniken Greve

I

One of the great challenges when interpreting Kafka's texts is to describe correctly the difficulties they pose for their reader. Another is to respond to these difficulties in a way that allows them to play a role in the texts' rhetorical design and communicative effect. Having discussed the problems arising from relying on "allegorical equations of Kafka's figures with abstractions drawn from other systems, be they theology, philosophy, psychoanalysis or 'textual self-reflexivity,'" Ronald Speirs and Beatrice Sandberg settle for a way of reading Kafka's three novels that takes them "as far as possible, at face value" (1997, 28). Taking this approach—with its important qualification "as far as possible"—as a guide to the reading of "Die Verwandlung" ("The Metamorphosis") (Kafka 1994) one may ask: Just how far does this face-value approach take us? How is the reader supposed to respond to the features of the text that show resistance to such a reading? Is there a way of responding to such features of the text as a part of its rhetorical design without resorting to an allegorical reading?

Let me start by outlining a reading that follows Speirs and Sandberg's example and progresses through the text intent on seeing it as "a description of the experience of one individual in his dealings with others" (1997, 28). The opening paragraph of the story is designed to involve the reader immediately, and with no preparation, in a huge crisis in Gregor

Samsa's life. He wakes up in his bed and finds himself transformed into some form of insect. The event destabilizes the entire life of the Samsa family, and the dramatic action revolves around the various ways in which Gregor and his family respond to and try to deal with this crisis. All the members of the family—Gregor's father, mother, and his sister, Grete, in addition to Gregor himself—seem to share one overall project: to re-establish normality by healing the rupture that the metamorphosis has caused. However, if the project is essentially shared, Gregor's and the family's strategies are markedly different and in conflict with each other. Gregor aspires from the first minute to heal the rupture by seeking to communicate his humanity to his family despite his new non-human bodily form so as to secure his place in the family as son and brother, while the other members of the family seek to re-establish normality by protecting themselves and their ordinary life from the social and emotional consequences of the outbreak of abnormality at the heart of family life by locking Gregor in his room.[1] The conflict between divergent strategies in dealing with the rupture of normality develops into a "territorial" struggle within the flat, a struggle that structures the dramatic action of the story. Each of the first three parts sees a build-up of dramatic tension that reaches its climax when Gregor tries to break out of his room, only to be driven back into this confined space. After his third attempt, he gives up, returns to his room, and lies down to die, finally to be swept up and disposed of as litter by the cleaning lady.

This reading of the story as a family drama is supported by the flashbacks in the opening sections of the story, through which we get a sense of Gregor's resentment prior to the metamorphosis—his resentment, more specifically, at the restrictions imposed on his social life and his love life by his role as the breadwinner of the family after his father's bankruptcy. The metamorphosis certainly offers no improvement of his situation; on the contrary, it ruins any hope of a wider and more satisfying engagement with other people. The metamorphosis also reinforces the pattern of power struggle and oppression that seems well established among the male members of the family. It is hardly a coincidence that the authoritarian father is the only one who never enters into the transformed Gregor's room, that he plays the most violent role in preventing Gregor from breaking out into the rest of the flat, and that he delivers the final blow to Gregor's deteriorating health. The suppressed sexual longings that fuel Gregor's general dissatisfaction with life before the transformation are brought out in a cruder form after his transformation, in his clinging to the picture of the woman with the fur boa, while the connection between the father's oppression of Gregor and Gregor's sexual needs is suggested by the apple the father throws at him and which slowly decays in the wound on his back.

The transformation also throws an unbearably ironic light on Gregor's willingness to make such sacrifices in his life prior to this catastrophic event. Now that he is unable to provide for the family, it appears not only that the economic situation was not as bad as Gregor was led to believe but also that his sacrifices have inhibited the rest of the family and prevented them from flourishing. They are liberated and revitalized by Gregor Samsa's death; they are able to realize capacities they did not recognize before. If he was the victim of their needs, they seem to have been the victims of his support. They all seem to have been locked in the destructive workings of family life, with its characteristic patterns of dependence and power, guilt and suppressed longings, sacrifices and mutual victimization.

According to such a reading, the narrative invites a readerly response that is based on the mimetic aspect of the characters,[2] Gregor included: We relate to them as people. Their conflicts and the story's inherent ironies make sense of and cast light on life as we know it. However, there is one serious snag to this way of responding to the story. It seems to depend on our forgetting or ignoring just how unheard of, how unacceptable and in effect unthinkable the metamorphosis is, how deeply and fundamentally it constitutes a breach with the world as we know it and with the logic of life. Being struck and puzzled by the metamorphosis as a rupture of the logic of life, the reader should ask: What claims to understanding Gregor's fate are we entitled to? Are we actually making sense of his situation, or are we just under the illusion that we are doing so? In order to normalize his situation, Gregor struggles to remain a member of the family inside the human circle. But is it not the case that he has also fallen outside human society as far as the reader is concerned?

II

At second thought, the face-value approach seems to run into trouble at the very beginning of the narrative. We are clearly invited to engage the story as a family drama, but this engagement leads to a frustration of the sense-making effort of the reader. The event of the metamorphosis constitutes an instance of ontological fuzziness that requires an effort of *naturalization* on the part of the reader, an effort of "bring[ing] it into relation with a type of discourse or model which is already, in some sense, natural and legible" (Culler 1980, 138). So what routes to naturalization are available to the reader of "Die Verwandlung"? Rimmon-Kenan distinguishes between two kinds of models of coherence available to the reader of narratives: the reality models, which "help naturalize elements by reference to some concept (or structure) which governs our perception of the world," and the literary models, which "make elements intelligible by reference to specifically literary exigencies or institutions" (2002, 125). Neither of these, however, is of much help in attempts at giving coherence to this particular story. First, the metamorphosis appears as the result of unknown forces or an agency that has no place in any model of reality as we perceive it. Second, even though the event of the metamorphosis has a rich array of literary forebears in fairy tales, folklore, and pre-realistic texts such as Apuleius's *The Golden Ass,* it is a salient feature of the metamorphosis as it is presented in Kafka's story that it is located in a world that otherwise operates according to the laws of the world as we know it. We are not in the world of fairy tales; nevertheless, fairy-tale events seem to happen here.

In its discursive treatment of the event, the text clearly and self-consciously acknowledges this. If we look at how the metamorphosis is described, we find that it is not in fact described. We are not told what happened; only the situation consequent to the event is presented to the reader. This indeterminacy is a logical necessity, given the nature of the event. It *cannot* be made determinate within the human universe on which it is projected. To regard it as a dream would be a way of bringing it within the logic of life as we know it, but that possibility is rejected immediately by the protagonist himself: "Es war kein Traum" (KAF, 1:93) ("It was no dream" [Kafka 1996, 3]). This instance of free indirect thought, reflecting and participating in Gregor's struggle to come to terms with his situation, has a function also on the axis of communication between implied author and reader. Marking the authorial recognition of the attentive reader's attempts to naturalize the event, the authorial message seems clear: the central event in "Die Verwandlung" defies explanation and refuses naturalization, at least along such tracks.

This message runs counter, however, to the spirit in which the story is told by the narrator, who is loyal to Gregor's attempt to play down the consequences of the transformation and relates the story in a fashion that assumes that there is no problem whatsoever connected with the logic of the event. This attitude is clearly fundamental to our initial engagement in the drama. We are invited to forget the shock of the metamorphosis as soon as it occurs and to give ourselves over to the narrative flow, which allows us to participate in Gregor's brave but eventually failed attempt to reintegrate himself in the normal life of the family despite his new conditions. However, the attitude of the narrator, his covering up the ontological fuzziness of the metamorphosis, is also fundamental to our growing sense of distrust in the sense we are invited to make. In his reporting function the narrator relates in an untroubled fashion something we simply cannot accept. Even if we follow the action primarily through Gregor's perspective, and even if his thoughts and aspirations are those of a human being, the reader is constantly reminded through the detailed description of his movements as an insect of Gregor's separation from human life as we know it, and thus his separation from us.

III

Seen thus, "Die Verwandlung" appears as a narrative with a rhetorical design that is rich in inherent contradictions. On the one hand, we are invited to forget the ontological fuzziness of the metamorphosis in our attempts at making sense of the story. On the other hand, our sense of puzzlement at this very event is stimulated by the text itself. How do we resolve these inherent contradictions in the response the story invites? Perhaps the best way to bring the story within the reader's comprehension is the most confrontational: to take what seems to be destructive of sense to be a potential source of its construction. Rather than ignoring the transformed Gregor's ontological fuzziness, we should take the deviation from mimetic demands to be central to the story's thematic concern and rhetorical effect; we should see the metamorphosis itself, the transformation of Gregor, as that which allows his fate to speak to us, albeit in terms that go beyond the mimetic aspect of his character.

To see this possibility more clearly, we have to return once more to the opening of the story, in which the nature and the immediate consequences of the metamorphosis are exposed. Perhaps the most shocking aspect of it is not the metamorphosis itself but rather the fact that the narrator's account assumes Gregor's inner human life to be *unaffected* by the transformation of his human body into some verminous creature. He wakes up thinking, believing, fearing, wishing, resenting, remembering, pondering, and planning in the manner of a human being, but he has a non-human body.

Looked at from the point of view of the history of philosophy, however, this thought does not seem shocking at all. Philosophical dualism sees the human being as divided between an outer and an inner being, a bodily being on the one hand and a mental or spiritual being—a soul—on the other. Whatever terms we prefer to use to denote the difference between the human body and the inner human life, dualism seems to assume that the inner human life constitutes the real human being, and that there is in fact no necessary relationship between the (outer) human body and the inner life. One's body is incidental to one's humanity. This idea may be theorized in various ways, the most famous and influential, perhaps, being that of René Descartes, whose distinction between the two substances—the immaterial *res cogitans* and the material *res extensa*—may be easily dismissed by most modern thinkers, but whose conception of the human being nevertheless continues to haunt us and to shape our coming to terms with what it is to be human.[3]

Taking the dualistic assumptions underlying the event of the metamorphosis as the starting point for another readerly progression through the text, it seems that the story invites the reader to engage in the narrative's exploration of the ontological repercussions of the metamorphosis. A major compositional feature of "Die Verwandlung" is the pattern of alternation between Gregor Samsa's being alone in his room and his facing the other family members. This allows for a dual perspective on the ontological repercussions of the metamorphosis: it creates a rhythmic shift between the first-person perspective and the third-person perspective through which the implications of Gregor's bodily change are explored.

How does the assumption of an external relationship between the inner and the outer human being hold up when it is explored through the first-person perspective in the narrative? In one sense it is confirmed, for Gregor does experience his body as external to his humanity. From the second he wakes up in his bed transformed into a new shape, his bodily being emerges as something out there, as something he first familiarizes himself with by looking at:

> Er lag auf seinem panzerartig harten Rücken und sah, wenn er den Kopf ein wenig hob, seinen gewölbten, braunen, von bogenförmigen Versteifungen geteilten Bauch, auf dessen Höhe sich die Bettdecke, zum gänzlichen Niedergleiten bereit, kaum noch erhalten konnte. Seine vielen, im Vergleich zu seinem sonstigen Umfang kläglich dünnen Beine flimmerten ihm hilflos vor den Augen. (KAF, 1:93)

> He was lying on his back as hard as armor plate, and when he lifted his head a little, he saw his vaulted brown belly, sectioned by arch-shaped

> ribs, to whose dome the cover, about to slide off completely, could barely cling. His many legs, pitifully thin compared with the size of the rest of him, were waving helplessly before his eyes.) (Kafka 1996, 3)

The distance between Gregor and the body he surveys is expressed in his tendency to view his body as having a life of its own. He watches it with concern: the legs are pitifully thin and are waving helplessly. That is, his body has become an object that he reaches out to through his thoughts; he has to learn to use his body in the way that one has to learn to handle a tool. This is made all the more difficult by the fact that the things around him—the tools ("die Zeuge," to use Heidegger's term from *Sein und Zeit*) that suit the human body perfectly—are sheer obstacles to him in his new bodily shape. He experiments with ways of moving his body out of bed and with ways of using his new mouth to turn the key: "Es schien leider, daß er keine eigentlichen Zähne hatte,—womit sollte er gleich den Schlüssel fassen?") (KAF, 1:106) ("Unfortunately it seemed that he had no real teeth—what was he supposed to grip the key with?" [Kafka 1996, 11]). Only with the greatest effort and concentration does he manage to maneuver his body out of the room and make himself visible to the others.

Gregor's object-relation to his new body, however, is clearly a consequence of the metamorphosis, and as such the transformation cannot confirm the assumption that there is no logical connection between the inner human life and the human body. Rather, the transformation seems to have severed the logical connection between Gregor's inner life and his body. Even if his inner life has survived his metamorphosis, the characteristic way in which the inner human life is related to the human body has not. The spontaneous flow of movement, the flow of intentional action and bodily movement that characterizes the human way of being in the world, has stopped. In Gregor's first attempt to withdraw to his room in response to his father's despair and fury, "und so begann er . . . sich nach Möglichkeit rasch, in Wirklichkeit aber doch nur sehr langsam umzudrehen" (KAF, 1:112) ("he began to turn around as quickly as possible, in reality turning only very slowly" [Kafka 1996, 15]. In this clause we see the working of the mind that is in effect detached from the working of the body.

In other words, Gregor's difficulties in making his body move in accordance with his will and intentions, the way in which his body has become objectified, sheds light on the way our body under normal circumstances evades objective thought. Being confronted with Gregor's thought-dependent movements, we are shocked into seeing what we normally take for granted. We see that we are not the decision-makers for our own bodies, manipulating it with our intellect into the right position in relation to things in the world. It is not because we have an *intellectual* grasp of the dimensions of the space and our body's size and position that we know how to move in inhabited space; our wanting something, intending something, thinking something—this is a bodily stance toward the world. Maurice Merleau-Ponty, a philosopher who has explored this problem in great detail, uses the term subject-body to indicate the way in which the inner human being is logically connected with the human body: "Consciousness is being-towards-the-thing through the intermediary of the body" (1989, 138–39). The ability to act in and on the world is grounded in our being a subject-body. As such we project ourselves toward the things in the world in a way that does not leave room for a purely instrumental relation to one's own body: "In the action of the hand which is raised towards an object is contained a reference to the object, not as an object represented, but as that highly specific thing towards which we project ourselves, near which we are, in anticipation, and which we haunt" (Merleau-Ponty 1989, 138). Gregor is no longer a body-subject in Merleau-Ponty's sense, and this very concept holds up a mirror in which we can see the distortions of Gregor's relation to his body. We see more clearly that the metamorphosis constitutes a departure from the characteristic human way of relating to one's own body, a fall from being a subject-body.

By positing the human being as a subject-body, Merleau-Ponty also criticizes the intellectualism inherent in Cartesian dualism: "Consciousness is in the first place not a matter of 'I think that' but of 'I can'" (1989, 137). The whole process of accessing the world is connected with this "I can":

> Our bodily experience of movement . . . provides us with a way of access to the world and the object, with a "praktognosia" [practical knowledge], which has to be recognized as original and perhaps as primary. My body has its world, or understands its world, without having to make use of my "symbolic" or "objectifying function." (Merleau-Ponty 1989, 140–41)

Far from having a body that "has its world," Gregor has a body that has lost its world, that no longer "understands" it. His inner life has become a matter of "I cannot"; the severing of the logical relation between consciousness and body is matched by a severing of the logical relation between body and world, and a loss of the bodily at-home-ness in the world that goes with the "I can."

We see this all the more clearly in Gregor's relation to his room as the story progresses. To some extent he manages to establish a relation to his new body that in turn makes him more at home in the world: he learns to crawl on the walls and enjoys hanging from the ceiling: "es war ganz anders, als das Liegen auf dem Fußboden; man atmete freier; ein leichtes Schwingen ging durch den Körper" (KAF, 1:126–27) ("it was completely different from lying on the floor; one could breathe more freely; a faint swinging sensation went through the body" [Kafka 1996, 23]). And even when he loses control of his upside-down body in the state of "fast glücklichen Zerstreutheit" (KAF, 1:127) ("the almost happy absent-mindedness" [Kafka 1996, 23]), his acquired at-home-ness in his new body is such that he is not hurt by the fall.

However, as Gregor gradually becomes more united with his new non-human body, he simultaneously becomes more detached from his humanity, and this affects his relation to his room. An important stage in his deterioration takes place when the furniture is removed from his room so as to simplify his moving about. Initially, he foresees this change as a change for the better, but he realizes soon that it is catastrophic to his sense of being human. It not only means that he becomes even more isolated in his room: "Denn in einem Raum, in dem Gregor ganz allein die leeren Wände beherrschte, würde wohl kein Mensch außer Grete jemals einzutreten sich getrauen" (KAF, 1:130) ("Into a room in which Gregor ruled the bare walls alone, no human being beside Grete was ever likely to set foot" [Kafka 1996, 25]). He also realizes that without the human room with its furniture he will no longer be able to remember his human past, and it seems absolutely clear to him that retaining the room in its former state is crucial to his survival:

> Nichts sollte entfernt werden; alles mußte bleiben; die guten Einwirkungen der Möbel auf seinen Zustand konnte er nicht entbehren; und wenn die Möbel ihn hinderten, das sinnlose Herumkriechen zu betreiben, so war es kein Schaden, sondern ein großer Vorteil. (KAF, 1:129)
>
> (Nothing should be removed; everything had to stay; he could not do without the beneficial influence of the furniture on his state of mind; and if the furniture prevented him from carrying on this senseless crawling around, then that was no loss but rather a great advantage.) (Kafka 1996, 25)

In other words, this characteristic feature of inner human life—that one relates to past events, that one's human past lives on in one's conception of oneself as a person and as a human being—is dependent on Gregor's relation to the human body he no longer has. The logical connection between being human and having a human body is confirmed, now mediated through the significance of "ein richtiges, nur etwas zu kleines Menschenzimmer" (KAF, 1:93) ("a regular human room, only a little on the small side" [Kafka 1996, 3]) that he looked at with appreciation the first morning he woke up as an insect.

Thus, rather than having survived the transformation, Gregor's inner life is transfigured into a consciousness in deterioration. Instead of confirming dualistic assumptions about the human being, the progression of the story is geared toward revealing dualism's philosophical distortion of it. In so far as we *think* it has survived, it may be because our own thinking suffers from the same distortion.

IV

If the scenes in which Gregor battles with his new bodily form bring out the logical relation between the human body and the inner human life, the scenes of confrontation between Gregor and his family explore the ontological repercussions of his metamorphosis by highlighting the connection between ontology and ethics in our dealings with one another. The story seems to reveal the potential conflict between psychological reactions and ethical demands: The members of the family know the verminous creature is Gregor; indeed, the fact that they know this is part of the horror of seeing him in this bodily form.

Grete's response to Gregor carries a huge moral weight. She continues to treat the creature as a human being and as her brother, as someone to whom she owes care and love. Is her response grounded in dualistic assumptions? Does she continue to treat him as a human being because she thinks his inner self is unscathed by the metamorphosis? Not necessarily. We may take her to accept that the vermin is Gregor, her brother, in virtue of his history; that is, she responds to the vermin as her brother not because she can recognize her brother in the creature, nor because she is able to give a plausible explanation for what has happened to him, but simply because she acknowledges that this transformation is something that has happened to *him,* her brother Gregor. This non-dualistic and non-reductive conception of the identity of the human being[4] brings out the continuity in the demands other people make on us quite independently of what changes they undergo, in ways we are familiar with in connection with people who undergo severe physical or psychic damage, for instance. In Grete's initial response, then, there seems to be no room for the thought that he is outside the human circle of care and concern. In his new bodily form, Gregor may not meet the ontological standards of human beings, but that is morally irrelevant because he did not qualify for her moral concern in the first place.

Viewed in this light, Grete's final denunciation of the vermin as Gregor, the son and the brother—"Ich will vor diesem Untier nicht den Namen meines Bruders aussprechen [. . .]. Du musst bloss den Gedanken loszuwerden suchen, dass es Gregor ist" (KAF, 1:149, 150) ("I won't pronounce the name of my brother in front of this monster. . . . You just have to try to get rid of the idea that it's Gregor" [Kafka 1996, 37, 38])—is to be regarded as a moral failure. But can the question be so easily settled? First, this view seems hardly to recognize the deep connection between the ethical and the psychological strands of our response: we develop our ethical responses to other people who have a recognizable human form, and although it is clearly a mistake to turn this recognizable human form into a criterion for moral concern, it is difficult to imagine a moral concern of the kind we owe human beings that is completely divorced from the habitual response toward beings with a recognizable human body. Second, there are important differences between the severely deformed person and Gregor Samsa. In the first case, there is a story of deformation that can be told. The story of Gregor's metamorphosis, however, cannot be told. The ontological fuzziness that is an obstacle to sense in the story pops up again, but now as an obstacle to holding on to the thought that the vermin is Gregor.

Trying to counter the deep-seated dualistic tendency in our thought about human beings, Wittgenstein says, "The human body is the best picture of the human soul" (2001, 152). How are we to understand "the best picture of"? Stanley Cavell offers us help in this gloss on the remark: "The human body is the best picture of the human soul—not, I feel like adding, primarily because it represents the soul but because it expresses it. The body is the field of expression of the soul, the body is *of* the soul; it is the soul's; a human soul *has* a human body" (1982, 356).

Without a human body that is the field of expression of his soul, Gregor fails to communicate with his family. Thus, contrary to the assumptions behind the dualistic conception, human understanding seems to depend on the live expressive human body. The meeting of minds is not so much hindered by the body as the dualist induces us to believe, but rather is made possible by or conditioned by the human body. The meeting of minds depends on the human being's natural expressiveness. To say that it is natural is not, however, to deny that it is conventional in some sense. The point is rather that we tend to work with a misleading conception of the relation between the natural and the conventional. In Cavell's words, "very little of what goes on among human beings . . . is *merely* conventional" (1982, 119).

V

If this progression through the text captures something important in the story, it still seems unclear how these philosophical concerns relate to the story as a family drama. Is it an allegorical reading of the text I have offered, the actual dramatic action being merely a vehicle for the discussion of philosophical problems? Such a conclusion seems to miss the communicative point of the interdependence and interaction of the two readerly progressions, the one engaging in the story as a family drama and the other exploring our ontological assumptions about the event that sets the drama in motion.

To see how deeply the ontological "drama" is embedded in the family drama, we need to return once again to the beginning of the story. As already mentioned, there is no description of how the metamorphosis took place, and this indeterminacy follows from the nature of the event: it simply cannot be made determinate within the world as we know it. However, the opening clause of the story is marked by another indeterminacy that at least allows the possibility of a causal connection between the metamorphosis and Gregor's life prior to it. The sequence of events referred to in the opening paragraph—his unsettling dreams *and* his waking up to find himself transformed into an insect—is in fact indeterminate between a consecutive and a consequential reading. His transformation may simply come *after* his unsettling dreams (*x* happened, then *y* happened) or there may be a causal connection between his unsettling dreams and the state in which he wakes up. Even if the first is the only reading with an indisputable basis in the text, the second is not ruled out.[5]

But how are we supposed to make sense of a causal connection between the unsettling dream and the metamorphosis? What kind of causal connection could there possibly be? One possibility is to see the metamorphosis itself as the result of an escape fantasy on the part of Gregor. There are several textual indications of a tie between the metamorphosis and Gregor's desire to escape. His deep dissatisfaction with his professional life, family life, social life, and love life lends credibility to the idea that he has entertained the thought of escaping it all. The image of a verminous creature is well suited to capture the combination of aggression toward a dominating father, suppressed sexual desire, and self-contempt that seems to make up his frame of mind prior to the metamorphosis. Fantasizing and escapism both belong to the world of dreams, but in this case the dreamer finds on waking up that the escapist dream has taken on the form of a nightmarish reality. This is perhaps the ultimate nightmare, or nightmare turned daymare: to wake up from acting out suppressed wishes in one's dreams and find oneself changed in accordance with those dreams.

The temptation to escape by means of bodily withdrawal also appears in the other piece of writing in which Kafka experiments with the motif of a man transformed into a vermin, the fragment "Wedding Preparations in the Country." The protagonist Raban imagines that he can send his human body into a situation that he is dreading. He remains in his bed and becomes a giant beetle. "Die Verwandlung" may be seen as the fantasy in which *this* fantasy takes on the form of reality.

Taking the metamorphosis to be the fatal outcome of an escape fantasy has the effect of embedding the ontologically fuzzy metamorphosis in the dramatic action, but it also requires a reconfiguration or reconstruction of the plot structure in "Die Verwandlung." One of the assumptions that governed the first progression through the text was that the opening of dramatic action coincides with the beginning of the discourse (i.e., that the first destabilizing event is the event of the metamorphosis). This assumption does not hold if we accept a consequential rather than a consecutive reading of the opening connective clause: it implies that we are faced with an *in medias res* opening in "Die Verwandlung," leaving the reader with the task of reconstructing the part of the plot that reaches back into the past. What is presented as background to the unfolding drama (Gregor's discontent and frame of mind) is in fact part of the causal chain of events. Again the reader is misguided by the narrator: while we are given the impression that we are entering the dramatic action exactly when it gets going, it turns out that we enter the dramatic action at a point when it is in fact far into the process of complication. The real start of the dramatic action, in this case, is Gregor's response of entertaining the escape fantasy.

It follows from this reconfiguration of the plot that Gregor has a considerable part in, and therefore responsibility for, his own misery. It is not the result of a hidden external agency but rather internally related to his handling of his life. The reconfiguration also sheds light on his curious and seemingly inappropriate response to his transformation. He is certainly distressed by his new bodily form, and he reflects on how he will be responded to, but quite absurdly he seems even more concerned with being too late for work. His refusal to recognize the seriousness of his situation makes sense if we see it in light of his unwillingness to acknowledge his responsibility: escapist, wishful thinking that prompted the metamorphosis carries over into the way his mind works after his temptation to depart from his human body has taken on the form of a nightmarish reality.

VI

Does my interpretation, with its postulation of a causal connection between Gregor's previous life and the metamorphosis, restore the face-value approach to the text? It clearly does not solve the problem of naturalization. According to our understanding of how the world normally works, we simply do not wake up from a dream and find ourselves transformed in accordance with those dreams. The crucial event in the story remains unacceptable and unheard of, and no psychological explanation of the escape wish (the wish to escape from obligations, an outbreak of suppressed sexual desire, a wish for revenge on his father, etc.) is able to do away with the ontological fuzziness of the metamorphosis.

However, perhaps naturalization is not the route to follow when trying to make sense of this story; seeing the significance of the story's resistance to sense is a better alternative. We seem to gain sense by allowing the story to revolve around the ontological problematic it contains. We should not take the story to be a vehicle for reflection on issues in philosophical anthropology, but rather see the unfolding of the dramatic action as an enactment of or fleshing out of the *temptation* of dualism. The temptation of dualism resides not only in the history of philosophy but also in us. I guess most of us have sometimes woken up hoping that Descartes was right—that the bodily creature we are, uneasy as any one of us may feel about it, is external to the human being that we are; that there are no essential connections. This may be due either to self-contempt or to an unwillingness to stand by human life as essentially shared with other bodily human beings. Exactly because dualism is conceived of in this story not primarily as a philosophical idea, but rather as a human temptation, or as an idea that is existentially grounded, we are able to find our feet with the transformed Gregor.

By acknowledging that dualism is an idea that resonates deeply with any human being who is alert to life's complexities and anxieties, we can see that Gregor's extraordinary ontological situation, his being human and yet not a human being, emerges as a fictional dramatization of the rather more ordinary and familiar struggle of coming to terms with the human condition and a reflection of our often half-hearted commitment to it. The image of Gregor transformed into something verminous is particularly suited to capturing the aspects of the temptation of dualism noted above: the aggression toward other people, the resentment of their demands on us, and the self-contempt that is likely to result.

In the fictional dramatization of this wish in "Die Verwandlung," the denial of the human condition turns out to be fatal, not least because Gregor is deprived of a comprehensible human language. Initially, he is unaware of his exclusion from linguistic communication. He thinks he speaks to his family in words, he hears his own sounds as words, but they can't hear words in the sounds he utters. He clearly recognizes the importance of conversation in order to stay human: his attempt at communicating is essentially an attempt at communicating his humanity to them, assuming that the inclusion in the human conversation sustains his inclusion "in den menschlichen Kreis" (KAF, 1:106) ("into human society" [Kafka 1996, 11]), and he regards his progressively lowered awareness of what is important to him as a human being to be a consequence of his being excluded from the human conversation. But contrary to the assumption on which the fantasy of dualism rests, this conversation—"Seit ein Gespräch wir sind," to use a phrase from Hölderlin—is a conversation the *whole* human being participates in. If we take conversation and communication as crucial to our being human, there is in no logical room for divorcing the human being that we are from our human body.

This focus on the importance of the human conversation also carries over to the text itself, as an act of communication. By taking such pains to frustrate the reader's attempts at making sense of the story, Kafka runs the risk of failing to communicate with his reader at all. Even so, the chief difficulty of "Die Verwandlung" is the nature of the story's concern—its probing into the role of the human body in our being human and our unwillingness to confront this issue, to participate in these probings. Hence the elusiveness of the communicative content of the story: the anguish connected with the temptation of dualism, with its reference to our wavering between acknowledging the human condition and our all too human wish to escape it, indicates the sense of anguish that the story gives voice to and the kind of truth it expresses. Speirs and Sandberg say of Kafka's fiction in general, "Such elusive, only intuitively graspable and yet indubitable 'truth,' rather than some rationally demonstrable 'sense,' is what Kafka hoped his fiction, at its best, could achieve" (1997, 18). For the reader of "Die Verwandlung," this communicative effect is captured not by abandoning the face-value approach but by following it to its limit and by seeking to recognize and optimize the significance of this limit. However, if the particular kind of anguish given expression in "Die Verwandlung" does not resonate with us, it is unlikely that we can see ourselves as spoken to by the story in this way. No matter how important the textual design is in shaping the reader's relation to the text, the readerly interaction with that design is still dependent on who the reader is and the sense of existence that is within the reader's reach. In that respect "Die Verwandlung" is a highly risky act of communication.

Its riskiness, however, does not detract from its importance as a contribution to a *philosophical* discussion. Participating in the fictional dramatization of the temptation of dualism, the reader is invited to *experience* the connection between the thesis of dualism and the ontological-existential anguish of the Samsa family: that of Gregor in particular, but also of the father, mother and sister. Such connections between ontological and existential issues are seldom vibrant in philosophical discussions, even if they are crucial to understanding what is at stake; why the discussion matters. Thus, experiencing the thesis fleshed out in the form of a narrative is also philosophically important in that it helps us reconnect the thesis with the anguish. To acknowledge this is to acknowledge that the narrative form of "Die Verwandlung" is crucial to the reader's engagement with and grasp of its philosophical concerns.

Notes

1. Note the nuances within the family's response: Grete accommodates for the fact that Gregor is still Gregor longer than do the mother and the father.

2. I employ the term "mimetic" here in accordance with James Phelan's use of the term. He distinguishes between three aspects of the literary character—the mimetic, the thematic, and the synthetic—and defines the mimetic aspect of the character as "that component of character directed to its imitation of a possible person" (2005, 216). Generally, the reading strategy adopted in my interpretation of "Die

Verwandlung" is indebted to Phelan's rhetorical approach to narrativity, especially the significance attributed to the progression of the story and to the readerly sense-making engagement in this progression.

3. The idea that there is only an external relation between the inner human being and the outer human body may be imagined in at least two ways. We may envisage the possibility that the human body is merely an automaton. What looks like a human being is in fact not that at all: despite the smile, the devious glance, the seemingly wholehearted dedication to other human beings, and other human characteristics, there may be in fact no inner life there to support the bodily and verbal expressions. Conversely, we may be asked to imagine that inside the body that does not look like a human being at all there is a rich inner human life unfolding—complete with intentions, hopes, and the capacity for planning, calculation, and dismay in the face of severe trouble—with no way of expressing this inner life in the concentration of a face, the hopeful glance, the beaten looks or, for that matter, in the posture of the human body, in dragging one's feet in despair. All these human feelings and cognitions are there, inside the non-human body, and the absence of a human body for them to be expressed in seems not to be detrimental to their reality. The way Gregor's transformation is described is premised on the second version of this dualistic picture of the human being.

4. For an extensive discussion of this conception of the identity of human beings, see David Cockburn, *Other Human Beings* (1990). My discussion of dualism owes a lot to Cockburn's work.

5. Our attitude to this indeterminacy may depend on our view of the reading process. Is it a matter of choice on the part of the reader whether we see a causal connection between the two events? Rimmon-Kenan seems to think so. In her comment on Forster's famous distinction between plot and story and his example of the latter ("'The king died and then the queen died'"), she holds that "there is nothing to prevent a causally-minded reader from supplementing Forster's . . . example with the causal link that would make it into an implicit plot" (Rimmon-Kenan 2002, 17). A more rhetorically oriented reader, however, will assume the possibility that this indeterminacy may be part of the rhetorical design of the text, assuming that our response to it should be constrained by considerations of the potential connections between this aspect of the text and others that together may contribute to the text's overall communicative effect.

Works Cited

Cavell, Stanley. 1982. *The claim of reason: Wittgenstein, skepticism, morality, tragedy.* Cambridge: Cambridge Univ. Press.

Cockburn, David. 1990. *Other human beings.* Hampshire/London: Macmillan

Culler, Jonathan. 1980. *Structuralist poetics: Structuralism, linguistics and the study of literature.* London: Routledge & Kegan Paul.

Kafka, Franz. 1994. Die Verwandlung. In *Ein Landarzt und andere Drucke zu Lebzeiten.* Vol. 1. Frankfurt am Main: Fischer Taschenbuch Verlag.

———. 1996. *The metamorphosis.* Trans. and ed. Stanley Corngold. New York: Norton.

Merleau-Ponty, Maurice. 1989. *Phenomenology of perception*. Trans. Colin Smith. London: Routledge.

Phelan, James. 2005. *Living to tell about it: A rhetoric and ethics of character narration*. Ithaca, NY: Cornell Univ. Press.

Rimmon-Kenan, Shlomith. 2002. *Narrative fiction: Contemporary poetics*. 2nd ed. London: Routledge.

Speirs, Ronald, and Beatrice Sandberg. 1997. *Franz Kafka*. London: Macmillan.

Wittgenstein, Ludwig. 2001. *Philosophische Untersuchungen / Philosophical Investigations*. Trans. G. E. M. Anscombe. Ed. G. E. M. Anscombe and Rush Rhees. Oxford: Blackwell.

3

"LIGHTNING NO LONGER FLASHES"

KAFKA'S CHINESE VOICE AND THE THUNDER OF THE GREAT WAR

Benno Wagner

Relations between the neighboring domains of literary scholarship and cultural studies have sometimes been less than cordial. In his speech of thanks for the Bavarian Grand Prize for Literature, for example, the eminent German literary critic Karl Heinz Bohrer (2005) fought to defend his "fatherland" (literary scholarship) against the barbaric nomads of today (cultural studies). I would like to take three of his statements as a point of departure for the following reflections. First, culture is always the outward form an age gives to its shared thought, action, and arts; it is a form of knowledge corresponding to a social norm. Literature, on the other hand, like painting and music, always refers to some incommensurable event, an anti-normative phenomenon. If I want to understand the *art* of a piece of art, Bohrer contends, I may not make use of the historical category of culture. Second, the reality displayed in the language of literature is ominous, and its referentiality needs to be questioned. Third, from these considerations results the a priori assumption of any literary scholarship worth its name—that is to say, the absolute and fundamental difference between history and reality on the one hand, and literature on the other (Bohrer 2005, 20).

In what follows I would like to question the severe alternative Bohrer offers literary scholarship: *either* the variety stage of cultural forms devoid of any true artistic value *or* the position adopted by the true aesthete, sitting in a rocking chair and gazing out of the window, hands in trouser pockets, a bottle of wine on the table. I shall look at the *cultural form* of modern propaganda, the *historical event* of World War I, and the *narrative strategy* in Kafka's Chinese stories of spring 1917, in order to demonstrate the intricate nexus between the "reality displayed," or rather hidden, in these stories, and the ominous referentiality of Kafka's poetic language. I shall argue, in other words, that the origin and the law of the "anti-normative" quality of Kafka's narratives are only conceivable through close analysis of precisely those cultural forms and historical events that surround them.[1]

Admittedly, mentioning the war seems to be the weakest possible foundation for any such claim. If we consult the currently available handbooks in German on the literature of war, we do not find a single reference to Kafka. This scholarly finding is of course immediately confirmed by one of the main sources for Kafka scholarship, namely Kafka's own diary. On July 31, 1914, the first day of the global catastrophe, we read (over and over again): "Ich habe keine Zeit. Es ist allgemeine Mobilisierung. K. und P. sind einberufen. . . . Nachmittag werde ich in der Fabrik sein müssen. . . . Aber schreiben werde ich trotz alledem, unbedingt, es ist mein Kampf um die Selbsterhaltung" (KKAT, 543) ("I have no time. General mobilization. K. and P. have been called up. . . . [So] I shall have to spend my afternoons in the factory. . . . But I will write in spite of everything, absolutely; it is my struggle for self-preservation" [Kafka 1964, 300]). And again, six days later: "Der Sinn für die Darstellung meines traumhaften inneren Lebens hat alles andere ins Nebensächliche gerückt und es ist in einer schrecklichen Weise verkümmert und hört nicht auf zu verkümmern" (KKAT, 546) ("My talent for portraying my dreamlike inner life has thrust all other matters into the background; they have dwindled dreadfully, nor will they cease to dwindle" [Kafka 1964, 302]). Could there be a clearer assertion of Bohrer's scholarly a priori, the irredeemable disjunction of history and literature? Could Kafka have expressed his indifference toward all things military more obviously than in his entry of August 2: "Deutschland hat Russland den Krieg erklärt.—Nachmittag Schwimmschule" (KKAT, 543) ("Germany has declared war on Russia.—Swimming in the afternoon" [Kafka 1964, 301])? But wait: here, in fact, we may just have found a nice example of that "ominous referentiality" about which Bohrer warns us. A sufficient quantity and quality of wine provided, it will occur to us that in Kafka's notebooks "swimming" is a prominent cipher for the condition of the writer, a model image connecting an existential situation (swimming as opposed to drowning)[2] to a publicly acclaimed skill or ability (competitive swimming for a world record).[3] So let us see if we can find out more about this ominous referentiality that links the war to the swimming school.

I

The beginning of the First World War, that "seminal catastrophe" (Kennan 1979, 3) of the twentieth century, also marks a turning point in the history of language and narrative. In the German-Austrian *Augusterlebnis* ("August experience") of 1914, the poets' yearning for a reunion of language and life—as expressed so beautifully in Hugo von Hofmannsthal's *A Letter* (a fictional letter, purportedly addressed to Philip Lord Chandos)—had been fulfilled, albeit in a doubly paradoxical way. First, the supposedly unreflecting, immediate experience of collective enthusiasm was in fact generated by an unparalleled, concerted effort of mass organization and the mass media. Referring to a public proclamation of war that he observed from his window, Kafka notes in his diary on August 6, "Organisiert war es gut. Es soll sich jeden Abend wiederholen, morgen Sonntag zweimal" (KKAT, 546) ("It was well organized. It is to be repeated every evening, twice tomorrow and on Sunday" [Kafka 1964, 302]). Second, the enhanced life described in the general narrative of the *Augusterlebnis* is always sacrificed life, the poetic cipher for the beginning of industrialized mass killing. This was the hour for the poets and intellectuals to proclaim what Gustav Roethe, a professor of German literature in Berlin, called "the immense experience [*das ungeheure Erlebnis*] that binds us together, purifies and elevates us" (1914, 18). Thus, *Erlebnis,* that child of fin-de-siècle German philosophy, with its triple narrative potential—embracing the biography of the individual, the collective social experience, and the higher plane of world history (see Horn 2000, 131)—had been summoned to report for active duty. In that summer of 1914, no one seemed to mind the gap between culture and artistic expression, Bohrer's a priori of literary scholarship. Of course, considered as a turning point in the history of public speech, the *Augusterlebnis* had not come out of the blue. As Friedrich Kittler has pointed out, the three German "wars of unification" between 1863 and 1870 had already posed a serious problem for the iconography of war: "Telegraph networks, military build-up plans, recruitment statistics, and ballistic tables—none of these would yield pictures any more. Their only reality is numbers. Yet mass armies could not be recruited with naked numbers alone. Hence a new politics of images was part of the new strategy of national wars" (2000, i).

Two further points need to be added. First, the challenge (the lack of immediate, manifest significance in technology and positive knowledge) was not restricted to the military field; second, the response (the production of new levels or layers of evidence) was not restricted to the visual media but applied to verbal imagery as well. In his anti-capitalist and anti-Semitic pamphlet, *Das Gesetz des Nomadentums und die heutige Judenherrschaft* ("The law of the nomad and today's reign of the Jews"),[4] for example, the Viennese Orientalist Adolf Wahrmund offered a reading of history as an eternal conflict between two human types: the sedentary, culturally productive Aryan, and the nomadic, destructive Semite, who made a living out of raiding Aryan culture (1919).[5] In order to justify his reductionist model, Wahrmund called for the creation of a visual form of historiography to counteract "meaningless" positivism and statistics. What was needed in order to understand history was not theory and the systematic organization of evidence; rather, only "real, which is to say natural powers of life should be looked at" ("ins Auge gefaßt werden"), the "eternal key figures of historical events" who could resist the technological-Semitic "collapse of culture" ("Kultursturz") (Wahrmund 1919, 4).

Clearly, Western society's current habit of invoking a "clash of cultures" as a remedy for the imminent "collapse of culture" (i.e., the practice of externalizing an immanent threat to one's way of life) is deeply rooted in modern metahistory. As Hegelian philosophy began to disintegrate, cultural types, freed from the treadmill of the dialectic, spread out across a variety of discourses, including those of scholarship, journalism, and propaganda. The application of typology could be located anywhere on a scale between two epistemic poles, an *essentialist* one, allegedly connected to depth and transcendental truth, and a *cognitive* one, connected to surface and positive knowledge. Wahrmund's Aryan-Semitic dichotomy obviously represents an extreme version of the essentialist option, with its discursive claim to penetrate the appearance of historical phenomena and grasp their essence. In the aftermath of the two world wars, conservative German historians argued that types of the second (cognitive) kind had to be distinguished clearly from such essentialist terminology. Types were to be considered as "approximative or accidental terms, approaching the essence of their historical object asymptotically . . . and naturally open to changes, additions, and amendments, not as to their form, but as to their content, creating space for a conflict of opinions from which the truly typical traits would then emerge" (Zittel 1967, 128; my translation). Seen thus, types functioned as cultural protocols for historical processes and events. While the recording or filing function of the accidental type was opposed to the expressive function of the essentialist type, it is precisely the paradoxical interplay of these two functions that created the remarkable discursive appeal of typology and brought about the typically German fascination with types.

In the summer of 1914, in a series of state-sponsored talks given in Berlin and distributed widely in cheap pamphlets (Wilamowitz-Moellendorf 1914), German professors contributed to the new politics of imagery by providing it with a set of pseudo-scholarly narratives that served as an enhancing cultural frame. For example, the political economist Werner Sombart (Max Weber's most notable scholarly opponent in the pre-war period) updated essentialist typology for military deployment. In Sombart's narrative, presented in a pamphlet published in 1915 and entitled *Händler und Helden* ("Traders and heroes"), world history is dominated by the conflict between traders (typically British) and heroes (typically Germans). Whereas the trader strives for a secure and comfortable life, a life they control by calculation, Sombart's hero "wants to give, he wants to waste himself, to sacrifice himself" (1915, 64) to call attention to the state at war and its life-devouring military machine. "Do people have a clue," exclaimed Karl Kraus, the foremost critic of this murderous typology, "about the kind of life to which the press gives expression? A life that has long since been the imprint [*Ausdruck*] of this very press" (1988, 16). In the face of an all-embracing war journalism that was capable of "transforming printer's ink into blood" (1988, 18), Kraus chose to turn to silence—albeit in his own paradoxical way, by proclaiming his famous anti-war tirade to be an inevitable commentary that distinguished his silence from tacit agreement.[6]

Kafka's famous remark of 1922—"mauscheln wie Kraus kann niemand" (Kafka 1975, 336) ("No one can 'mauscheln' like Kraus" [Kafka 1978, 288])—represents a case of extreme modesty. In response to the challenge of war propaganda, Kafka too, just like Kraus, falls back on *mauscheln,* an untranslatable term for the anti-Semitic notion that there exists a typically Jewish, or rather Yiddish, *modus loquendi,* allegedly a fraudulent language that combined vivid gesticulation with hidden meaning. Unlike Kraus, however, Kafka creates a narrative voice that conceals even the traces of its own *mauscheln,* thereby combining silence with utmost eloquence.

II

In the spring of 1917, when the multi-ethnic Hapsburg Empire believed itself to be surrounded by an alliance of foreign and barbaric enemies while facing, on the domestic front, the choice between returning to authoritarian centralism or being swept away by the strong and multiple movements toward national independence in its constituent territories, Kafka was invited to join an artists' association for "Greater Austria." He declined the invitation on the grounds that he was "nicht imstande, mir ein im Geiste irgendwie einheitliches Groß-Österreich klarzumachen und noch weniger allerdings, mich diesem Geistigen ganz eingefügt zu denken, vor einer solchen Entscheidung schrecke ich zurück" (KKANI, 336) ("incapable of envisaging a homogeneous Greater Austria and even less capable of imagining myself completely integrated into that spiritual whole; from such a decision I shrink back") (my translation). This rejection implies the initiating factor in all of Kafka's writings: an assignment.

On the very next page of his notebook Kafka sets out to write down two stories about the Chinese Empire. The first and longer fragment, "Building the Great Wall of China," reflects the interplay between national defense against barbarous nomads on the one hand and the domestic issue of the administrative and imaginary organization of political leadership and unity on the other. While the story's first sentence—"Die chinesische Mauer ist an ihrer nördlichsten Stelle beendet worden" (KKANI, 337) ("The Great Wall of China was finished at its most northerly point" [KSS, 113; translation modified])—seems to proclaim the completion of the defensive wall, it soon becomes clear that, as the Chinese master of torture in Octave Mirbeau's novel *Torture Garden* had whispered in Kafka's ear, "Something is rotten in the state of China" (1997, 152).[7] The flaw lies in the system of partial construction that leaves wide gaps in the wall and creates doubts about the accountability of the Chinese High Command. By the end of the account, however, these very doubts, together with the manifold representations of the Emperor himself in the various provinces and villages, are acknowledged precisely to be the foundation of the Empire's political constitution. The second fragment, "A Page from an Old Document," proves this conclusion wrong, however, as it describes the situation after the failure of national defense, when the capital has been invaded by the nomads while the Emperor looks on helplessly. The diegetic frame (the document is alleged to be a fragment of an old manuscript damaged by fire) seems to place it in the historical past of the first account.

At first glance, we are dealing here with a neat historical analogy linking China with Austria, wrapped up in a literary image. On the one hand, Kafka's Chinese account corresponds with the facts of Chinese history in its key elements and even in many striking details. The first long narrative could be located around 1435 when, at the cultural peak of the Ming Dynasty, the Great Wall was completed. The second account could be connected to the nomad invasion in the thirteenth century when the Chinese capital of Nanking, unlike Beijing in later centuries, was still located far from the border, as an important detail of the shoemaker's account has it. On the other hand, Austria enters the picture via a letter in which Talleyrand, after the battle of Austerlitz, reminded Napoleon that "the Hapsburg monarchy is an accumulation of states fitting together badly, completely different in language, customs, creed, and constitution, which only have in common the person of their Emperor. Such a power cannot but be weak; but it is a suitable bulwark against the barbarians—and a necessary one" (Cooper, 186). This image of the "necessary bulwark" against the barbaric Slavs was of course revitalized in German-Austrian war propaganda time and time again.

Yet the correlation between Kafka's China and the Austria of 1917 cannot simply be reduced to the semiotic scale, to the mere analogy between two Empires on the verge of being invaded. Rather, it needs to be located and analyzed on a pragmatic level, namely as Kafka's reaction to and intervention in political discourse by the aesthetic means of narration. Allow me to unfold this hypothesis in three steps.

If we look at the diegetic frame of Kafka's narrative, we note that his narrated world stands in close proximity to the typological thinking of his day. In nineteenth-century typology, "China" was used as shorthand for the cultural condition that the German conservative sociologist Arnold Gehlen was later to term "crystallized" in his critique of the administrative social state on both sides of the iron curtain (1962, 311–28). In Hegel's *Lectures on the Philosophy of History,* the crystallized culture of the Chinese—a system of strictly top-down administrative and intra-family hierarchies and the complete absence of subjective inwardness and responsibility—represented the cultural other of a dynamic and progressive Western culture based on individual responsibility and reason. It was only later in the nineteenth century, in Nietzsche's criticism of Western culture and the Bismarckian welfare state, that the possibility of filing the case of Europe itself under the rubric of "Chinese affairs" was first discussed at some length. In *The Gay Science,* Nietzsche wrote, "Socialists and the state idolaters of Europe, with their measures for making life better and safer, could easily establish Chinese conditions and Chinese 'happiness' in Europe too, if only they could first extirpate the sicklier, more tender, more feminine dissatisfaction and romanticism that are still superabundant here at present" (2001, sec. 1, 25). In the first version of his *Protestant Ethic* (1904), even Max Weber spoke of the "'Chinese' petrifaction" of modern culture", in the revised edition, published after the end of World War I, this regressive use of typology was wisely changed to "mechanical petrifaction" (1996, 154, 202; my translation). In Wahrmund's anti-Semitic pamphlet, it is the "petrified" Semitic culture that threatens to undo Europe's efforts to tear itself away from the influence of Asia during the classical age. Conversely, Martin Buber, one of the founding fathers of "cultural Zionism," with its center in Prague, contends that only Oriental culture is capable of granting unity and unquestionable meaning, of creating those "metaphors of the nameless" (1963b, 56; my translation) that would be able to reconcile what Buber called the "Asian crisis" (1963b, 64) of the age, its lack of a unifying myth, as craved by the artists' association of "Greater Austria" that Kafka declined to join. In Buber's Zionist cultural script, it is precisely and exclusively "the Jew" to whom this mission must be assigned, since he alone had always "remained an oriental" (1963b, 62).

Kafka certainly *knew* the cultural "China" file to the extent that it is displayed here, and far beyond. When he started writing about China at the turning point of the First World War, however, he not only imitated a complex semiotic structure but also inscribed his writing into a series of pragmatic speech acts. In the years following the constitutional crisis of 1848, when the unity of the Hapsburg Empire was threatened by the desire of its various peoples for self-determination, Karel Havlíček Borovský, a founding father of the Czech political press, was exiled to Tyrol. From there he wrote, in the guise of a foreign correspondent, critical reports about the domestic affairs of Ireland and China, reports that could be related approximately or accidentally to the Hapsburg Empire.[8] Withdrawing to a setting in order to reflect critically on the present need not, however, simply be a reaction to repression and censorship. It can also be an active move to create space for contemplation in the face of overwhelming events. Kafka's Chinese reflections also participate in the tradition of this other gesture, as instanced most notably by Nietzsche's retrospective foreword to *The Birth of Tragedy:* "As the thunder of the Battle of Wörth rolled across Europe, the brooder and lover of riddles who fathered the book was sitting in some corner of the Alps . . . writing down his thoughts about the *Greeks* . . . " (1999, 3). Kafka, in turn, as the first and foremost among those readers Nietzsche had been craving all his life,[9] found the precise formula for his sidestep to Asia in the opening section of the fourth *Unfashionable Observation,* where Nietzsche invokes the example of Alexander the Great to characterize the Wagnerian perspective on contemporary culture: "We know that in moments of extraordinary danger or when making important decisions about their lives, people compress all their experiences in an infinitely accelerated process of introspection and are able to perceive once again with uncommon sharpness the nearest and the most distant things. What might Alexander the Great have seen in that moment in which he had Europe and Asia drink from one and the same cup?" (1995, 262).

Shifting focus from the diegetic frame to the narrative instance, we can now establish that the latter, in terms of contemporary cultural typology, truly is Chinese. "The Chinese," Hegel writes in his *Lectures on the Philosophy of History,* "have as a general characteristic a remarkable skill in imitation, which is exercised not merely in daily life, but also in art" (1900, 144). Right from its first breath, in other words, Kafka's Chinese voice is infected with literacy. Not only does it produce nothing but imitations but it emerges from an act of imitation itself, appearing simply to echo Hegel's Chinese typology, including its subsequent changes, additions, and emendations. This narrative voice keeps oscillating between the nearest and the most distant things, as Nietzsche put it, tensed as it is between inwardness and identity on the one hand, and exteriority and multiplicity on the other. Accordingly, the narrator of the "Great Wall" fragment is at once in the position of a detached observer of the defense venture and involved in it (as a subordinate leader). He thus operates on both sides of the distinction between a heterodiegetic and a homodiegetic narrator, while the diegetic world is at once a "narrated world" and a "discussed world."[10] As we are discussing a story by Franz Kafka, this narratological distinction, or rather indecision, between detachment and involvement already occurs on the level of the narrative itself. Thus, the Chinese narrator repeats the movement of his Bohemian author when he stresses that "Meine Untersuchung ist doch nur eine historische, aus den längst verflogenen Gewitterwolken zuckt kein Blitz mehr" (KKANI, 346) ("my investigation is purely historical; lightning no longer flashes from the long since vanished thunderclouds" [KSS, 117; translation modified]). At the same time, the narrative structure that creates this peculiar indecision, which is to say a rudimentary matrix narrative bringing forth an extended and complex, multi-level hyponarrative, is a defining feature of the multifarious reports on safety measures Kafka, the insurance clerk, had to write for the Austrian authorities. Here, too, the genre requires the reporter's detachment from the content of the report, while official responsibility grants continuous involvement. The specific difference between those Bohemian reports and the Chinese report lies in the fact that in the latter case the matrix narrative does not precede the report, but is embedded in it, thus confronting the reader with an uninitialized hyponarrative. At both levels of writing, the detached style of the report may be interrupted by quoted statements of actors involved in the field. Within Kafka's office writings, his long report on "Umfang der Versicherungspflicht der Baugewerbe und baulichen Nebengewerbe" (Kafka 2004, 54–69, 70–73) ("the Scope of Compulsory Insurance for the Building Trades" [Kafka 2009, 54–73]) represents a vivid example of just such an orchestration of voices by the insertion of third-degree narratives.[11] In the same vein, his Chinese narrator eschews the perspective of *Erlebnis* ("experience") in favor of the perspective of historical events but easily shifts to the opposite mode of expression when he quotes the rhetoric and spirit of the *Augusterlebnis* in the following description of the building operations: "jeder Landsmann war ein Bruder, für den man eine Schutzmauer baute. . . . Einheit! Einheit! Brust an Brust, ein Reigen des Volkes, Blut, nicht mehr eingesperrt im kärglichen Kreislauf des Körpers, sondern süß rollend und doch wiederkehrend durch das unendliche China" (KKANI, 342) ("Every fellow countryman was a brother for whom one was building a wall of protection. . . . Unity! unity! breast on breast, a round dance of the people, blood, no longer locked up in the cramped circulation of the body but rolling sweetly and yet returning through the infinity of China" [KSS, 115; translation modified]).

This oscillation between involvement and detachment, this amalgamation of the nearest and the most distant things, becomes even more crucial when we try to get to know the narrator. His peculiar double qualification as an expert on nomad prevention and "vergleichende Völkergeschichte" (KKANI, 48) ("comparative ethnography" [KSS, 118]) betrays a certain kinship with Kafka, the Bohemian expert on accident prevention and writer of stories about China whose confessed desire was to "die ganze Menschen- und Tiergemeinschaft zu überblicken, ihre grundlegenden Vorlieben, Wünsche, sittlichen Ideale zu erkennen, sie auf einfache Vorschriften zurückzuführen" (Br, 755) ("know the entire human and animal community, to recognize their fundamental preferences, desires, and moral ideas, to reduce them to simple rules" [Kafka 1974, 545]). It is a kinship, though, that is less a case of personal similarities than of common skills, despite a number of correspondences in educational and career matters. Any Kafka scholar interested in narratology would do well to listen closely the Chinese narrator's clue that "es gibt bestimmte Fragen denen man nur mit diesem Mittel gewissermaßen an den Nerv herankommt" (KKANI, 348) ("there are certain questions whose nub, so to speak, one can get to only by this method" [KSS, 118]), namely by linking comparative ethnography (Kafka's definition of his writing project) to issues of public safety.

The interplay between literature (on one side of Bohrer's gap) and the Great War and industrial accident insurance (on the other) goes far beyond a number of random allusive references. In the wake of the excitement triggered by the Chernobyl disaster, it has been suggested that historians should adopt some of the methods of accident research in order to understand better the emergence and course of major armed conflicts.[12] Kafka's response, as it were, has been waiting patiently for this challenge to be made. A glance across to the "cultural" side of Bohrer's gap to the desert of Kafka's office writings, reveals that the narrative arrangement of his Chinese-nomadic typology owes a considerable debt to the discourse of accident prevention and accident insurance. In fact, we find the key problems of Kafka's Chinese narrative prefigured in two speeches Kafka composed in 1913 as a ghostwriter for his Institute's presentation at the Second International Congress for Rescue Service and Accident Prevention in Vienna (see Kafka 2004, 860.). To begin with, the difference between a complete defense wall and the inexpedient system of piecemeal construction points to the distinction between accident prevention in the German Reich and in Austria, whereas in Germany the organization of accident insurance by trade associations (specific branches of production) permitted a systematic method of accident prevention: "[war] die territoriale Organisation [in Österreich] . . . viel zu umfassend . . . um mit der Unfallverhütung zweckmäßig verbunden zu werden" (Kafka 2004, 278) ("the territorial organization [in Austria] was much too broad . . . to be coupled with accident prevention in a purposeful way" [Kafka 2009, 269]). This led to the very system of piecemeal construction on which the narrator comments: "Aber der Teilbau war nur ein Notbehelf und unzweckmäßig. Bleibt also nur die Folgerung, dass die Führerschaft etwas Unzweckmäßiges wollte. Sonderbare Folgerung, gewiß" (KKANI, 345) ("But partial construction was only a makeshift and unsuited to its purpose. The conclusion that remains is that the leaders wanted something unsuited to its purpose. An odd conclusion, certainly" [KSS, 117]). The first Vienna speech on Bohemian accident prevention also anticipates the strategic crux of the Chinese construction project—adapting the construction of the wall not only to the continuous development of building technology but also to the nomads' permanent shifting from place to place: "die Unfallverhütung [ist] in fortwährender Umbildung begriffen . . . da sie einerseits der Entwicklung der Industrie und Maschinentechnik, andererseits jener der Unfallverhütungstechnik folgen soll" (Kafka 2004, 277) ("accident prevention is in the process of continuous reformulation, since it must follow both the development of industry and machine technology as well as the developments of accident prevention technology" [Kafka 2009, 251]).[13] Like the Chinese in Kafka's story, his expert colleagues on accident insurance in Prague were well aware of the fact that they could learn from the accidents/nomad movements how best to organize their defense against them. In 1916 Alois Gütling, the head statistician of the Prague institute, with whom Kafka shared an office, suggested applying Charles Frederick Taylor's *Principles of Scientific Management* to accident prevention. By breaking down the process of production into its most basic steps, it would soon be possible to establish statistically the precise accident risk of every single movement made by an individual worker (Gütling 1916, 189).[14] As contemporary war reporting on the strategy of battlefront development was organized according to the same basic conflict—between a defense effort that followed a spatial logic and an enemy whose movements in space seemed to be incalculable—Kafka's Chinese-nomad scenario offers its readers a space for an interdisciplinary dialogue on accidents in industry and history.

The presence of extra-literary forms and procedures at the very center of the aesthetic becomes even more undeniable when we look at the overall arrangement of narrative voices. Like his office writings, Kafka's "Chinese protocols" depend on a narrative source that brings forth a variety of voices, among which the voice of the expert does not claim privileged credibility or authority, thereby exposing the void space of a metanarrative instance, or rather, the metanarrative instance as a void space.[15] Thus, the Chinese architect cites a number of legends from Chinese folk wisdom, thereby insisting on the superiority of public opinion over the scholarly knowledge of historians and finally underlining the fact that it is precisely the polyphonic constitution of imaginary unity that is the foundation of the Chinese Empire. Yet there is a most significant multi-vocality at work here that transgresses even the diegetic frame of the architect's report. When Kafka abandoned his first Chinese fragment, the next thing he wrote was the first few lines of the story about a trader who prematurely shuts down his shop in the afternoon out of disgust at his business (KKANI, 357). On the very next page of Kafka's notebook we witness the opening of another story and another shop: "Ich habe eine Schusterwerkstatt auf dem Platz vor dem kaiserlichen Palast. Kaum öffne ich in der Morgendämmerung meinen Laden, sehe ich schon die Eingänge aller hier einlaufenden Gassen von Bewaffneten besetzt. Es sind . . . offenbar Nomaden aus dem Norden" (KKANI, 358)

("I have a shoemaker's shop on the square in front of the Imperial Palace. No sooner do I open my shop at dawn than I see armed men occupying the openings to all the streets that run into the square. . . . they are evidently nomads from the North" [KSS, 66]).

The connection between the architect's report on nomad prevention and the shoemaker's report on nomad invasion is much stronger than this. It goes far beyond the opposition between two strategic scenarios—a shop closed in the afternoon and a shop opened in the morning, "the most risky time of the day" (cf Vogl 1994, 745)—and far beyond the order of pages in Kafka's notebook. In fact, Kafka has taken the interplay between the two irreconcilable narratives and voices (those of the architect and the shoemaker) straight from his downtown office at the Accident Insurance Institute up to his "shoemaker's shop"[16] to the *Alchimistengasse* (right in front of the Prague Royal Palace), where he wrote his after-hours protocols at that time. The two narrative perspectives on the nomad issue reflect precisely the two discourses on industrial accidents that collided almost day by day, week by week, on Kafka's office desk. On the one hand, there is the discourse of the expert on accident prevention, speaking in the name of an institution, arguing from a wide angle and multiple perspectives with knowledge of technology and manpower management, conceiving the accident as an eventuality, a mere probability—a risk related to the life of a population. On the other hand, there is the discourse of the accident victim, with all the features of a typical incident report (*Hergangsbericht*) as prescribed by the official form for a compensation claim.[17] In the latter case, an individual faces the post-accident situation with an unequipped mind, incapable of remembering the actual event—"Auf eine mir unbegreifliche Weise sind sie bis in die Hauptstadt gedrungen, die doch sehr weit von der Grenze enfernt ist" (KKANI, 358) ("In a manner incomprehensible to me, they have penetrated to the capital, although it lies a long way from the border" [KSS, 66])—and describes a fate as it relates to the life of an individual. Moreover, in the shoemaker's account the Chinese architect's *Erlebnis* scenario, the supposedly immense and elevating experience of a collective *communio sanguinis,* is inverted, for the imagined liberation of the blood actually comes about quite literally as a live ox is torn to pieces by the bloodthirsty nomads who congregate in the name of cruelty and havoc. What is more, the witness/victim not only finds himself abandoned by those responsible for nomad prevention but also finds that the third narrative dimension of the *Erlebnis,* the plane of world history, has been cancelled. As the Emperor watches the scene from his Palace with his head bowed, unable to take action, all are abandoned, even by nomad insurance. The traders and craftsmen, following Sombart's typoscript, establish an elementary mutual insurance scheme as a substitute for heroic state action by pooling their money to support the butcher whose free home delivery of raw meat to the nomads is intended to still their thirst for blood. Alas, this procedure has as much influence on the nomads as accident insurance has on the occurrence of accidents: "Bekämen die Nomaden kein Fleisch, wer weiß was ihnen zu tun einfiele, wer weiß allerdings, was ihnen einfallen wird, selbst wenn sie täglich Fleisch bekommen" (KKANI, 360) ("If the nomads were not to get meat, who knows what would occur to them to do; who knows, for that matter, what will occur to them even if they do get their daily meat" [KSS, 67]). There is neither an "event" nor decisive action in the endless leagues of China; it is a traders' world devoid of those heroes who could turn this whole affair into what First World War propaganda would consider a proper narrative: "Uns Handwerkern und Geschäftsleuten ist die Rettung des Vaterlandes anvertraut; wir sind aber einer solchen Aufgabe nicht gewachsen; haben uns doch auch nie gerühmt, dessen fähig zu sein. Ein Mißverständnis ist es und wir gehn daran zugrunde" (KKANI, 361) ("To us craftsmen and businessmen the salvation of the fatherland is entrusted; but we are not up to such a task; certainly we have never boasted of being capable of it. It is a misunderstanding, and it is driving us to our ruin" [KSS, 67]). This is how Kafka responds *post festum,* in the spring of 1917, to Sombart's invocation of heroism at the outset of the war.

In his analysis of Kafka's narrative voice, Joseph Vogl argues that the *eventum tantum,* the purely virtual event beyond empirical time with its linear flux, the event that has always happened already or has not happened yet, organizes the unique narrative space of Kafka's stories (see Vogl 1994, 754). As I have just shown, the status of the accident in insurance discourse is marked precisely by this oscillation between prematurity and belatedness, between the "not yet" of accident prevention and the "no more" of the accident report.[18] Thus, Kafka the poet and Kafka the clerk are obviously guilty of smuggling on a grand scale across Bohrer's forbidden border. Yet this matter is even more scandalous, and even more complicated. The gap between Kafka's narrators and the event they elaborate on, Vogl continues, opens up the impersonal space of a form of indirect speech, a *discours indirect libre* that sets the scene for an assemblage of voices, voices not emerging from subjects but in turn creating a fluid matrix for multiple subjectivities (1994, 755). In contrast to the intra-diegetic multi-vocality discussed so far—the voices reported by the architect, his insistence on the Emperor's manifold imaginary existence, the *différend* between the architect and the shoemaker—this other, glossolalic multi-vocality is radically transdiegetic, transtextual, or, rather, transmedial.

III

I believe that it is precisely at this apparently abstract point of my analysis that an assignment for philology comes into play. Kafka, as Vogl argues convincingly, developed his "fourth person" (1994, 747) narrative voice right from the start in his *Beschreibung eines Kampfes* (*Description of a Struggle*) and "Hochzeitsvorbereitungen auf dem Lande" ("Wedding Preparations in the Country"). But it is only after the summer of 1914, when the *Erlebnis* of the first-person plural, the nationalist "We feeling" (*Wir-Gefühl*), makes its murderous presence felt, that Kafka begins to think about occupying strategically the unmarked space of the "fourth person." In his stories from the First World War, Kafka deploys his "urge to imitate" (Kafka 1964, 157)—to build a literary machine that simultaneously copies and destroys the machinery of war propaganda. Thereafter, his narratives, word by word and scene by scene, down to their most incommensurable and incomprehensible passages, seem to consist of the rich prey of Kafka's truly nomadic raids in writing.

To begin with a random example, the treacherous first sentence of this pseudo-foundational narrative ("The Great Wall of China was finished at its most northerly point" [KSS, 113; translation modified]) could well be seen as "inspired by" or "copied from" the first sentence of the preface to the proceedings of the Second International Congress for Rescue Service and Accident Prevention, which, in its Bohemian section, was so closely connected to the fragmentary organization of the Chinese security effort. The volume that made Kafka an international, if anonymous, author on insurance begins, "With the Second International Conference which took place between 9 and 13 September 1913 within the walls of the friendly Imperial Capital of Vienna, a great and significant work has been completed" (Charas 1914, iii). If we shift our focus onto the rhetoric of the fatherland and philosophical subtleties, such as the difference between mythological time and historical time, as in a speech titled "Social Welfare and the German Will to Victory" delivered by the president of the German Imperial Insurance Bureau, Paul Kaufmann, to the attentive staff of Kafka's Prague agency, we find the following: "A century ago patriotic men had confidently drawn attention to Germany's eternal calling (*Ewigkeitsberuf*), which is to set the final stone on the obelisk of history" (Kaufmann 1915, 23). In the same fall, Kafka might have stumbled across the proclamation in Rudolf Kjellén's geopolitical writings that the "final stone" was about to be added to another "building," namely the German bridge between Berlin and the Orient, which was the providential project of the Baghdad Railway that Germans had been looking forward to so enthusiastically since the summer of 1914 (Kjellén 1916, 39; my translation). If you have a sensitive ear for the newsflash quality of Kafka's famous opening sentence, you might hear yet another voice omnipresent in Kafka's writings, the voice of Theodor Herzl, who advertised his project of a Jewish state to his sponsors as a "defense wall of Europe against Asia, an outpost of civilization as opposed to barbarism." Later in his fantasy, Herzl went on: "Once the Jewish Company has been constituted the news will be carried in a single day to the remotest ends of the earth by the lightning speed of our telegraph wires. And immediate relief will ensue" (1943, 110). At this point, Kafka's seemingly displaced Chinese fragment, "In diese Welt drang nun die Nachricht vom Mauerbau. Auch sie verspätet etwa dreißig Jahre nach ihrer Verkündigung" (KKANI, 356) ("News of the building of the Wall now penetrated into this world. It, too, was delayed by some thirty years after its proclamation" [KSS, 123]), an announcement made by a boatman to the narrator's incredulous father, seems to move more to the center of the narrative. But even if you are more interested in the contradictory potential of that opening sentence, you do not necessarily need to read on in Kafka's story to uncover it. For its contradictions are already virulent in what seems to be its "source material." In 1910, when he was getting more involved in Zionist issues, Kafka (and other readers of Herzl's *The Jewish State*) were informed, as members of the audience allegedly listening enthralled to Martin Buber's Prague speeches on Jewry, that "the Jews have not even begun their work" (Buber 1963a, 17), since this work was not plain and simple nation-building but a brotherhood based on a community of blood. If we remember that Kafka is a writer by assignment, we only need to turn a few pages in Paul de Lagarde's *Deutsche Schriften* ("German writings") to find the gist of his response to the Writers' Association for Greater Austria. "The church," so de Lagarde asserts in his essay titled "The Religion of the Future," "satisfied men's minds for as long as it was under construction. Once it was completed, people left it. Should we not, then, find our satisfaction in building, since the centuries have shown us that the only thing humans can ever achieve is to begin and to continue; when it comes to finishing things, they tire of the completed work and start all over again" (1891, 232; my translation).

IV

How are we to make use of this mess for narrative theory? Obviously, a "materialist" approach to text—as a montage of elements or a web of motives—would inevitably bring to light the business of a most bizarre "patch-up job," a literature very much resembling the man inhabiting the present-day "Land of Culture" of Nietzsche's Zarathustra:

> Written all over with the signs of the past that are daubed over in turn with new signs: thus you have hidden yourselves well from all interpreters of signs!
>
> . . . You seem to be baked from colours and out of scraps of paper glued together.
>
> All ages and peoples gaze motley out of your veils; all customs and all beliefs speak motley out of your gestures.
>
> He who tore away from you your veils and wraps and paint and gestures would have just enough left to frighten the birds. (Nietzsche 2003, 142)

This is precisely the "culturalist" scenario Bohrer warns against—and it would be hard to deny a certain similarity between Nietzsche's Alexandrine "present day man" and the object of half a century of Kafka scholarship. Meanwhile, to be sure, post-structuralism has warned against assuming that there is a difficult recalcitrance in first-rate works of art, a resistance to understanding that calls for masterful interpretive reconstruction. But does that condemn us to leave the rich life of Kafka's multivocality behind, to abandon it for the sake of the inexorably recurring insight into the impossibility of perfection, unity, and truth? Or could we hope to assume a case of "textual stubbornness" here,[19] after all, a narration resisting our efforts to interpret the text and yet having a production within a larger purpose?

Shifting focus from "meaning" to "production," we then would no longer reduce Kafka's text to an organized set of signs representing this or that meaning or transcribing this or that source material. Beyond the stubborn imperfection of those signs, we would trace a set of *signals* evoking multitudes of voices,[20] producing an indeterminacy that would aim to counteract the murderous determination implied in the propaganda-based national identities of Kafka's time. What creates the movement of this kind of literature is not the simple difference between a hypotext and a hypertext that "transforms" the hypotext (as suggested by Genette [1992, 15]) but rather the complex difference between the series of echo texts triggered by a matrix text—very much in the way that the manifold imaginings of the Emperor define the life of the Chinese people, while the Emperor himself, like the scripture, remains unalterable. While at any point the unalterable text of Kafka's protocol may be used to introduce a temporary order into the chaos of echoes, the echoes will keep coming back and intensifying with each new reading of the protocol.

In the conceptual frame developed so far, we can describe this phenomenon as being yet another instance of Kafka the writer borrowing skills from Kafka the clerk, of a cultural skill becoming effective in the very heart of the aesthetic. At any given point in the syntagma of Kafka's poetic protocols, his unique terminological shorthand, by its mere power of allusion (or "approximation"), "records" and "files" a paradigm of (often conflicting) expressive voices. By short-circuiting the essentialist and the approximative poles of German typological thinking, Kafka transforms propagandistic types from images of dissociation (designed to create a "them against us" plot) into images of association, thereby undermining their polemic potential. Hence the next step of my analysis—reaching far beyond the scope of this article—would require me to show in detail how, in the course of his Chinese reports, the Chinese-nomad constellation would simultaneously or intermittently "approximate" the threat that the Czechs represented to the Germans, the Germans to the Czechs, the Jews to the anti-Semites, the anti-Semites to the Jews, the so-called *Ostjuden* to the *Westjuden,* and, at the end of the day, the threat presented by any of the warring parties in the eyes of the other.[21] If we conceive of reading as a matter of multiple acts performed by multitudes (as suggested by Roland Barthes) rather than as the unique act of an individual, then Kafka, the eternal shipwreck and great swimmer, provides his contemporaries with a semiotic Noah's Ark, offering, as the "larger purpose" postulated above, a common ground for any individual and any people precisely on the basis of their common habit of using polemics to distinguish themselves from one another.

V

Such "Kafkaian negotiations," as we may summarize in the specific context of this volume, are by no means restricted to the level of "competing representations" (Greenblatt 1990, 7) to the topical or figurative level of speech. As we have seen, they also comprise the level of narrative form and strategy. Even these apparently purely poetic features are informed (or, as Karl Heinz Bohrer or Jochen Vogt[22] might prefer to say, infected) by non-literary discourses, such as administrative reports on legal and technological aspects of public insurance; and in turn, ever since the discursive event called "Kafka," bureaucratic formats have been infected with the virus of multi-vocality. If literature, to conclude with another of the provocations Bohrer hurled into the face of his audience, is "too tall an order" (2005, 20) for today's students, this is not because of its *remoteness* from the cultural context but because of literature's *rootedness* in and its indebtedness to just such a context. This is the tall order I have in store for all readers of Kafka: instead of coming to know themselves by ceaselessly going over, word for word, the decrees of the Highest Leaders, or musing endlessly over the intentions and plans of the Emperor, I invite them to take the trajectory of the Chinese architect—that is, to explore the soul of all the provinces, to listen to the stories and legends of all the village-dwellers of all ages. For it is *between* these narratives that the immeasurable wealth and wisdom of Kafka's leaderless Empire of letters can be found.

Notes

1. In other words, and on a larger scale, I am aiming to revise a new historicist approach to literary texts and cultural context by reconstructing such misty metaphors as the "circulation of social energy" and "negotiations" between text and context (Greenblatt 1990, 67), the specific writing strategies, techniques, and procedures a given author employs, and the specific set of documents processed by them.

2. See the "bachelor" fragment, posthumously "restored" by Max Brod (Kafka 1964, 25).

3. See the "great swimmer" fragment in KKANII (254–56). For an English translation of this fragment, see http://www.grandstreet.com/gsissues/gs56/gs56e.html (accessed March 29, 2009).

4. First published in 1887, Wahrmund's book became an anti-Semitic "bestseller" when it was re-published after World War I.

5. "Der Jude als Razziant an arischem Geistesgut" ("The Jew as a raider of Aryan intellectual property") (Wahrmund 1919, 112–13).

6. "At this great time you may expect to hear from me no words of my own. None apart from these, which are still just about able to prevent silence from being misinterpreted" (Kraus 1988, 9; my translation).

7. This novel (*Le Jardin des Supplices*), first published in German in 1901 and immediately confiscated by the censor, challenges European civilization by comparing

it to excessive "Asian" cruelty. While it has been identified as a major source for Kafka's 1914 story "In the Penal Colony" (see Zilcosky 2003, 110), its far-reaching echoes in his "Chinese voice" remain to be discovered.

8. After the war, Kafka made private use of the fade-over between Havlíček's biography and his own. Long-exiled in a Tyrolean village in the spring of 1920, ink-wooing his Vienna based translator Milena Jesenská, and constantly suppressing the desire to board the next train to the capital, he instead book-travels to a Tibetan village, only to ink-sigh over its distance from Vienna, adding: "What I call foolish is the idea that Tibet is far away from Vienna. Would it really be far?" (Kafka 1953, 45).

9. On Kafka as Nietzsche's first reader, see Wagner (2006a).

10. For this distinction see Weinrich (2001).

11. For my terminology of narrative levels and a useful conversion of concepts developed by Gérard Genette, Mieke Bal, and others, see Jahn (2005).

12. See, for example, Jäckel's reading of World War I as an "accident at the maximum limit of credibility" and his remark "it is astonishing that historians have never learned from accident experts. For both face the task, again and again, of clearing up catastrophes" (1996, 154; my translation).

13. "Those sections of the wall left abandoned in barren regions can easily be destroyed, over and over, by the nomads, especially since at that time these people, made anxious by the construction of the Wall, changed their dwelling places with incomprehensible rapidity, like locusts, and so perhaps had a better overview of the progress of the Wall than even we ourselves, its builders" (KSS, 113; translation modified).

14. For details, see Wagner (2009, 40–41).

15. Gerhard Neumann's chapter in this volume focuses on this procedure. For its role in Kafka's office writings, see Wagner (2003).

16. For the association of writing with the craft of a shoemaker, see Kafka's diary entry of June 5, 1922, where he notes his "Talent für 'Flickarbeit'" (KKAT, 922) ("talent for 'botch work'" [Kafka 1964, 421]).

17. On the impact of accident forms on the narrative structure of Kafka's stories, see Wagner (2006/2008).

18. For a sophisticated analysis of the status of the event in accident insurance, see Schäffner (2000).

19. See James Phelan's chapter in this volume, esp. pp. 32–34.

20. For a similar use of the concept of "signal" in Joyce studies, see Topia (1984, 109).

21. For a detailed reconstruction, see Wagner (2006b).

22. In his epilogue to the (belated) German translation of Genette's *Discours du récit,* Vogt argues that in the structuralist and poststructuralist decades (i.e., 1960–1990, roughly speaking) it was more difficult for a theory of literature based on the idea of aesthetic autonomy to cross the Rhine than to make the passage across the Atlantic. However, as we have seen, even at the level of form the aesthetic text is deeply indebted to its cultural context. Therefore, poetological analysis may very well (and actually needs to) make use of discourse analysis without falling guilty of downgrading literature to the level of mere "ideology or Ersatz philosophy" (Vogt 1998, 299).

Works Cited

Bohrer, Karl Heinz. 2005. Literatur ist nicht Kultur: Zur Verteidigung einer Disziplin. *Süddeutsche Zeitung* 251 (October 31–November 1): 20.

Buber, Martin. 1963a. Das Judentum und die Juden. In *Der Jude und sein Judentum: Gesammelte Aufsätze und Reden,* 9–18. Cologne: Melzer.

———. 1963b. Der Geist des Orients und das Judentum. In *Der Jude und sein Judentum: Gesammelte Aufsätze und Reden,* 46–65. Cologne: Melzer.

Charas, H. 1914. Vorwort. In *Bericht über den II. Internationalen Kongreß für Rettungswesen und Unfallverhütung,* ed. H. Charas, ii–vii. Vienna: Verlag der Kongreßleitung.

Cooper, Duff. 1935. *Talleyrand.* Leibzig: Insel.

Gehlen, Arnold. 1962. Über kulturelle Kristallisation. In *Studien zur Soziologie und Anthropologie,* 311–28. Neuwied: Luchterhand.

Genette, Gérard. 1992. *Palimpseste: Die Literatur auf zweiter Stufe.* Frankfurt am Main: Suhrkamp.

Greenblatt, Stephen. 1990. *Shakespearean negotiations: The circulation of social energy in Renaissance England.* Oxford: Clarendon Press.

Gütling, Alois. 1916. Beiträge zu den Themen Unfallverhütung und Unfallstatistik. In *Österreichische Zeitschrift für öffentliche und private Versicherung,* 153–92.

Hegel, G. W. F. 1900. *Lectures on the philosophy of history.* Trans. J. Sibree. London: George Bull & Sons.

Herzl, Theodor. 1943. *The Jewish state: An attempt at a modern solution of the Jewish question.* New York: Scopus.

Horn, Eva. 2000. Erlebnis und Trauma: Die narrative Konstruktion des Kriegsereignisses in Psychiatrie und Kriegsroman. In *Modernität und Trauma: Beiträge zum Zeitenbruch des Ersten Weltkrieges,* ed. Inka Mülder-Bach, 131–62. Vienna: WUV—Universitätsverlag.

Jäckel, Eberhard. 1996. *Das deutsche Jahrhundert: Eine historische Bilanz.* Stuttgart: Deutsche Verlags-Anstalt.

Jahn, Manfred. 2005. *Narratology: A guide to the theory of narrative.* Cologne: Univ. of Cologne. http://www.uni-koeln.de/~ame02/pppn.htm (accessed April 12, 2008).

Kafka, Franz. 1953. *Letters to Milena.* Trans. Tania Stern and James Stern. London: Secker & Warburg.

———. 1964. *Diaries 1910–1923.* Ed. Max Brod. London: Penguin Books.

———. 1974. *Letters to Felice.* Trans. James Stern and Elizabeth Duckworth. Ed. Erich Heller and Jürgen Born. London: Secker & Warburg.

———. 1978. *Letters to friends, family and editors.* Trans. Richard Winston and Clara Winston. London: John Calder.

———. 2004. *Amtliche Schriften.* Ed. Klaus Hermsdorf and Benno Wagner. Frankfurt: Fischer.

Fragments. *Grand Street,* http://www.grandstreet.com/gsissues/gs56/gs56e.html (accessed March 29, 2009).

———. 2009. *Franz Kafka: The office writings.* Ed. Stanley Corngold, Jack Greenberg, and Benno Wagner. Trans. Eric Patton, with Ruth Hein. Princeton, NJ: Princeton Univ. Press.

Kaufmann, Paul. 1915. *Soziale Fürsorge und deutscher Siegeswille.* Berlin: Vahlen.

Kennan, George. 1979. *The decline of Bismarck's European order: Franco-Prussian relations, 1875–1890*. Princeton, NJ: Princeton Univ. Press.

Kittler, Friedrich. 2000. Krieg im Schaltkreis. *Frankfurter Allgemeine Zeitung*. Beilage *Bilder und Zeiten,* November 25, i–ii.

Kjellén, Rudolf. 1916. *Die politischen Probleme des Weltkriegs*. Leipzig: Teubner.

Kraus, Karl. 1988. In dieser großen Zeit. In *Weltgericht I,* ed. Christian Wagenknecht, 9–24. Frankfurt: Suhrkamp.

Lagarde, Paul de. 1891. Die Religion der Zukunft. In *Deutsche Schriften: Gesammtausgabe letzter Hand,* 217–47. Göttingen: Dieterich.

Mirbeau, Octave. 1997. *Torture garden*. Trans. M. Richardson. Sawtry, Cambridgeshire: Dedalus.

Nietzsche, Friedrich. 1995. *Unfashionable observations*. Trans. Richard T. Gray. Stanford: Stanford Univ. Press.

———. 1999. *The birth of tragedy and other writings*. Trans. Ronald Speirs. Cambridge: Cambridge Univ. Press.

———. 2001. *The gay science*. Trans. J. Nauckhoff. Cambridge: Cambridge Univ. Press.

———. 2003. *Thus spoke Zarathustra: A book for everyone and no one*. Trans. R. J. Hollingdale. London: Penguin Books.

Roethe, Gustav. 1914. Wir Deutschen und der Krieg. In *Deutsche Reden in schwerer Zeit,* ed. Wilamowitz-Moellendorf, 15–46. Berlin: Heymann.

Schäffner, Wolfgang. 2000. Das Trauma der Versicherung: Das Ereignis im Zeitalter der Wahrscheinlichkeit. In *Modernität und Trauma: Beiträge zum Zeitenbruch des Ersten Weltkrieges,* ed. Inka Mülder-Bach, 104–20. Vienna: WUV-Universitätsverlag.

Sombart, Werner. 1915. *Händler und Helden: Patriotische Besinnungen*. Munich: Duncker & Humblot.

Talleyrand-Périgord, Charles-Maurice de. Quoted in Münch 1949, 663.

Topia, André. 1984. The matrix and the echo: Intertextuality in *Ulysses*. In *Poststructuralist Joyce: Essays from the French,* ed. Derek Attridge and Daniel Ferrer, 103–27. Cambridge: Cambridge Univ. Press.

Vogl, Josef. 1994. Vierte Person: Kafkas Erzählstimme. *Deutsche Vierteljahresschrift für Literaturwissenschaft und Geistesgeschichte* 68:745–56.

Vogt, Jochen. 1998. Nachwort des Herausgebers. In Gérard Genette, *Die Erzählung,* 299–303. Munich: Wilhelm Fink.

Wagner, Benno. 2003. "Beglaubigungssorgen": Zur Problematik von Verfasserschaft, Autorschaft und Werkintegration im Rahmen der *Amtlichen Schriften* Franz Kafkas. *Editio: International Yearbook of Scholarly Editing* 17:155–69.

———. 2006a. Insuring Nietzsche: Kafka's files. *New German Critique* 33:83–119.

———. 2006b. "Sprechen kann man mit den Nomaden nicht": Sprachenpolitik und Verwaltung bei Otto Bauer und Franz Kafka. In *Sprache und nationale Identität in öffentlichen Institutionen der Kafka-Zeit,* ed. M. Nekula and A. Greule, 109–28. Vienna: Böhlau.

———. 2006/2008. Paris, 9-11-1911: Kafka's poetics of accident. Pts. 1 and 2. *Journal of The Kafka Society of America,* New International Series, 30 (2006): 1–2; (2008): 52–62.

———. 2009. Kafka's office writings: Historical background and institutional context. In *Franz Kafka: The office writings,* ed. Stanley Corngold, Jack Greenberg, and Benno Wagner, 19–48. Princeton, NJ: Princeton Univ. Press.

Wahrmund, Adolf. 1919. *Das Gesetz des Nomadentums und die heutige Judenherrschaft.* Munich: Deutscher Volksverlag.

Weber, Max. 1904/1996. *Die protestantische Ethik und der "Geist" des Kapitalismus.* Ed. K. Lichtblau and J. Weiß. Weinheim: Beltz / Athenäum.

Weinrich, Harald. 2001. *Tempus: Besprochene und erzählte Welt.* Munich: Beck.

Wilamowitz-Moellendorf, Ulrich von, et al. 1914. *Deutsche Reden in schwerer Zeit.* Ed. Zentralstelle für Volkswohlfahrt and Verein für volkstümliche Kurse von Berliner Hochschullehrern. Berlin: Heymann.

Zilcosky, John. 2003. *Kafka's travels: Exoticism, colonialism and the traffic of writing.* New York: Palgrave Macmillan.

Zittel, Bernhard. 1967. Der Typus in der Geschichtswissenschaft. In *Methoden der Politologie,* ed. R. H. Schmidt, 124–37. Darmstadt: Wissenschaftliche Buchgesellschaft.

4

THE ABANDONED WRITING DESK

ON KAFKA'S METANARRATIVES, AS EXEMPLIFIED BY "DER HEIZER"

Gerhard Neumann

> Ich will nicht daß er es allen erzählt. ("I do not want him to tell everyone".)
>
> —Kafka, *Der Verschollene* (KKAV, 39)[1]

> Aber auch abgesehen davon sind in Deiner Rede einige Fehler enthalten gewesen, d.h. ich meine, es hat sich in Wirklichkeit nicht alles so zugetragen. ("But apart from that there were some errors in your account; that is, I think that not all of it really occurred in that way".)
>
> —Kafka, *Der Verschollene* (KKAV, 43)

> Du mußt Dich aber zur Wehr setzen, ja und nein sagen, sonst haben ja die Leute keine Ahnung von der Wahrheit. ("But you must defend yourself, say yes or no—otherwise people have no inkling of the truth".)
>
> —Kafka, *Der Verschollene* (KKAV, 49)

I

Kafka's writings focus particularly on something that he once called "den riskantesten Augenblick im Tag" ("the most risky moment of the day").[2] It is the focus of attention on the transition from sleep to waking, on the act of birth from the mother's womb into the bosom of the family, and finally on the exit from the family and the entry into society. It is this last transition to which Karl Roßmann's American uncle refers when he explains that "die ersten Tage eines Europäers in Amerika [seien] einer Geburt vergleichbar" (KKAV, 56) ("the first days of a European in America are comparable to a birth"). Kafka's story "The Stoker" likewise revolves around this act of birth into a strange society, around this most hazardous moment of the transition from the familiar to the alien. Adhering to the conventional structure of the novel of individual development, Kafka gives his story the traditional focus on the inception of a twofold career, stemming from a scenario of origins: there is, on the one hand, a beginning in sexual experience, and, on the other, in vocational life.[3] But for such a career to get under way successfully, there needs to be—as I mentioned—an opening scene, a story that may be narrated as an origin and that generates from out of itself a continuing life-narrative.[4] In the case of the protagonist of "The Stoker," Karl Roßmann, it is an erotic episode that serves as a narrative of origin—no rarity in stories of individual development. It is the episode of Karl Roßmann's being seduced by the cook, Johanna Brummer, a servant in his parents' apartment.[5] This scene of seduction is modeled on the mythical template of the Fall from Grace. Yet in stark contrast to the myth, it reveals itself to be the embarrassing failure of a scene of recognition between the sexes: a scene Karl is incapable of putting into narrative, since it involves too much shame and helpless incomprehension. After his metamorphosis, Gregor Samsa asks in comparable terms, "Was ist mit mir geschehen?" (KKAD, 115) ("What has happened to me?"); and it is said of Josef K. at the end of *The Trial:* "es war, als sollte die Scham ihn überleben" (KKAP, 312) ("it was as if his shame were destined to survive him").

In no sense can Karl draw on support for his future career from the narration of this "primal scene." Thus his situation is the opposite of that which occurs in many nineteenth-century novels, where a sexual initiation opens the portal to a process of maturity. Kafka's story "The Stoker" tells of the crisis of the individual's "second birth" into the world and then relates the problems that result from the fact that the scene of origin simply cannot be narrated.[6] In this sense, Kafka conducts an experiment with the possibility or impossibility of beginnings that provide or do *not* provide the foundation for a life-narrative.

And yet if we cast only a cursory glance at Kafka's story, we *do* get the impression that a life-narrative of this kind could readily be told in two short sentences. The novella begins as follows:

> Als der siebzehnjährige Karl Roßmann, der von seinen armen Eltern nach Amerika geschickt worden war, weil ihn ein Dienstmädchen verführt

> und ein Kind von ihm bekommen hatte, in dem schon langsam gewordenen Schiff in den Hafen von Newyork einfuhr, erblickte er die schon längst beobachtete Statue der Freiheitsgöttin wie in einem plötzlich stärker gewordenen Sonnenlicht. Ihr Arm mit dem Schwert ragte wie neuerdings empor und um ihre Gestalt wehten die freien Lüfte. (KKAV, 7)
>
> (When, at the age of seventeen, Karl Roßman, who had been sent to America by his poor parents because a servant-girl had seduced him and borne a child as a result, sailed into New York harbour on board a ship that was gradually losing way, he suddenly saw the statue of the Goddess of Liberty, on which he had had his eyes for some time, as if in a flash of brighter sunlight. Her arm with the sword was raised aloft as before and the free breezes played about her figure.)

Here we find the blueprint for a whole life and the template for a career, such as one might find in any book. From this point the narrative could flow with perfect freedom, telling of the primal scene of the Fall from Grace, of the story of his sexual initiation (a story that he has brought with him to the New World of the virtual allegorizing of the scene from the perspective of guilt and punishment, discipline and justice—all in the radiance of an aura of destiny. But an interpretation of the text in this sense as the nucleus of a story with a quite predictable future development would be entirely misguided. As Karl is about to leave the ship, it turns out he has made two mistakes. He has forgotten his umbrella and he has also left behind the suitcase entrusted to him by his father.[7] These two errors will deflect Karl from the straight and narrow path and lead him back into the labyrinthine belly of the ship. He wanders along corridors, hurries through an empty room "mit einem verlassenen Schreibtisch"(KKAV, 8) ("with an abandoned writing desk")—a detail whose importance will become clear later—and ends up knocking on "eine beliebige kleine Türe" (KKAV, 8) ("a random little door") behind which he meets the stoker, who—of course—gives the story its title. The adolescent boy and the man of mature years try to get to know each other and to communicate about their respective situations.

The stoker says he has just been dismissed from his job on account of some misdemeanors he is supposed to have committed, and he intends to complain about this to the captain. Karl has been compelled to emigrate to America, so they have both, in a sense, been sent into exile. But when the stoker inquires: "Warum haben Sie denn [nach Amerika] fahren müssen?" ("Why did you have to travel to America?") Karl refuses to tell his story. Rather, the text tells us: "'Ach was!' sagte Karl und warf die ganze Geschichte mit der Hand weg" (KKAV, 12) ("'Not worth mentioning!' said Karl, and dismissed the whole story with a gesture"). To this the stoker replies, "Es wird schon einen Grund gehabt haben" ("Oh yes! There'll have been a reason, all right"), and the narrator observes, "[daß man nicht recht wußte] ob [der Heizer] damit die Erzählung dieses Grundes fordern oder abwehren wolle" (KKAV, 12) ("that it was not clear whether the stoker wanted to demand this reason be revealed or prevent any disclosure of it"). By means of this ambiguity, the stoker (and through him the narrator) gives us a clue as to how the rest of the story might best be read. Our attention is meant to focus on the constant alternation of demands that, on the one hand, stories be told, and on the other hand, the rejection or refusal of narrative.

When Karl and the stoker finally end up in the Captain's cabin, Karl tries in two ways to block the narration of his own story—for naturally he believes he has "thrown it away." His first attempt is to present his passport to confirm his identity, but the purser reacts—as the text says—by flicking it away with two fingers, precisely as Karl had previously "flicked aside" his own life-story. Karl's second strategy to avoid telling how he had been seduced consists in taking sides with the stoker, then usurping the other's life-story and reciting it to the impatient gentlemen in the cabin. In order to achieve what we might term an *indirect* narration of himself, he vicariously tells the stoker's story—with the secret desire of casting the tale of his own Fall from Grace into oblivion: "Wenn ihn doch seine Eltern sehen könnten," ("If only his parents could see him now") the text runs "wie er im fremden Land vor angesehenen Persönlichkeiten das Gute verfocht" (KKAV, 33) ("fighting for the good in a foreign land before persons of repute").

At this point the reader's attention is drawn to the man with the bamboo cane, who has, up till now, been present in the cabin merely as an observer. He approaches Karl and asks—not once but twice—the question that implicitly demands the narration of his true life-story: "Wie heißen Sie denn eigentlich?" (KKAV, 31, 35) ("What *is* your real name?") Through this exchange it slowly comes to light that the stranger is Karl's rich American uncle. The cook, Johanna Brummer, who had seduced Karl, has written him a letter that arrived faster than the ship and informed him of Karl's "love story." The uncle has copied a summary description of Karl from the letter into his notebook and has now recognized Karl by comparing his appearance with the notes.

During this recognition scene[8]—virtually an anagnorisis in the drama of Karl's quest for an identity—Karl for a second time resists narrating his story. For when, according to the account in the cook's letter, the uncle sets about retelling the story of Karl's seduction, Karl says quietly to himself "ich will nicht daß er es allen erzählt" (KKAV, 39) ("I do not want him to tell everyone"). This does not in the least prevent the uncle from doing precisely that, namely reciting the history of Karl's seduction, announcing as he does so that he will later give his nephew the letter his seductress has written, so that he "den Brief, wenn er mag, in der Stille seines ihn schon erwartenden Zimmers zur Belehrung lesen kann" (KKAV, 41) ("can read it for his edification in the quiet of the bedroom that has already been prepared for him"). Thus, Karl would be not once but twice the recipient of the story he himself refuses to tell at any price: in the version contained in the cook's letter and also in his uncle's recounting of that text "for his edification."

At this moment during the "narrative" of the cook's "narration" of his story, the dialogue-scene in the Captain's cabin suddenly jumps—in the *novella*— into a kind of indirect speech that reflects Karl's stream of consciousness:

> Karl hatte aber keine Gefühle für jenes Mädchen. Im Gedränge einer immer mehr zurückgestoßenen Vergangenheit saß sie in ihrer Küche neben dem Küchenschrank, auf dessen Platte sie ihren Elbogen stützte. (KKAV, 41)

> (But Karl felt nothing for that girl. In the crowded scenes of his past, that were being pushed ever further back, he saw her in her kitchen next to the kitchen-cupboard, with her elbows propped up on its marble top.)

It was this sequence and its indirect speech that, as early as 1914, delighted Robert Musil in his review of the story; Musil considered it a mode that one could scarcely designate as "narrative," yet one that nonetheless gives voice to the dull murmur of experience.[9] Karl's indirect speech ends with the following words:

> Weinend kam er endlich nach vielen Wiedersehenswünschen ihrerseits in sein Bett. Das war alles gewesen und doch verstand es der Onkel, daraus eine große Geschichte zu machen. (KKAV, 43)

> (Weeping, Karl reached his own bed after receiving many assurances from

> her that she wanted to see him again. That was all it had been, and yet the uncle was managing to make some great story out of it.)

Here the problem of the metanarrative that is Kafka's central concern in "The Stoker" appears with the greatest clarity. The "big story" told by the uncle is superimposed on the *petit récit* that unfolds—without Karl's grasping its significance—in the sequence of indirect speech. To borrow a term from Giorgio Agamben (2002), the "grandiose program" of literary narrative is played off against the dull, half-conscious murmuring of "naked life."

When the audience fails to laugh at his uncle's "big story" as Karl had feared—probably out of respect for the uncle's dignified presence—Karl turns once again to the story of the stoker, which he had taken over once before at the beginning of the *novella*. He now tries to give the stoker a lesson—in, of all things, the correct and true way to recount life-stories. For in the meantime, the stoker—trying to tell his own sob-story to the Captain—has literally talked himself out of his job, by making what the text describes as a "trauriges Durcheinanderstrudeln" (KKAV, 27) ("pitiful mishmash") of his own arguments. "Sie müssen das einfacher erzählen, klarer, der Herr Kapitän kann das nicht würdigen so wie Sie es ihm erzählen" (KKAV, 28) ("You must tell everything more simply, more clearly—the way you are telling it, the Captain cannot appreciate the facts")—thus Karl's admonition to the stoker at the beginning of the scene in the cabin. To this he adds, "Ordnen Sie doch Ihre Beschwerden, sagen Sie die Wichtigste zuerst und absteigend die andern. . . . Mir haben Sie es doch immer so klar dargestellt" (KKAV, 28) ("Put your complaints in an orderly manner, state what is most important first and then the rest in descending order. . . . You always put it so clearly to me"). Then, right at the end, when he takes leave of the stoker, Karl warns him again: "Du mußt Dich aber zur Wehr setzen, ja und nein sagen, sonst haben ja die Leute keine Ahnung von der Wahrheit" (KKAV, 49) ("But you must defend yourself, say yes or no—otherwise people will have no inkling of the truth"). Even when confronting his uncle, Karl assumes the manner of a teacher of rhetoric: "[abgesehen davon] sind in Deiner Rede einige Fehler enthalten gewesen, d.h. ich meine, es hat sich in Wirklichkeit nicht so zugetragen" (KKAV, 43) ("there were some errors in your account; that is, I am of the view that in reality not all of it occurred in that way"). Karl, who is incapable of narrating the originary scene of his own life-history and who—perhaps because of this—tries to suppress it, paradoxically assumes the posture of instructor to his fellow narrators so as to conceal his inability to tell his own story.

II

Keeping in mind that this novella is at the same time the opening chapter of a novel, it seems to be Kafka's intent to demonstrate the impossibility of narrating the one scene that is the inception of a developing life-story. The method he chooses is to intertwine narratives of narratives and observe their continual failures. Karl suppresses the story that marks the commencement of his exile and "throws it away." But this suppressed story overtakes him on his voyage to America in the form of a letter written by his seductress, the cook, and is transformed by his uncle through the process of narration into a kind of *text* of recognition and *test* of identity—and thus turned into a "big story" (as Karl describes it) or "grand narrative" (as it might be described in literary theory). Karl's muted consciousness then narrates the whole again to himself as a *petit récit,* as the murmuring of an almost inarticulate experience. Finally, Karl adopts a kind of alibi-narrative, namely the stoker's story. Instead of attempting to make his own story credible according to the rules of "reasonable" narratives, he tries to infuse this alibi-narrative with credibility and to rehearse it as a cover-narrative of his own story, which cannot be told; we might say that the cover-narrative is the true narrative's double. In this way Karl's own erotic story is overlaid by that of the stoker's career—painted over, as it were.

Here we confront Kafka's unique narrative construct that has the following implications: the story of one and the same "experience" is conveyed from one narrative voice to another, and assumes in the process the qualities of a "suppressed," "written," "retold," "withheld," and "translated" narration. What remains a mystery is the vantage point *from* which this play of narrative and metanarrative, of telling and of telling-upon-telling is actually directed. For the "authorial" narrator, who occasionally flits through the text, remains a very weak presence. He has surrendered virtually all his authority to the characters who tell and retell the story. One indication of this specifically Kafkaesque metanarrative construct—that is, the absence of a dominant narrator—seems to me to be given by the detail I emphasized previously. When Karl, lost and disoriented, traverses the labyrinth of the empty ship looking for his umbrella, he passes a "verlassenen Schreibtisch" (KKAV, 8) ("abandoned writing desk") in an empty room. This clue points to the authorial narrator who has abandoned his place at the writing desk and thereby abandoned the individual characters to their own narrative fates—namely to those modes of telling that are transformed in their passage from one narrative voice to another— transmitted, translated, transnarrated—through the medium of the letter and the notes.

One is tempted to call this an extremely daring game with vicarious narration. It takes the form of the unstoppable telling of the stories of others. The cook vicariously narrates Karl's story. Karl vicariously narrates the stoker's story. The uncle, in turn, vicariously retells Karl's story. These narratives are "recapitulations" and "overlays" that translate, correct, falsify, displace, magnify and reduce, but they do not reveal the nucleus that is the primal scene from which everything else proceeds. This must be left a mystery.

These narrative constructs, with whose conditions and possibilities the story experiments, seem to crystallize out of three distinct fields of discourse and their respective codes. *First,* there is the field of the authorial narrator—weakly contoured as he may be—who at no point engages in metafictional reflections about his own narrative. *Second,* there is the level of utterance by the characters who carry the story and who frequently indulge in vicarious narration. The text itself betrays an awareness of this. When Karl begins narrating the miserable tale of the stoker, taking it over from its "owner," the reproach is made that the stoker has brought with him an "eingelernten Stimmführer" (KKAV, 24) ("pre-rehearsed mouthpiece"). But the characters in the text are not just vicarious narrators—they also assume the posture of critics and rectifiers, indeed almost of instructors, with regard to the narratives of other figures. *Third,* there is the mode of "indirect speech" as a narrative strategy, reflecting not only Karl's half-awareness but also, at one point, that of the stoker. This strategy may be read as a move on the part of that authorial narrator who has cleared his desk, who has abandoned the responsibility for narrating the story and left it to the half-awareness of his characters—characters who can do no more than entrust themselves to what cannot be told, what is experienced dimly and with no transparency, whether this be the enigmatic seduction to which Karl falls victim—or else the wrong that the stoker has to suffer uncomprehendingly.

Kafka thus interweaves the narrative fields of the authorial narrator, of what the characters tell one another, and of indirect speech. I propose that we consider the complex intertwining of these three realms of narrative authority as a game with metanarrative strategies. If metalanguage is that second language which speaks about a first,[10] then we could say metanarrative is that second narrative which overlays a prior one. In doing so it demonstrates the conditions that govern the possibility that "the telling of life-stories"—within a given historical and cultural situation—can be rendered intercommunicative (that is, achieved by mutual understanding). What makes Kafka's text unique, I imagine, is that the game with different narratives is no longer played by the authorial narrator but that the latter smuggles interference into the narrative voice of the text—hence a game of retellings, of a narrative that doubles itself and allows what is told to be subverted by the very act of telling. So it is that we are no longer dealing with the self-reflection of an authorial narrator who thinks aloud about how and in precisely what narrative guise he is to present the story he has in mind—something Thomas Mann is fond of to the point of embarrassment. Rather, we must here be receptive to a voice that cuts across the process of narrative, harmonizing—as it were—with the utterances of one narrator after another but directed by no discernible, dominant narrative authority.

In this sense it is, perhaps, more accurate *not* to describe what is effected in Kafka's prose as an overlaying of narrative processes but to see it rather as an oscillation and alternation within the narrative process itself. We might call it a vibration of the narrative thread, which—released from the control of the authorial narrator—has different narrative voices within the text align their frequencies with itself, or, better still, assigns to them in turn its own resonance. Kafka's narrative strategy thus creates something like a free-floating tissue of narration, for which no one voice accepts lasting responsibility and which ultimately splits into several separate strands. It is almost as if Kafka intended to allow a freedom of space in which a story could narrate itself in several voices—a story that can by no means leap over the abyss between inarticulate life and the norms of discourse, between "naked life" and "sovereign law," but still it "shows" that the gap is there. "The Stoker" is a novella which tells of what determines the possibility that, in a world of ironclad norms of discourse, it might once more be possible to establish narratives as a way of telling about lives.

III

Now, in these terms we should of course ask ourselves why Kafka, at first sight, seems to use such simple patterns of narration. There has long been talk of Kafka's "obstinate" manner of story-telling. And yet he develops such complicated patterns of narratives and of the doubling of narratives. Clearly, this complexity of narrative structures is related to the question of whether it is possible at all to relate the history of the "modern" subjectivity, which developed around 1900. If it is possible, how it might be done? For this unfortunate entity strives to find its proper place among three different codes that are mutually incompatible. First, there is the code of public existence, which is determined by politics and institutions (Habermas 1962); second, there is the code of private or familial existence, which is dictated by paternal authority; third, there is the code of intimacy (Luhmann 1982), which involves the basic improbability that emotions may be communicated between individuals and presupposes that the uniqueness of each individual is an inalienable quality.[11] What faintest possibility might there be that any authorial agency should succeed in creating a unified narrative within the field of interplay between these three discrepant codes? How could the kernel of intimacy in any human life ever be articulated and transmitted in acts of narrative under such circumstances?

Storytelling, as Kafka sets out to illustrate in "The Stoker," demonstrates that the task of narrating the event within the field of tension that exists between the withholding and forcing-out of the same story can simply not be performed. No code exists in which its "as suchness" can be expressed. There remains only the resort to interrogations and confessions. If the event of intimacy can be glimpsed at all, then it can be only in the gap that yawns between the law and "naked life." The catch-22 situation in which narrative here has to try to sustain itself is the irresolvable, compulsive alternation between being interrogated—thus the uncle's question, "Wie heißen Sie denn eigentlich" (KKAV, 31) ("What *is* your real name?")—and being forced to an admission—thus Karl's "ich will nicht daß er es allen erzählt" (KKAV, 39) ("I do not want him to tell it to everyone"). Lastly, there is the lapse into inarticulacy, which somehow finds its place in the gap between the other two. For Kafka there is no other mode of telling than a "narrative under condemnation." Jacques Derrida's formulation of this is memorable: the law with all its strategies of oppression invariably pre-exists narrative; but, contrariwise, the telling of a life in total exposure invariably precedes the law and can find no way of entering into it.[12] Only in this gap between the two extremes can the trace of the narrative voice, passing from mouth to mouth, inscribe itself: sometimes as a corrective, sometimes as a retelling, sometimes vicariously.

On the basis of this insight, we might now make the attempt to show the literary status of the text "The Stoker" among varieties of narrative in a more precise manner. Is it a novella in its own right, or should we rather see it as the opening chapter of a novel? To all appearances Kafka has, in the opening scenes of this novel, put the problematic variations of literary narration to the test—and taken them to absurd lengths. Just as Karl's route *should* lead straight from the ship into America's open spaces but gets tangled right at the start and takes him back into the labyrinth of the ship's belly, so the narrative traces, which *should* make tangible Karl's originary narrative, as the seed from which his future will sprout, become knotted and confused. Just as the direct route takes him farther and farther into the labyrinth; just as the main portal becomes some random little door on which he chances to knock;[13] just as—to draw a final analogy—the *diretissima* bifurcates into a rhizome, in all these ways syntagmatic narrative—at the very beginning of a novel, of all places!—suddenly flips into a kind of paradigmatic narration, into a *perpetuum mobile* of stories that bifurcate and overlay one another.[14] One might venture to call such storytelling "stereometric." In any event, it is overgrown with metanarratives. Storytelling that is vicarious and that constantly corrects itself becomes increasingly an interweaving of narrative acts, narrative repetitions, and their mutually critical interactions. But all this occurs without the intervention of an omniscient narrator or even the establishment of a hierarchy of narrative levels. Such an absence of a conventional hierarchy may help explain the apparent contradictions in Kafka's narrative manner and the mutability of his narrative modes. Viewed from one perspective, "The Stoker" is a novella; viewed from another, it is the beginning of a novel that could have no proper end. The ordering power of the omniscient narrator is conspicuous by its absence, and this absence manifests itself in the intricate layering of ambivalences behind façades of narrative simplicity.

Kafka has used his *novella* "The Stoker" as a means of setting out the question that is characteristic of all his work—or, rather, he has set it before our very eyes in narrative form. This question is, of course, whether there are still any narratives available for the telling of individual uniqueness, for the recounting of that inalienable "naked life." Thus, I conclude that he has given us, with this *novella,* his version of that poetological primal scene which prefigures his art as a novelist, together with all the irresolvable contradictions active within it.

(Translated by Anthony Stephens)

Notes

1. All translations by Anthony Stephens.

2. A textual variant in *The Trial*: "Darum sei auch der Augenblick des Erwachens der riskanteste Augenblick im Tag, sei er einmal überstanden, ohne dass man irgendwohin von seinem Platze fortgezogen wurde, so könne man den ganzen Tag über getrost sein" (KKAP, 169) ("Therefore the moment of waking is the most perilous moment of the day—once you have survived it without being forcibly dislocated from your proper place, you can face all the rest of the day with confidence").

3. In *Wilhelm Meister* this scenario is presented as a paradigm; on the reading of love relationships as patterns of identity, see Luhmann (1982). On the construction of individuality, see Luhmann (1994, 191–202).

4. In *Wilhelm Meister* this function is fulfilled by the marionette theatre, Tankred and Chlorinde, Mariane, and the fisher-boy.

5. This was a cliché in literature around the turn of the century, for example in Schnitzler's "Der Reigen."

6. Something similar is attempted by Rotpeter, the ape turned human, in Kafka's "Ein Bericht für eine Akademie."

7. "Als ihm der Vater den Koffer für immer übergeben hatte, hatte er im Scherz gefragt: Wie lange wirst du ihn haben?" (KKAV, 14) ("When his father had entrusted him with the suitcase for ever, he had asked jokingly, How long will you manage to keep it?").

8. The stoker explicitly refers to it as "Wiedererkennung" (KKAV, 47) ("recognition").

9. According to Musil (1914), Kafka showed himself as "a very conscious artist" (1170) whose narrative style is characterized by "total dissolution and total control" (1169). The protagonist's actions are "entirely matters that can never be brought to an end that, from the perspective of the external world, dangle into it like broken off wires, and his thoughts are such as he can never think through to a conclusion" (Musil 1914, 1170). "It is deliberate naivety . . . something indirect, complicated, accomplished . . . a moral sensibility . . . of a refined and penetrating irritability" that "makes visible peculiar overlaps" (Musil 1914, 1170).

10. Roland Barthes terms this strategy "metanarrative, because it is a second language in which one speaks about the first" (1978, 115). Above all, I refer to Genette (1969, 1982, 1994).

11. Kafka's short autobiographical text "Jeder Mensch ist eigentümlich . . . " (KKANII, 7) ("Each person is unique . . . ") is of great significance in this context. See also the chapter by Hillis Miller in this volume.

12. It is rewarding to consider slightly different expressions of this insight. See Derrida (1983; 1984, 88; 1992a; 1992b).

13. There are three doors in the narrative, the "kleine Tür" (KKAV, 8) ("little door") before the stoker's berth, the "heillos unvorbereitet (KKAV, 33) ("fatally unexpectedly") opened door to the Captain's cabin, and the "Türchen" (KKAV, 52) ("little door") through which Karl and his uncle leave the ship by way of a set of stairs, possibly a gangway.

14. The twin concepts of syntagm and paradigm have been extensively used by Rainer Warning in his studies of Proust, following on from the narrative theory of

A. J. Greimas. For a discussion of the metaphor of the rhizome as a structural characteristic of Kafka's narratives, see Deleuze and Guattari (1997).

Works Cited

Agamben, Giorgio. 2002. *Homo sacer: Die souveräne Macht und das nackte Leben.* Frankfurt am Main: Suhrkamp.

Barthes, Roland. 1978. *Mythologies.* Trans. Annette Lavers. New York: Hill & Wang.

Deleuze, Gilles, and Félix Guattari. 1997. *Kafka: Toward a minor literature.* Trans. Dana Polan. Minneapolis: Univ. of Minnesota Press.

Derrida, Jacques. 1983. Préjugés. In *Spiegel und Gleichnis: Festschrift für Jacob Taubes,* ed. Nobert W. Bolz and Wolfgang Hübner, 343–66. Würzburg: Königshausen & Neumann.

———. 1984. Devant la loi. In *Philosophy and Literature,* ed. A. Phillip, 173–88. Cambridge: Cambridge Univ. Press.

———. 1992a. Before the law. In *Acts of literature,* ed. Derek Attridge, 181–220. New York: Routledge.

———. 1992b. Préjugés. In *Vor dem Gesetz,* ed. Peter Engelmann. Wien: Passagen-Verlag.

Genette, Gérard. 1969. *Figures II.* Paris: Éditions du Seuil.

———. 1982. *Palimpsestes. La littérature en second degré.* Paris: Éditions du Seuil.

———. 1994. *Die Erzählung.* Munich: Wilhelm Fink.

Habermas, Jürgen. 1962. *Strukturwandel der Öffentlichkeit: Untersuchungen zu einer Kategorie der bürgerlichen Gesellschaft.* Neuwied: Luchterhand.

Kafka, Franz. 2002a. *Schriften.* Vol. 1 of *Tagebücher,* ed. Jürgen Born et al. Kritische Ausgabe [Critical Edition]. Frankfurt am Main: Fischer.

———. 2002b. *Tagebücher.* Vol. 2 of *Tagebücher,* ed. Jürgen Born et al. Kritische Ausgabe [("Critical Edition]"). Frankfurt am Main: Fischer.

Luhmann, Niklas. 1982. *Liebe als Passion: Zur Codierung von Intimität.* Frankfurt am Main: Suhrkamp.

———. 1994. Kopierte Existenz und Karriere: Zur Herstellung der Individualität. In *Riskante Freiheiten: Individualisierung in modernen Gesellschaften,* ed. Ulrich Beck and Elisabeth Beck-Gernsheim, 191–202. Frankfurt am Main: Suhrkamp.

Musil, Robert. 1914. Literarische Chronik. *Die freie Bühne* 25 (*Die neue Rundschau*): 1169–1170.

Warning, Rainer. 2000. *Proust-Studien.* Munich: Wilhelm Fink.

5

THERESE'S STORY IN *DER VERSCHOLLENE*

Gerhard Kurz

I

This discussion of *Der Verschollene* (*The Man Who Disappeared*) begins by making some introductory observations on the narrative structure of Kafka's uncompleted novel. I then proceed to analyze a particularly interesting example of embedded narrative, namely Therese's story in chapter five, entitled "Im Hotel Occidental."[1]

The central plot of the novel concerns the story of Karl Roßmann. Having been seduced by a maidservant and given her a child, Karl has been cast out of his family's home in Prague and sent to America. According to his uncle, Karl has been "einfach beiseite geschafft . . . wie man eine Katze vor die Tür wirft, wenn sie ärgert" (38) ("simply got rid of, the way you put the cat out if it's making a nuisance of itself"). This expulsion is only the first in a catechism of repudiations that serve to establish the novel's narrative pattern. This pattern is embedded in the overarching narrative scheme of a journey: literally, the crossing from Europe to America, the arrival in New York, the trip to a country house on the outskirts of the city, the "march" to the city of Ramses, the period spent in the Hotel Occidental, and then the ride to Clayton, where Karl is admitted to the "Nature Theatre of Oklahama" under the name of "Negro." As in other narratives by Kafka, however, the literal journey is given overtones of another, larger and spiritual journey, of which the movements of the figures are examples.

The narrative pattern of journeying bears a wide range of associations in Kafka's oeuvre. K.'s arrival, after a long walk, at the bridge leading to the village constitutes the beginning of the novel *Das Schloß* (*The Castle*), in which the protagonist will undertake numerous, fruitless attempts to communicate with the authorities who are assumed to occupy the castle overlooking the village. By the end of *Der Proceß* (*The Trial*), it emerges that another kind of journey (one that leads to death) started with the arrest of Josef K. at the beginning of the novel. The waiting of the man from the country in the story "Vor dem Gesetz" ("Before the Law"), which Kafka incorporated in *The Trial,* is presented as a stage in a journey toward The Law. In *The Man Who Disappeared,* the pattern of journeying includes passages describing communication through various media, technical devices, writing situations, work sequences and, above all, traffic. America is perceived and described as a domain in which humans, means of transportation, and information are incessantly chasing one another.

In this novel, journeying can be described more accurately as a pattern of temporary or illusory inclusion alternating with expulsion, via the (repeated) cycle of seduction, lapse, condemnation, and banishment. This pattern emerges mainly from the interactions of the protagonist Karl with seductive females on the one hand and authoritative figures on the other, such as his parents and uncle, the Head Waiter, the Head Porter, and the female Head Cook who all pull and push him in various directions. As we shall see, Therese's story is integrated into the overall composition by the way it represents a revealing variation of this pattern of inclusion and exclusion, as a sub-plot in which someone is brought to the reader's attention as an expellee in need of help from others—including Karl himself. If the novel shows Karl being expelled and others failing to help him, Therese's story shows Karl in turn failing to help another person, who is just as much in need of help as he is. Karl was expelled by his parents, Therese was abandoned by her father and then by her mother. Karl's self-image as an excluded victim of circumstance is thereby contrasted with an image of him as one of the excluders.

The first seduction of Karl Roßmann in the family home by the maidservant or "Köchin" Johanna Brummer results in his condemnation and subsequent expulsion by his parents. Karl's second seductress is Klara, daughter of Pollunder. Acting against his uncle's wishes, Karl has let himself be coaxed by Mr. Green into visiting a country house near New York. Karl experiences the meeting with Klara as a seduction; he resists it and calls Klara "eine tolle Katze" (91) ("wildcat"); in his view, her room bears the traits of a "recht gefährlichen Höhle" (90) ("rather dangerous lair"). As his uncle had earlier compared Karl to a cat being turned out of the house (38), the encounter underscores the ferocity of relations in a world of hunters and prey. After midnight on the day of Karl's visit to Pollunder's country house, the uncle (repeating the pattern that began in the parental home) communicates his own condemnation and expulsion of Karl by letter, according to which his nephew's lapse stems from his decision "vom Onkel fortzugehen" (123) ("to leave his uncle"). The third seduction of Karl, ostensibly into the role of adopted child, is undertaken by the maternal and obese Head Cook at the Hotel Occidental, Grete Mitzelbach, who hails from Vienna. Here again Karl's lapse is marginal and apparently involuntary. He leaves his workplace at the elevator for a brief moment in order to help a comrade. Nevertheless, the condemnation by the Head Waiter and the subsequent "execution" by the Head Porter are effected. Karl is accused of having left his "Posten" without permission (225) and of having "gelogen, gelumpt, gesoffen und gestohlen" (259) ("lied, debauched, drunk and stolen"). With the introduction of the fourth woman encountered by Karl it becomes evident that most of the female characters have been designed as a serial type. Her name, Brunelda, faintly echoes that of "Brummer," the name of the family maidservant, and may allude ironically to Brunhilde, the mythical figure of Germanic saga and of Wagner's opera.

The fifth and last "Verlockung" (388) ("lure") is effected by a poster offering admittance to the "große Theater von Oklahama." "'Jeder war willkommen,' hieß es" (388) ("'Everybody was welcome,' it said"). Hundreds of seemingly gigantic women are standing at the entrance to the grounds of the racecourse where recruiting to the theater takes place. Alternating with male devils, the women figure as a line of angels. Karl recognizes one of these women as Fanny, an "alte Freundin" (393). To him she appears as "fast die höchste" ("almost the tallest") of women. It is Fanny who enables him to make his way to the place of admission. Her name may allude to Cleland's pornographic novel *Fanny Hill,* but the link is not elaborated.

In this pattern of seduction and expulsion, the experience of sexuality opens repeatedly onto encounters with death. During his sexual intercourse with Johanna Brummer, Karl, suffocating, shakes: "Kopf und Hals aus dem Kissen heraus" (43) ("Karl's head and neck leapt out of the pillows"). The next dominatrix, Klara, threatens to slap Karl in the face and says "Und vielleicht bist du ein Ehrenmann—ich möchte es fast glauben—und wirst mit den Ohrfeigen nicht weiterleben wollen und dich aus der Welt schaffen" (92) ("Maybe you're a man of honor—I almost think you are—and you won't be able to go on living after you've been slapped and you'll have to do away with yourself").

The series of female characters opens with the maidservant, introduced in the very first sentence of the novel. Immediately thereafter we are told how Karl sees the Statue of Liberty in New York harbor. As she is furnished not with a torch but with sword, this "goddess of freedom" appears to have been transformed into a figure alluding both to the goddess of justice and to the cherub with the flaming sword who guards the gate of Paradise (Gen. 3:24). As the semantic switch from "die schon längst beobachtete Statue" ("the statue which had already been in view for some time") to "erblickte" ("suddenly saw") and "wie neuerdings" ("only just") indicates, this description is not made by an objective narrator. Rather, it is a focalization of Karl's perception. He perceives, or imagines, the statue as a figure whose arm with the sword rises up while the "freien Lüfte" (7) ("unchained winds," verbatim: "free winds") are blowing around it.[2]

This entangling of a realistic and an imaginary perception establishes from the outset a realistic and at the same time an allegorical dimension of meaning for the entire novel. In the narrative process, the elements of the opening sequence—seduction, expulsion, journey—are picked up again, elaborated, and integrated into a spiralling network of motives. This is quite characteristic of any traditional novel. The statue's sword, for example, recurs as the uncle's stick and several subsequent hints and allusions to the military ("comrade," "post," and "execution," for example). The direction of the sword-arm, "empor" ("aloft"), commented on by Karl—"So hoch" (7) ("So high")—is mirrored in Karl's path, which on the one hand leads spatially upward from station to station, always a little farther up: from the uncle's house to the house in the country, to the hotel, to "solche Höhe" ("such heights") in the theater of Oklahama, while at the same time leading downward socially.

In an attempt to brush aside his uncle's account of his seduction and expulsion, Karl uses the words "große Geschichte" (43), translatable verbatim as a "big story" or "a great story." Yet within the novel's allegorical dimension (introduced by the sword of the goddess), this "big story," which Karl wishes to reject, evokes the seduction of Adam by Eve and the expulsion from paradise. Given that their expulsion entails the change from immortal to mortal existence, in which the continuity of life is only assured by procreation (the consequence of the "original sin"), this expulsion has the character of a birth or re-birth. When Karl's uncle compares the crossing from Europe to America with a "Geburt" (56) ("birth"), involving the passage "vom Jenseits in die menschliche Welt" ("entering the human world from the beyond"), he is invoking precisely this "große Geschichte" to impose a particular, culturally familiar meaning on Karl's arrival in the New World. At the same time, this journey into the human world is fraught with allusions to death: The pattern of the passage to America itself alludes to the mythical Acheron: the passage to death. The officials at New York harbor wear black uniforms, Karl applies at the Theatre of Oklahoma under the name of "Negro." The cold and loneliness of the abandoned Therese and her mother in New York and the deliberate death of Therese's mother will take up the same motif again.

II

On his way to Ramses with two mysterious characters, the tramps Robinson and Delamarche, Karl arrives at the Hotel Occidental. The Head Cook takes to him and employs him as a lift-boy. Therese, typist and secretary to the Head Cook, befriends Karl. However, one cannot say that Karl befriends her in equal measure. "Sie hatte keine Geheimnisse vor ihm" (195) ("she had no secrets from him"), we are told, but nothing is said about Karl revealing his secrets to her. On the contrary, she has to submit to Karl. From Karl's perspective the following arrogant statement is added: "Es wäre auch nicht gut möglich gewesen, nach ihrem Besuch damals am ersten Abend noch Geheimnisse vor ihm zu haben" (195–96) ("and indeed it would have been difficult for her to have any secrets after her first visit to him that first evening").

Therese is an illegitimate child; the father, a builders' foreman, had emigrated to New York, leaving Therese's exhausted mother to follow him with her daughter. Yet he deserted them shortly after their arrival without much explanation, moving on to Canada. The "Zurückgebliebenen" heard no more of him—"zum Teil auch nicht zu verwundern . . . denn sie waren in den Massenquartieren des New Yorker Ostens unauffindbar verschwunden" (196) ("which wasn't all that surprising as they were hopelessly lost in the cramped ghetto in the Eastern part of New York"; "unauffindbar": verbatim: "not to be found"). This father is "verschollen," they are "verschollen." The term "verschollen" is applied to people whose whereabouts are known to no one, of whom there are no tidings, of whom no one knows whether they are still alive. This story contains a twofold reflection of Karl's story. Like Karl, bereft of his family, the mother has lost her husband and the child has lost her father and her mother while they themselves are lost in New York. Conversely, the father has left his only child behind, voluntarily, just as Karl seems to have forgotten about his own child. At any rate, his consciousness betrays no trace of it.

Therese's story begins thus: "Einmal erzählte Therese—Karl stand neben ihr am Fenster und sah auf die Straße—vom Tod ihrer Mutter" (196) ("Once—Karl was standing next to her at the window, gazing down on the street—Therese had talked about the death of her mother"). Obviously she relates this event in considerable detail because it is "spät" (202) ("late") when she finishes. The reference to looking out of the window down at the street is of some importance. Previously, the uncle had warned Karl not to look down at the street from the balcony, since this action would give rise to confusion and would lead anyone "der hier bleiben will" ("who wants to stay here") to his "Verderben" (56) ("doom"). The situation at the window is a situation occurring, ominously, at a threshold.

Therese's story is not the first embedded narrative or narrated narrative in the novel. In the first chapter, the uncle, while being entertained in the captain's cabin, relates the story of Karl's seduction and expulsion, mentioning the maidservant's letter that announces Karl's arrival in New York. The uncle tells this story to explain a "kleine Familienszene" (37) ("little family scene"), since Karl has questioned their relation. In this account, more of the events predating Karl's arrival in New York are revealed. Furthermore, the uncle's narrative has such a profound effect on Karl that the episode of his seduction returns to the forefront of his consciousness "Aus dem Gedränge einer immer mehr zurückgestoßenen Vergangenheit" (41) ("in the crush of an ever-receding [verbatim: 'repelled'] past").

Besides the acts of saying, talking, asking, answering, inquiring, interrogating, and admitting, the act of narrating is of importance. Throughout the novel, narrations are demanded or warded off.[3] Karl asks the stoker to narrate "einfacher . . . klarer" (28) ("more clearly and simply"); he tells the uncle about life at home; he has to tell the Head Cook about Europe; the Head Waiter tells about Karl's misdeeds (240). In her narration, Therese tells of the death of her mother ten years ago, when she was about five years old. Together with Therese, the mother is in desperate search of accommodation in wintry New York. The mother has no employment, no money, nothing left to eat, no "Plätzchen," (198) ("place") only the prospect of work on a construction site, starting the next morning. As she feels dead tired and has already coughed up blood, she tries to "irgendwo in die Wärme zu kommen und sich auszuruhen"

(197) ("get in the warm somewhere and rest"). As if "in einem Wahn" (196) ("possessed") she rushes through the streets during a snowstorm, a situation her child is not wholly able to understand: "das Ganze schien damals für seinen Unverstand nur die Erklärung zu haben, daß die Mutter von ihm weglaufen wolle" (199) ("in her incomprehension the only explanation she could find for the whole thing was that her mother was trying to run away from her").

They seem to be refused admittance everywhere, but they do not step inside any building even though the gates and doors are not locked. After midnight, the mother stops addressing anyone and does not want rest anymore. In the morning, they reach the construction site where the mother is supposed to start working. Like a Native American preparing for fighting, she ties a colored rag around her head, then she climbs the scaffolding and plunges herself over the edge. Seen from Therese's viewpoint, the mother has escaped into death. "Die letzte Erinnerung Thereses an ihre Mutter war, wie sie mit auseinandergestreckten Beinen dalag in dem karierten Rock, der noch aus Pommern stammte, wie jenes auf ihr liegende rohe Brett sie fast bedeckte, wie nun die Leute von allen Seiten zusammenliefen und wie oben vom Bau irgendein Mann zornig etwas hinunterrief" (202) ("Therese's last memory of her mother was of her lying there with legs apart in the checkered skirt she had brought with her from Pomerania, the rough plank on top of her, almost covering her, people running together from all directions, and from up on the site some man angrily shouted something").

Embedding narrations is a familiar enough technique of novel writing. Embedded narrations can mirror and condense fundamental aspects of the novel as a whole. Kafka already employs this technique in *Beschreibung eines Kampfes* (*Description of a Struggle*) and also in his two other novels: "Before the Law," which is the "legend" in *The Trial,* and Olga's story about Amalia's secret in *The Castle.* Both have similar mirroring functions. Therese's story reflects Karl's story, while the mother's restless hunt through the streets exemplifies the pace of the American world of industry and labor he encounters elsewhere. The Head Cook only sleeps for a few hours each night; the student Joseph Mendel does not sleep at all; the elevator-boys sleep standing on their feet in order to manage their twelve-hour-shifts; Karl and Therese carry out their errands in a great hurry. However, in Therese's memory this great hurry might well have been "in Wirklichkeit ganz gut auch bloß ein Schleichen" ("and perhaps in reality it was no more than a mere crawl"). "Therese wußte auch nicht, ob sie von Mitternacht bis fünf Uhr früh in zwanzig Häusern oder in zwei oder gar nur in einem Haus gewesen waren" (199) ("Nor could Therese be sure whether they had tried their luck in twenty houses between midnight and five o'clock, or two or even just one"). The fruitless search appears to go on for an eternity; it seems that mother and child are refused entry everywhere—and for all time.

The mother's climb up the scaffolding, whose vertical bars soared into the blue sky, takes the same direction as the sword raised aloft by the Statue of Liberty; it also mirrors Karl's progress through a series of ever-higher destinations. This detail is particularly important to Therese: "Sie hatte ausführlich erzählt, wie es sonst nicht ihre Gewohnheit war, und gerade bei gleichgültigen Stellen, wie bei der Beschreibung der Gerüststangen, die jede für sich allein in den Himmel ragten, hatte sie mit Tränen in den Augen innehalten müssen" (202) ("It had been unusually detailed for her, and, especially in unimportant places, for instance the description of the scaffolding poles each soaring into the sky, she had to stop with tears in her eyes"). The expression "gleichgültige Stellen" (202) ("unimportant places") is semantically ambiguous, since it can also mean "gleich gültige Stellen" of the story, i.e. passages of equal importance.

At first glance, the story told by Therese about her mother is a tale of hunger, sickness and despair, ending in the mother's lethal fall from the scaffolding. It seems to be a tale of the deadly coldness and indifference of a capitalist society in the tradition of the social novel à la Dickens or Hugo. However, the situation also bears apocalyptic traits transcending the social dimension. The passage describing the "rauchigen Dunst, der wie durch einen Brand verursacht, die Zimmer erfüllte" (198) ("the haze that filled the rooms like smoke from a fire") conjures an image of the tenement halls as an apocalyptic world. The hotel dormitory is likewise filled with smoke (149) and the uncle is somber with satisfaction when Karl, sharing his place by the window, recites his first American poem, "die Darstellung einer Feuersbrunst" (62) ("the account of a conflagration").[4]

Much the same as her memory is not reliable, Therese's narration also is ambiguous because it is intertwined with a conflicting voice telling a different story. In the narration two voices are blended. From a certain moment onward, the mother is no longer looking for an accommodation for herself and her child; instead, already "totmüde" (197) ("dead tired"), she is looking for death. With hindsight it appears to Therese that the mother "nur in den ersten Stunden ernstlich einen Platz suchte" (198) ("had only been serious in her search for the first few hours"). The child's incomprehension can only give the whole thing the seeming

"Erklärung," ("explanation") "dass die Mutter von ihm weglaufen wollte" (199) ("that her mother was trying to run away from her"). In this context the expression means more than merely running away. They do not join any of the groups of people they encounter but count themselves "glücklich" (200) to escape them. They are no longer looking for accommodation.

The mother's fall seems at first glance to be an accident. But it is no accident. There are indications that she resolutely plunges herself into death: for her climb, she has decorated herself with the aforementioned "colored rag" like an Indian.[5] She moves purposefully, with a sureness and authority she did not have before. "Nun kam aber die Mutter auf ihrem Gang zu einem kleinen Ziegelhaufen, vor dem das Geländer und wahrscheinlich auch der Weg aufhörten, aber sie hielt sich nicht daran, ging auf den Ziegelhaufen los, ihre Geschicklichkeit schien sie verlassen zu haben, sie stieß den Ziegelhaufen um und fiel über ihn hinweg in die Tiefe" (157) ("Then her mother came to a little pile of bricks marking the end of the railing and probably the path as well, but she didn't stop, she walked up to the bricks, her sure-footedness seemed to have deserted her, she kicked over the bricks and fell with them over the edge"). In this sentence, one voice recounts the mother's death as a deliberate act, while another voice presents the death as an accident caused by clumsiness. The expression "ging auf den Ziegelhaufen los" also means a determined attack by the mother against the obstacles in her path. In her narration, Therese both understands and misunderstands "the whole thing," marveling at her mother's "sure-footedness" in "ihrem Dusel" (201); "Dusel" means drowsiness or daze as well as stupendous, unexpected good fortune. The ambiguity plays both on the mother's numbed subjection to circumstance and on her determined pursuit of release from her situation.

Enhanced by semantic allusions and ambiguities, the intensity of Therese's narration establishes a parabolic meaning. It can be understood as "proof" of the impossibility of finding "Unterkommen"—accommodation as well as a sustaining position—in life. The men in the doorways of the houses not only deny entry to Therese and her mother by their mute presence or a curt word. They prove, as it is said, the "Unmöglichkeit des Unterkommens"—the impossibility of finding shelter, or, indeed, a place in life: "trat nur die Gestalt irgend jemandes hervor, der im Türrahmen stand und entweder durch seine stumme Gegenwart oder durch ein kurzes Wort die Unmöglichkeit eines Unterkommens in dem betreffenden Zimmer bewies" (198) ("a human figure would loom in the doorway, and either with a curt word or by its mute presence prove the impossibility of finding shelter in that particular room"). Strikingly, the phrase mentions the fact that there is "immerfort Leben" (199) ("always life"), thus life per se. The houses where people meet at every turn can stand for life in general. Thus, one possible meaning of "immerfort Leben" is that there is always life, evermore, continuous. Another meaning of the phrase is "life that always is already gone, permanently lost": *immer fort.*

A proof to whom? To Therese? She is shown in the narrative as a character who does not understand and yet at the same time understands "the whole thing." To Karl? Should he, or can he understand the story as proof of a previous statement or experience? Does he already understand the story as such a proof? Or should we say that the employment of "proved" betrays a subconscious understanding? In any case, the word indicates a proof to the addressee of the narration: Karl on one level, the reader on another.

III

How is Therese's story presented? It is the classic storytelling situation. Somebody, Therese, in her room one evening, is telling somebody else, Karl, on some occasion and for some purpose, that something happened: the death of her mother. The story is framed by indicating an act of narration: "Once . . . Therese had talked about . . . " and by a concluding narrative comment on the narration (202). Retrospectively, Therese tells of an incident that occurred "damals"(197) ("then"), ten years earlier; she must have been five years old, as she says. Her narrative commentary asserts that she can recollect everything—"ganz genau" (202) ("every detail"). And yet the use of the modal particles "wohl" ("arguably") or "vielleicht" ("perhaps") and the phrase "schien es jetzt im Rückblick" (198) ("had a dim memory, verbatim: "seemed in retrospect") indicates the uncertainty of her recollection. Thus, Therese's story is a subtle example of Kafka's technique of producing narrative uncertainty and of blending different narrative voices, different perspectives.

Originally, Kafka had written Therese's narration as a passage related by a first-person narrator (KKAVA, 195). He then changed it into a third-person narrative, thus making it congruent with the narrative discourse of the whole novel. He proceeded similarly with the beginning of *The Castle.* The adoption of a third-person narrative allows for interferences and the shifting of voices and perspectives. As is well known, the narrative perspective in Kafka's novels and stories is closely related to the main character's perspective. Moreover, adapting Therese's story to the novel's overall narrative discourse creates an intriguing bond between Karl's perspective and the perspectives adopted by the narrator. The following sentence is an illustrative example of these shifts and interferences: "Karl hatte noch keinen Winter in New York mitgemacht" (196) ("Karl hadn't yet experienced a winter in New York"). The narrative voice could be Therese addressing Karl, presented or transposed as third-person narration. Or the voice could be that of a heterodiegetic narrator. Or, if we link the sentence to Karl's perspective, the narrative voice can merge with Karl's voice, thus constituting a variant of free indirect speech influenced by Therese's description.

Thus two—or, given the possibility of Karl's voice being heard, three—narrative instances are blended together: Therese's—narrating, as we have seen, with two voices—Karl's, and the one reporting, transposing, and narrating Therese's speech. As readers who are considering the narrative situation—Therese as narrator, Karl as her audience standing close to her—we get the impression that this narrator's voice is blending into the filter of Karl's awareness or consciousness. Hence we also get the impression that Karl is deeply affected by Therese's story.

In the narrative discourse, four levels of speech are integrated: reported direct speech, free indirect speech, transposed speech, and narrated speech. The discourse alternates between scenic immediacy and narrative mediation, between past and present tense. Consider the first sentence: "Wie die Mutter und sie an einem Winterabend—sie konnte damals etwa fünf Jahre alt gewesen sein—jede mit ihrem Bündel durch die Straßen eilten, um Schlafstellen zu suchen" (196) ("The way that one winter evening her mother and herself—she must have been five at the time—each carrying a bundle, chased down the stree, looking for a place to sleep"). This is a beginning *in medias res.* The transposed speech indicated by the third-person narration and the past tense switches to free indirect speech due to the absence, the deletion of a narrative act (i.e., "Therese erzählte.") Narrating and experiencing, or reliving, converge. The inserted sentence, "sie konnte damals etwa fünf Jahre alt gewesen sein" ("she must have been five at the time"), is being told from the distance of an external focalization.

Immediacy and mediation of the narrative presentation also change in the following three sentences: "Und diese Schneestürme in den langen geraden Newyorker Straßen!" (196) ("And the snowstorms in the long straight streets of New York!"): free indirect speech, reported speech. "Karl hatte noch keinen Winter in New York mitgemacht." (196–97) ("Karl hadn't experienced a winter in New York"): reported speech, reported thoughts of Karl or utterance of an external narrator. "Geht man gegen den Wind, und der dreht sich im Kreise, kann man keinen Augenblick die Augen öffnen, immerfort zerreibt einem der Wind den Schnee auf dem Gesicht, es ist etwas Verzweifeltes." (197) ("If you walk into a swirling headwind, you can't open your eyes even for a second, the wind is incessantly rubbing snow in your face, you walk and walk and get nowhere, it's quite desperate"): reported direct speech.

With what intention does Therese tell Karl the story about her mother's death? Therese's narration has a mirroring, parabolic-reflexive, "proving" function in the novel's discourse. In the narrated world of the novel, the narration has diverse functions as well: Therese tells of her mother's death since she does not want to keep any secrets from Karl. With this narration, she confides in Karl and thereby asks for his reliance, friendship, and affection. She also explains her personal situation, particularly her relationship with the Head Cook who takes on the role of a substitute mother.

Another important purpose is specified directly. This purpose is what Therese is interested in at the end of her story: "weil der Anblick ihrer Mutter oben im halbfertigen Erdgeschoß das letzte Andenken an das Leben der Mutter war und sie es ihrem Freunde gar nicht genug deutlich überantworten konnte, wollte sie nach dem Schluße ihrer Erzählung noch einmal darauf zurückkommen, stockte aber, legte das Gesicht in die Hände und sagte kein Wort mehr." (202–3) ("because the sight of her mother up on the partly finished ground floor was her last memory of her mother's life, and she couldn't relate it clearly enough to her friend, she wanted to go back to it again after the end of her story, but she faltered, buried her face in her hands and didn't say another word"). This is odd phrasing: "das letzte Andenken an das Leben der Mutter . . . überantworten"—that is, to commit or hand over the last memory, the last mental souvenir to Karl. The last sight does not really refer to the actual last sight, the dead mother on the ground, but to the mother's behavior on the scaffolding, to the mother's life. "Überantworten" can mean to bequeath, to entrust, to deliver; it connotes giving ownership, responsibility, and consequences. Something of importance is judiciously entrusted to the care and responsibility of another.

Which message does Therese want Karl to understand by telling her story? What consequence is the bequest of the "last memory" of the mother's life supposed to have for Karl? Which kind of *Antwort* ("answer") is he supposed to give? Is it supposed to be a recognition of death, of one's own mortality, of the responsibility for one's own death?

The sentence "Sie hatte ausführlich erzählt, wie es sonst nicht ihre Gewohnheit war und gerade bei gleichgültigen Stellen, wie bei der Beschreibung der Gerüststangen, die jede allein für sich in den Himmel ragten, hatte sie mit Tränen in den Augen innehalten müssen" (202) ("The story had been unusually detailed for her, and, especially in unimportant places, for instance the description of the scaffolding poles each soaring into the sky, she had to stop with tears in her eyes") symbolically emphasizes that the human being is alone in this situation. The poles rise up to the sky "jede allein für sich" ("each on its own"), conveying the sense that one must take responsibility for living and dying. Therese narrates this while crying. For her, this part of the story is anything but unimportant. The phrasing "gleichgültige Stellen" ("unimportant places"), in contrast, focalizes Karl's perception of what she describes so vividly, or rather, his incomprehension. Yet why does Karl so emphatically perceive these passages to be unimportant? The end is ambiguous: Therese falters and rests her face in her hands. This could convey that she is overwhelmed by her own feelings, or it could be an expression of her desperation, since she cannot reach Karl; this communicative journey too has led into emptiness. The chapter ends without Karl giving an answer.

Notes

1. My work on this essay has been aided by studies by Kurz (1980, 152–58), Nicolai (1981), Neumann (1985, 43–65), Kremer (1994, 238–53), Plachta (1994, 75–97), Speirs and Sandberg (1997, 29–62), Godé and Vanoosthyse (1997), Scheffel (1999/2000, 279–95), Greiner (2003, 637–58), Metz (2004, 646–71), and Schillemeit (2004, 211–24). Textual references are to the critical edition of *Der Verschollene* (KKAV). Quotations in English from this edition refer to the translation by Michael Hoffman: *Franz Kafka. The Man Who Disappeared (Amerika).* London: Penguin Books 1996. I thank Daniel Randau for help with the translation of this essay.

2. At this point in the manuscript, Kafka deleted the following sentence: "Er sah zu ihr auf und verwarf das über sie Gelernte" (KKAVA, 123) ("He looked up at her and discarded all that he had learned about her").

3. See Gerhard Neumann's discussion in chapter 4.

4. Cf. the apocalyptic image of New York: "Und morgen wie abend und in den Träumen der Nacht vollzog sich auf dieser Straße ein immer drängender Verkehr . . . und alles dieses würde erfaßt und durchdrungen von einem mächtigen Licht, das immer wieder von der Menge der Gegenstände zerstreut, fortgetragen und wieder eifrig herbeigebracht wurde und das dem betörten Auge so körperlich erschien, als werde über dieser Straße eine alles bedeckende Glasscheibe jeden Augenblick immer wieder mit aller Kraft zerschlagen" (55) ("In the morning and evening, and in his dreams at night, that street was always full of swarming traffic . . . and all

this was held and penetrated by a mighty light, that was forever being scattered, carried off and eagerly returned by the multitudes of objects, and that seemed so palpable to the confused eye that it was like a sheet of glass spread out over the street that was being continually and violently smashed").

5. The motif of the Native American Indian as a figure of liberty recurs throughout Kafka's work. Illustrative examples include "Die Abweisung" and "Wunsch, Indianer zu werden."

Works Cited

Godé, M., and M. Vanoosthyse, eds. 1997. *Entre critique et rire: "Le Disparu" de Franz Kafka: Kafkas Roman "Der Verschollene."* Montpellier: Bibliothèque d'études germaniques et centre-européennes.

Greiner, B. 2003. Im Umkreis von Ramses: Kafkas *Verschollener* als jüdischer Bildungsroman. *Deutsche Vierteljahresschrift für Literaturwissenschaft und Geistesgeschichte* 77: 637–58.

Kafka, Franz. 1996. *The man who disappeared (Amerika).* Trans. Michael Hofmann. London: Penguin Books.

Kremer, D. 1994. Verschollen. Gegenwärtig. Franz Kafkas Roman *Der Verschollene.* In *Text + Kritik Sonderband: Franz Kafka,* ed. H. L. Arnold, 238–53. Munich: Edition Text + Kritik.

Kurz, Gerhard. 1980. *Traum-Schrecken: Kafkas literarische Existenzanalyse.* Stuttgart: Metzler.

Metz, J. 2004. Zion in the West: Cultural Zionism, diasporic doubles and the "direction" of Jewish literary identity in Kafka's *Der Verschollene. Deutsche Vierteljahresschrift für Literaturwissenschaft und Geistesgeschichte* 78: 646–71.

Neumann, Gerhard. 1985. Der Wanderer und der Verschollene: Zum Problem der Identität in Goethes *Wilhelm Meister* und in Kafkas *Amerika*-Roman. In *Paths and labyrinths,* ed. J. P. Stern and J. J. White, 43–65. London: Institute of Germanic Studies.

Nicolai, R. R. 1981. *Kafkas Amerika-Roman "Der Verschollene": Motive und Gestalten.* Würzburg: Königshausen & Neumann.

Plachta, B. 1994. *Der Verschollene.* In *Franz Kafka. Romane und Erzählungen,* ed. M. Müller, 75–97. Stuttgart: Reclam.

Scheffel, M. 1999/2000. Ins Endlose angelegt: Franz Kafkas Romanprojekt *Der Verschollene* aus narratologischer Sicht. *Runa,* 279–95.

Schillemeit, J. 2004. *Kafka-Studien.* Göttingen: Wallstein.

Speirs, Ronald, and Beatrice Sandberg. 1997. *Franz Kafka.* London: Macmillan.

6

THE SENSE OF AN UN-ENDING

THE RESISTANCE TO NARRATIVE CLOSURE IN KAFKA'S *DAS SCHLOSS*

J. Hillis Miller

The Castle's Challenges to Narratology

The narratological presuppositions of *The Castle* are (1) that none of the characters have direct or verifiable access to the minds of other characters and (2) that the narrative voice is limited to partial access to the protagonist's mind, without any direct access to the minds of other characters. *The Castle*'s narrative is governed by these presuppositions; they hold true in all of the segments and fragments we have of this incomplete novel. This essay explores the novel from the perspective of these controlling assumptions.

This essay has as its guiding path a question: how useful are narratological modes of analysis in reading and understanding Kafka's *Das Schloß?* An impressive body of theoretical and practical work exists in the discipline that calls itself "narratology." Though narratologists differ among themselves, their general goal is to establish an agreed-upon set of terms and distinctions that will allow an objective and verifiable analysis of narrative technique in a given work. Their correct assumption is that technique participates in the production of meaning. Some narratologists, skittish about the word "meaning," would prefer to say "production of effect."

The narrative techniques Kafka employed have inspired the more or less unpredictable and variable performative effects of reading his work. By "performative effect," I mean a decision, brought about by the reading, to do something; for example, to teach the novel or to write about it, but also perhaps to change one's behavior in everyday life. Evidence of the variability of these effects is the distressingly contradictory ways of reading Kafka that have developed over the years. Readings of many different kinds—religious readings, autobiographical readings, psychoanalytical readings, political readings, sociological readings, intrinsic readings, and allegorical readings—have proliferated, each claiming to "have Kafka right."

Two conspicuous features of *Das Schloß* are *prima facie* challenges to a narratological reading, though they do not forbid such a reading: (1) The novel is unfinished and (2) it is discontinuous, not a straight narrative line going from beginning to middle to end. *Das Schloß* is made up of a sequence of more or less detached segments or fragments that do not follow from one to the other in a linear narrative leading toward some ending that ties all the threads together. Kafka apparently improvised the various sections of the novel as he went along and as episodes for it occurred to him. Only in retrospect did he assign chapter numbers and establish a definite narrative sequence. That was never done for the later segments, so we do not know just what order they would have had, nor do we know what never-written sections might have intervened. In spite of hints that Kafka made to his friend Max Brod we do not really know how the novel would have ended. Brod said that Kafka told him, "The ostensible Land Surveyor was to find partial satisfaction at least. He was not to relax in his struggle, but was to die worn out by it. Round his death-bed the villagers were to assemble, and from the Castle itself word was to come that though K.'s legal claim to live in the village was not valid, yet taking certain auxiliary circumstances into account, he was to be permitted to live and work there" (Kafka 1951, 329–30). This ending would have been ambiguous enough. K. was to die at the moment he was given permission, so to speak, to live. Kafka did not live to write this or any other ending. Moreover, he may have been sugarcoating the story for his good friend Brod who had trouble accepting the ironically comic bleakness of Kafka's work.

The Castle's Narrator

The *donnée,* as Henry James would have called it, of *Das Schloß* is simple enough. A young man, who is called "K." by the narrator, arrives on a snowy night in a village at the foot of a Castle hill. He claims that he has an official appointment from Count Westwest, the Castle's sovereign, as Land Surveyor for the village. The novel's segments recount various attempts by K. to get accepted by the Castle and by the village. Initial telephone calls to the Castle yield ambiguous information. First the Castle authorities say no, and then they say yes.

I turn now to my first narratological question: what presumptions are made in *The Castle* about the way the protagonist, K., is related to other people in the village and to those he encounters who purport to be from the Castle? The early chapters of *The Castle* were initially written in the first person. Kafka then decided to write the novel in the third person. He went back through the manuscript to change "Ich" to "K." Maurice Blanchot, perhaps Kafka's best reader, has noted, in "Kafka et la littérature," that Kafka says he became a writer when he changed "*Ich*" to "*Er,*" "I" to "he" (Blanchot 1981, 86). The effect of this change is to double the narrative line and to make that double line vibrate with uncertainty. The doubling into free indirect discourse from first-person discourse, in the case of *Das Schloß,* gives the reader not only the way things seem to K. but also, at the same time, the effaced narrator's dry, objective report. That report enigmatically ironizes what K. says, thinks, and feels. I call the ironizing "enigmatic" because the narrator never explicitly passes judgment on K.'s judgments. K. may be right or he may be wrong. The narrative voice never says anything about that. Indeed, it never says anything at all on its own hook. The narrative voice just transposes first-person present-tense narration into third-person past-tense narration, *Ich bin* into *Er war.*

That narrator, moreover, does not fit very well into any of the usual narratological pigeon-holes. Far from being imaginable as any kind of person with one or another focalization, and identifiable as reliable or unreliable, the "narrator" of *Das Schloß* is almost completely impersonal. The narrative voice has somewhat restricted access to K.'s thoughts, perceptions, and feelings. This narrative voice is hardly amenable to evaluation as remaining the same from one time of narration to another, so dependent is it on K. Moreover, K. does not remain the same from one narrative segment to another. Nor do the characters. A spectacular example of this variability is what Olga tells K. about Klamm, K.'s chief intermediary for access to the Castle: "They say he looks completely different [*anders*] when he comes into the village and different when he leaves it, different before he has had a beer, different afterwards, different awake, different asleep, different alone, different in conversation, and, quite understandably after all this, almost utterly different [*fast grundverschieden*] up there at the Castle" (Kafka 1997, 216; Kafka 1998, 176. I have interpolated in the English translations here and throughout some words and phrases from the German original, when they help indicate the nuances of what Kafka wrote).

Ironic discourse is, notoriously, pace Wayne Booth, undecidable in its meaning (Booth 1974; de Man 1996; Miller 2001). The doubling of the protagonist by the narrative voice, as it functions in this particular case, makes *Das Schloß* ironic through and through. The narrator in *Das Schloß* is no more than a strange, disembodied power of narration, a linguistic energy of articulating (or disarticulating) K.'s experiences, thoughts, and feelings. This linguistic energy modulates from episode to episode. The narrative is hardly an "organic unity," such as some narratologists expect from a good literary work. Of course, someone might object that my claim that no globally unified reading is possible is a globally unified reading. I agree, but I would answer that this is a conspicuously Kafkaesque aporetic formulation. It is like, for example, what Kafka says about despair: "Don't despair, not even over the fact that you don't despair" (Kafka 1976, 224).

Forms of Narration in *The Castle*

Second narratological question: what mixture of ways of narration characterizes the words on the pages? The narrative texture of *Das Schloß* is made up, for the most part, of three linguistic registers: (1) dialogue between K. and the characters, reported with minimal objective or descriptive commentary (as opposed to interpretation) by the anonymous narrator, (2) interpretative speeches to K. by one of the characters, sometimes going on for many pages, to which K. responds, almost always in disagreement, with interpretative comments of his own (examples are the long speeches to K. by the landlady, by Frieda, by Olga, by Bürgel, and by Pepi), and (3) the report in free indirect discourse by an unnamed, impersonal narrator of things that go on inside K. (thoughts, feelings, interpretations, and sensations). This narrator's access is limited. The narrator often seems not to know things about K. that the reader would like to know—for example, whether or not K. is lying when he says he has an appointment as Land Surveyor.

The strict rule of the narration, as I have said, is that neither K. nor the narrator ever has direct access to the minds, feelings, or bodily sensations of the other characters. The landlady boastfully, and I believe fal laciously, asserts at one point that she can read K.'s thoughts. ("Wenn ich mir viel Mühe gebe," she says," kann ich mich ja hineindenken in Ihre

Gedanken" [Kafka 1997, 104]). ("If I make an effort, I can even think my way into your thoughts, which make no sense here but are perhaps valid in the foreign lands you come from") (Kafka 1998, 83). Even if she were able to think her way into K.'s thoughts, they would not make sense. They would seem like the babble of a foreigner speaking in a foreign tongue about strange customs and assumptions. More in correspondence with the evidence is the possibility of generalizing K.'s assertion that "ihre Beweggründe hält Amalia in ihrer Brust verschlossen, niemand wird sie ihr entreißen" (Kafka 1997, 242) ("Amalia keeps her motives sealed within her breast, and nobody can drag them from her" [Kafka 1998, 198]).

An immense part of the dense local texture of narration in *The Castle* is made up of dialogue between K. and one or another of the characters, sometimes punctuated by long stretches of free indirect discourse recording K.'s thoughts and feelings as he confronts that other person, looks him or her in the face, and listens to what that other person says. The law of these encounters is that K. cannot understand the other, nor can the other person understand him. Good examples of the registration in free indirect discourse of K.'s weird thoughts, as well as good examples of the way K. changes from scene to scene, are the long conversation in contretemps with Frieda in chapter 14, titled "Frieda's Reproach" (Kafka 1998, 151–61), and K.'s fantasy in the next chapter of what might have happened if he had not encountered Schwarzer at the inn on the night of his arrival. What he is reported to think to himself in his imaginings, however commonsensical those imaginings are, completely contradicts his claim in the opening pages that he has an appointment from Count Westwest. He thinks of "K. himself knocking on the door at the council chairman's during office hours the following day and registering as a foreign journeyman [*fremder Wanderbursch*] who had already found a place to sleep at a local citizen's [*bestimmten Gemeindemitglied*] and would probably continue his journey the next day, unless, and this was most unlikely, he found work here, but then only for a few days, since he hadn't the slightest intention of staying longer. This is what would have happened, or something of that sort, had it not been for Schwarzer" (Kafka 1997, 203; Kafka 1998, 165).

The word "verschlossen" ("sealed") in the passage about Amalia's secrecy reminds the reader of what is implied by the German word for Castle, "Schloß" ("a sealed enclosure"). The characters of *Das Schloß* are sealed off from one another. Each dwells in a private castle. Other people's thoughts and feelings must be inferred, always doubtfully and uncertainly, from what they say and from how they look. The result is that no verification of K.'s assumptions about what the other person is thinking or feeling is possible. This law of unverifiable "analogical apperception," as Husserl called it (1960), and the consequent uncertainty of interpretation, apply just as much to K.'s reading of the people in the village as to his (mis)understanding of people hypothetically connected to the Castle or representing it. What K. sees or hears or reads may mean this or it may mean that. No possible way exists to tell for sure. Nevertheless, an urgent need to make correct interpretations defines K.'s situation throughout. His life depends on it.

Interpreting Others and Digressive Narration

The result of the difficulty or perhaps even impossibility of understanding others is that *The Castle* is made up to a considerable degree of acts of interpretation (by K. or by others) that often contradict one another in the midst of a sentence. If what K. sees, hears, and reads were easy to understand, no lengthy work of interpretation would be necessary. The novel has scores of examples of the law of contradiction that governs interpretation in *Das Schloß*. Unverifiable and inconsistent "exegesis" forms the basic stylistic fabric of the novel. The narrative is not so much the straightforward telling of a story that might be interpreted narratologically as it is the staging of situations that are permanently inconclusive acts of reading, always in excess of the data they attempt to read. These readings are, perhaps, allegorical representations of the readers' own acts of interpretation.

The acts of interpretation within the novel exist on many different levels. They may take the form of a contradictory interpretation by K. or by another character based on some apparently trivial detail in another person's appearance, behavior, or speech, such as Frieda's hands, an example discussed below. The contradictions may take the form of extended dialogues in which K. and some other character—Frieda, the village chairman, the landlady, Hans Brunswick, Momus, Barnabas, Olga, Pepi, or others—argue at length and inconclusively about some aspect of K.'s situation or about someone else's "connection" to the Castle. These contradictory acts of exegesis may take the form of inconsistencies between the chapters. K. does not seem to be able to stick to any promise or commitment, as he tries, always unsuccessfully, way after way to reach Klamm, and to go beyond Klamm to the Castle itself. "Weg," German for "path," "road," or "way," is a key word in the novel. "Weg" might be taken as an ironically inappropriate name for the novel's narrative sequence, as it wanders this way and that, always starting over again from the beginning and never getting any closer to the Castle.

K.'s actions are perversely contradictory and self-destructive. He promises fidelity to Frieda but then betrays her by turning to Olga, Barnabas, and Amalia. He says at one point that he has left a wife and a child at home, but that does not keep him from promising to marry Frieda after he has slept with her. He repudiates the landlady's advice but later depends on her for information. Instead of getting him closer to the Castle, his dilatory wavering gets him farther and farther off course, or away from his "Weg," as the novel works its way toward stopping in the middle of a sentence. This sentence was about to report the speech of an apparently peripheral and inconsequential character, Gerstäcker's mother, after previous digressions to Pepi and then to Gerstäcker. It is even doubtful if the word "digression" may legitimately be used to describe *The Castle*'s narrative structure, since no identifiable straight or crooked path to the goal exists, and since we have no certainty even about the nature and location of the goal. A given "digression" might suddenly reach the goal, as exemplified by the proverbial law that "the longest way round is the shortest way home." As a narrative sequence open to clear and unambiguous interpretation, *The Castle* is most unsatisfactory.

The most extensive connected sequence (several chapters long) is made up by the "digression" of a story within a story. This is the narrative of the ostracism, by what Olga explicitly calls "die Gemeinde" (Kafka 1997, 254) ("the community" [Kafka 1998, 208]) of Barnabas's family after Amalia's refusal of a sexual advance from Sortini, an official from the castle. The novel, in specific scenes and as a whole, has the narrative rhythm of one of those dreams characterized by endless delay and a slowing down of time, as though one were trying to make one's way through deep snow, as K. indeed does early in the novel. Readers feel, to boot, as if they are getting farther and farther away from a constantly receding destination. When K. does finally get an interview with someone from the Castle—Bürgel, who says that he would be irresistibly tempted to help K., and who explains to K. just what he should do to get to the Castle—K. falls asleep at the crucial moment, so long-winded has Bürgel's discourse been. This may be an oblique warning to the reader to keep wakeful, even though the novel does not seem to be getting anywhere. One remembers the notorious occasion when Christ's disciples went to sleep: "What, could ye not watch with me one hour?" (Matt.

26.40, King James version). Reading *Das Schloß* is a most exasperating, perhaps even sleep-inducing, experience.

The Impossibility of Verifiable Interpretation as a Consequence of Others' Opacity

Many locutions that take the form "*x* and not *x*," or "*x* and at the same time *y*," or "perhaps this but also perhaps that" occur throughout *Das Schloß,* in many different ways and at many different scales. These expressions of unresolved contradictions, of negations without dialectical negativity or possible sublation, are either within speeches by one or another of the characters or within reports in free indirect discourse of something K. thinks to himself. The people who dwell in the village beneath the Castle are caught in the double bind of a permanently unverifiable either/or—or maybe this/perhaps that, or both this and that—though matters of the utmost importance, to the characters at least, are at stake in these undecidable oscillations between contradictory interpretations. The characters in *Das Schloß* all waver this way and that, often in a single sentence, because they can find no solid external ground for deciding one way or the other. The notorious run-on sentences that make up much of *Das Schloß,* long sequences of phrases or complete sentences bound together by commas or perhaps by semicolons, a stylistic feature that Max Brod "corrected" in the first edition and that was also suppressed in the Muir translation, mimics this side-by-sideness in non-hierarchical and non-dialectical dispersal of contradictory judgments or interpretations, just as I have mimicked this dispersal in this sentence.

This limitation in human possibilities of knowledge can be defined as the impossibility of verifiable interpretation. This impossibility, paradoxically, is what generates the narrative. Strangely enough, interpretative uncertainty, for Kafka, makes the world go around and keep its balance, as one passage asserts in a characteristically ironic and contradictory way, "So korrigiert sich selbst die Welt in ihrem Lauf und behält das Gleichgewicht. Das ist ja eine vorzügliche, immer wieder unvorstellbar vorzügliche Einrichtung, wenn auch in anderer Hinsicht trostlos" (Kafka 1997, 326) ("That is how the world corrects its course and keeps its equilibrium. It's certainly an excellent arrangement, always unimaginably excellent, even if in certain other respects hopeless" [Kafka 1998, 271]). Well, which is it, unimaginably excellent or hopeless ("trostlos")? One would like to know.

In an important entry in the *Diaries,* a characteristically strange and hyperbolic notation made on November 20, 1911, Kafka reflected on his fateful penchant for "antitheses," as well on as his distaste for them. "My repugnance for antitheses is certain," he says. He then goes on, predictably, to express this antipathy in a spectacular example of the way his thinking proceeds by way of (or rather, gets hung up on) antitheses that turn around and around. Though this circling seems to lead to endless vistas, Kafka's antitheses always conclude by turning back on themselves in a self-enclosure that offers no leads for going farther in any direction. No dialectical synthesis is possible for Kafka's antitheses. They just proliferate in a cascade of antitheses. The "wheel of life," a note in the *Diaries* explains, is "a toy through the aperture of which one perceived the successive positions of a figure affixed to a revolving wheel. It thus created the illusion of motion" (Kafka 1976, 495). The wheel of life was a primitive motion picture machine. It went round and round, repeating the same illusory motion:

> My repugnance ("Widerwillen") for antitheses is certain. They are unexpected, but do not surprise ("überraschen nicht"), for they have always been there; if they were unconscious, it was at the very edge of consciousness. They make for thoroughness ("Gründlichkeit"), fullness, completeness, but only like a figure on the "wheel of life" ("Lebensrad"), we have chased our little idea around the circle. They are as undifferentiated as they are different, they grow under one's hand as though bloated by water, beginning with the prospect of infinity ("Aussicht ins Grenzenlose"), they always end up in the same medium size. They curl up ("rollen sich ein"), cannot be straightened out, are mere clues ("geben keinen Anhaltspunkt"), are holes in wood, are immobile assaults, draw antitheses to themselves, as I have shown. If they would only draw all of them, and forever. (Kafka 2004b, not paginated; Kafka 1976, 122)

Performative Naming of Frieda's Hands

Yes, if we could just gather all antitheses in one sequestered bundle and let them keep quietly circulating there forever. Unfortunately, in Kafka's writing new antitheses are constantly appearing, outside the circle. Reading *Das Schloß* is certainly exasperating! It is exasperating because it skips from one antithesis to another, while remaining still stuck in the same place the narrative begins—in the village, at the foot of the Castle's hill.

Why so much equivocation? Why so little narrative progress? Let me look into a little detail at one apparently trivial such passage. K. reflects, when he first meets Frieda, that "Ihre Hände allerdings waren klein und zart, aber man hätte sie auch schwach und nichtssagend nennen können" (Kafka 1997, 50) ("Her hands were indeed small and delicate, but they could also be called weak and expressionless" [Kafka 1998, 37]). The effect of such sentences on the reader is extremely odd. Well, which is it, small and delicate, or weak and expressionless? Why cannot K., or the narrative voice, which here speaks for K. in free indirect discourse, make up their minds? It seems important to know, since K. is about to enter into a long-term liaison with Frieda. The odd effect is generated to a considerable degree by that phrase "man hätte sie . . . nennen können," "one could have called, or named, them. . . . " Called by whom? Named by whom? K.? The narrator? Kafka? Anyone under the sun ("one"; "man")?

Kafka himself, the reader may suddenly reflect, is ultimately responsible. He is making the whole thing up. He could call Frieda's hands whatever he likes, small and delicate, weak and expressionless, or anything else he chooses. The language of *Das Schloß* is not constative or referential, since no extra-linguistic referent exists against which it can be measured, but performative or constitutive. The word "nennen" calls attention to the constructive power of performative language in a literary fiction. It calls attention indirectly to the way the whole novel represents examples of the perpetual either/or or both/and of performative interpretation. Since no possible access to any external referent exists, you, K., the narrator, "man" in general, can call those imaginary hands anything you or they like. The situation of the characters, K. especially, doomed as they are to perpetual undecidable acts of interpretation, mimics the reader's own situation. The reader too is engaged in a difficult, or perhaps impossible, act of exegesis. The storyline generates the reader's attempt to understand as it pursues its wandering and discontinuous way through the novel.

Secular Imitation of Talmud and Midrash

It is as if, in *Das Schloß,* the famous nitpicking rabbinic interchanges of Talmudic or Midrashic readings had been applied to the give-and-take of ordinary human intercourse (Blanchot 1981, 192–95). The difference is that Talmudic or Midrashic interpretations are even more extravagant. Their exegesis, moreover, is often applied to passages from Jewish sacred scripture, not to specific secular details, so the assumption is that Jehovah must have meant something definite, even though that something may be hard to interpret. In addition, the goal of Talmud and Midrash, often at least seemingly reached, is reconciliation, harmony, elucidation, resolution of apparent contradiction.

The transfer of something like Talmudic or Midrashic procedures to K.'s never-successful attempt to understand the people around him, to find out how to get an audience with Klamm and how to get through Klamm to the Castle, produces something exceedingly strange and unsettling. An interminable interrogation of the evidence appears destined not to reach a verifiable conclusion, since no access is possible to solid, extratextual, authoritative evidence that would justify deciding one way or the other.

Much attention in *Das Schloß* is paid to written documents and to the difficulty of interpreting them. In one salient example, not only K. but also the village chairman and his wife read Klamm's letter to K. They never agree on the right way to read it. Is it an official letter or an unofficial one? Which would be better for K.? Is it friendly or unfriendly? Does it give K. an authorized position in the village or not?

The hardworking Castle authorities and their representatives in the village spend much time producing, storing, and interpreting huge assemblages of documents. An example is the comic description of the search for one document that may be lost in the closet full of documents in the chairman's room. The chairman's wife, Mizzi, and K's two assistants search there for the Castle's original decree stating that a Land Surveyor is needed (Kafka 1998, 60–62). This is followed by the seriocomic account of what happened to the misdirected file about the decision to hire or not to hire a Land Surveyor (Kafka 1998, 62–64). Another example is the putative description by the chairman of Sordini's office (necessarily putative because no one the reader encounters from the village has actually been there or ever seen Sordini), with its piles of documents that are constantly falling down (Kafka 1998, 66).

Sordini's office reminds me of Borges's story "The Library of Babel." That story, in turn, reminds me of the mind-boggling proliferation of databases, files, e-mails, and websites on the Internet, and of the never-wholly-successful attempts by Google and Yahoo! to keep them searchable. The World Wide Web in 2005 already had more than 600 billion pages (Kelley 2005, 96). It must have many billions more by now. A similar problem exists in *The Castle*. The Castle officials not only fail to keep up with the piles of new documents but also fail on most occasions to find documents that go astray. Files sent on the World Wide Web, such as e-mail attachments, are broken up into relatively short "packets," then routed through different trajectories and nodes to their destination, where they are reassembled in order. One can imagine a packet that gets lost and circulates endlessly in cyberspace without ever reaching its goal. Something like that happens to the village chairman's response to word from the Castle that a Land Surveyor should be appointed. The village chairman consults with the village citizens and responds that the village has no need of a Land Surveyor. That document, however, is mistakenly sent to Department B rather than to Department A. Department B has no idea what to do with it. The folder is mysteriously empty anyway. Years and years go by before the mix-up is sorted out. The delay is exacerbated because no mechanism exists in this bureaucracy, in a way similar to many bureaucracies, for admitting that an error has been made, even though a Control Department exists. This endless delay in getting documents sent to their right addressees is one example of the nightmarish temporality I mentioned earlier as a basic feature of narration in *Das Schloß*.

The reader of *The Castle,* faced with all this treatment of documents and their interpretation, may suddenly at some point realize that he or she is at that moment engaged in an act of interpretation that is mirrored by those in the novel. The text of *Das Schloß* and its various translations are by no means unequivocal. Kafka died leaving the novel unfinished. It stops in the middle of a sentence. It is plausible to believe that it was in principle impossible to finish. K. makes no headway at all in getting closer to the Castle. If anything, he is farther away at the end than he was at the beginning. The chapters do not progress chronologically toward a pre-determined or pre-existing goal. They move laterally, as K. encounters one dead end after another, only to retrace his steps and start again. It may be that Kafka gave up writing the novel because he was committed to writing as a way to make headway toward the goal of his own salvation and discovered to his dismay that writing cannot be used in this way. Literature, he may have come to believe, only leads to endless wandering.

Rejection of Mediation and Failed Attempts at Passage

For Kafka, as for Derrida, "Between my world, the 'my world'; what I call 'my world,' and there is no other for me, every other world making up part of it, between my world and every other world, there is initially the space and the time of an infinite difference, of an interruption incommensurable with all the attempts at passage, of bridge, of isthmus, of communication, of translation, of trope, and of transfer" (Derrida 2002/2003; my translation). *The Castle,* no reader can doubt, is a potentially endless variation on the theme of failed "attempts at passage." K. wants, or says he wants, to come face-to-face with the highest Castle authorities, with Count Westwest himself, in order to demand and get official authority to practice in the village his "calling" of Land Surveyor. He repudiates every mediation in the name of unmediated direct encounter. His sin is impatience. He wants to find a pathway to the interior of the Castle. He finds over and over again that he can attain only mediated access by way of people who have some sort of equivocal distant "Verbindung" ("connection") to the Castle, or perhaps only appear to do so.

"Verbindung" is a key word in the novel. It occurs again and again in different contexts; for example, strikingly, in Bürgel's description of himself as "Verbindungssekretär" (Kafka 1997, 313) ("a connecting secretary" [Kafka 1998, 259]). Bürgel is a self-proclaimed mediator, a connector. K., however, refuses, over and over, to have anything to do with such intermediaries. He recognizes, correctly, that all such intermediaries are also "blocking agents," obstacles in the pathway. K. discovers that, as one of Kafka's crucial aphorisms puts it, "Es gibt ein Ziel, aber keinen Weg; was wir Weg nennen, ist Zögern" (Kafka 2004a, no. 26) ("There is a goal but no way; what we call the way is only wavering" [Kafka 1946, 283]).

This pattern is repeated over and over in the incomplete novel. It might have gone on being repeated interminably in more and more chapters, without ever reaching that hypothetical deathbed scene with which Kafka, perhaps with an intention to mislead, told Max Brod he intended to end the novel.

It is not so much contrariness as an instinctive rejection of all mediation that leads to K.'s refusals. As the narrator says, apropos of one of those refusals, speaking for K. in free indirect discourse, "far be it from him to feel admiration or even envy [for Momus] since it was not closeness to Klamm in itself that was worth striving for but rather that he, K., and he alone, not anybody else with his wishes, or anybody else's, should approach Klamm, and approach him "nicht um bei ihm zu ruhen sondern um an ihm vorbeizukommen, weiter, ins Schloß" (Kafka 1997, 138) ("not so as to rest there with him but to get past him and go on into the Castle" [Kafka 1998, 111]).

Conclusion

The genius of *Das Schloß* is to have shown that the sad situation of its hero is the result of not having direct access to other people's minds and feelings. This means that, for Kafka, our situation vis-à-vis other people is the confrontation of a proliferating network of signs. The interpretation of those signs, or, more precisely, our reading and exegesis of them, is both urgently necessary and at the same time impossible or, even more precisely, always possible, but not ever possible to verify. We can read the signs others emit, but we can never be sure we have read them right. That is what Isabel Archer, by way of the narrator's indirect discourse, says to herself about Gilbert Osmond in Henry James's *The Portrait of a Lady:* "she had not read him right" (James 1909/1979, 192). James, however, reassuringly implies that Isabel has finally read Osmond "right," whereas Kafka never gives the reader that kind of reassurance.

This impossibility of verifiably correct reading is correlated with the special narrative devices, such as the effaced narrator, the narrative discontinuities, and the impossibility of finishing the story, that are distinguishing features of *The Castle.* I have focused throughout this essay on the relation between narrative conventions and problems of interpretation. Especially important have been questions having to do with the narrator, with the narrator's knowledge of the characters, and with their knowledge of one another. *The Castle* dramatizes the consequences of not being sure what other people are thinking and feeling, whatever they say and whatever their eyes, faces, and gestures seem to indicate. These consequences include the difficulty, perhaps the impossibility, of finishing any narrative, of giving a story narrative continuity and rounding it off with a satisfactory ending.

Works Cited

Blanchot, Maurice. 1981. *De Kafka à Kafka.* Paris: Gallimard.

Booth, Wayne. 1974. *A rhetoric of irony.* Chicago: Univ. of Chicago Press.

De Man, Paul. 1996. The concept of irony. In *Aesthetic ideology,* ed. Andrzej Warminski, 163–84. Minneapolis: Univ. of Minnesota Press.

Derrida, Jacques. 2002/2003. *La bête et le souverain (deuxième année).* J. Hillis Miller's personal computer files, gift from Jacques Derrida to him.

Kafka, Franz. 1946. *The Great Wall of China: Stories and reflections.* Trans. Willa Muir and Edwin Muir. New York: Schocken Books.

———. 1951. *The castle.* Trans. Edwin Muir and Willa Muir. New York: Alfred A. Knopf.

———. 1976. *Diaries 1910–1923.* Ed. Max Brod. Trans. Joseph Kresh and Martin Greenberg, with the cooperation of Hannah Arendt. New York: Schocken Books.

———. 1997. *Das Schloß.* Ed. Malcolm Pasley. Frankfurt: Fischer Taschenbuch Verlag.

———. 1998. *The castle.* Trans. Mark Harman. New York: Schocken Books.

———. 2004a. *Aphorismen.* The Kafka Project. http://www.kafka.org/index.php?aphorismen (accessed August 18, 2008).

———. 2004b. *Tagebücher.* The Kafka Project. http://www.kafka.org/index.php?h3 (accessed August 17, 2008).

Kelley, Kevin. 2005. We are the Web. *Wired,* August.

James, Henry. 1909/1971. *The portrait of a lady.* Vol. 4 of *The novels and tales of Henry James. 26 vols.* Fairfield, NJ: Augustus M. Kelley.

Husserl, Edmund. 1960. Fifth meditation: Uncovering the sphere of transcendental being as monadological intersubjectivity. In *Cartesian meditations: An introduction to phenomenology.* Trans. Dorion Cairns, 89–151. The Hague: Martinus Nijhoff.

Miller, J. Hillis. 2001. Friedrich Schlegel: Catachreses for chaos. In *Others,* 5–42. Princeton, NJ: Princeton Univ. Press.

7

STARTING IN THE MIDDLE? COMPLICATIONS OF NARRATIVE BEGINNINGS AND PROGRESSION IN KAFKA

Beatrice Sandberg

Reading Kafka in the critical and the facsimile editions deepens one's sense of how much he struggled to create continuity and connectedness (*Zusammenhang*) once he had started to write from a given beginning or to find the right point of ingress in order to follow a thread that would lead him through a story he wanted to tell. Whenever he found such a beginning, as in "The Metamorphosis," "The Stoker," and especially in "The Judgment," he felt overwhelming joy at having achieved coherence in a complex story. What he experienced while writing "The Judgment" represented his ideal: "Nur so kann geschrieben werden, in einem solchen Zusammenhang, mit solcher vollständigen Öffnung des Leibes und der Seele" (KAF, 10:101) ("This is the only possible way to write, in such a connected way, with such complete opening of body and soul").[1] This experience set a standard he strove to meet throughout his life but seldom attained, according to his own rigorous criteria. Usually the critics have agreed about the success of these narratives, but some have disagreed, such as Hans Dieter Zimmermann, who expresses doubts about "The Judgment," a novella that he believes to be overestimated with regard to its formal qualities and its elaboration of motifs.[2]

Zimmermann is not the only critic to have pointed out various deficiencies and inconsistencies, which are possibly attributable to the fact that the story was conceived of and executed in the course of a single hectic night.[3] According to Kafka's own testimony, however, the story had great importance for him because it represented the liberation of his ambitions as a writer. It also has a fascinating enigmatic obscurity as a story that welled up from a hard-pushed writer's mind in a more or less uncontrolled way after many unsuccessful attempts at producing literary texts. Yet Kafka could also be harsh about stories his readers admired when the stories did not meet his own standards. Even if he usually argues too negatively because of his high ambitions and his low self-esteem, such criticism of weaknesses in his texts is not always unwarranted. He mentions his feelings of bitterness, for example, while listening to Max Brod's reading aloud of his "kleine Automobilgeschichte" (KAF, 9:177) ("little automobile story"):

> Die ungeordneten Sätze dieser Geschichte mit Lücken daß man beide Hände dazwischen stecken könnte; ein Satz klingt hoch, ein Satz klingt tief wie es kommt; ein Satz reibt sich am andern wie die Zunge an einem hohlen oder falschen Zahn; ein Satz kommt mit einem so rohen Anfang anmarschiert, dass die ganze Geschichte in ein verdrießliches Staunen geräth. . . . Ich erklare es mir damit dass ich zu wenig Zeit und Ruhe habe um die Möglichkeiten meines Talentes in ihrer Gänze aus mir zu heben. Es kommen daher immer nur abreißende Anfänge zu Tage, abreißende Anfänge z. B. die ganze Automobilgeschichte durch. Würde ich einmal ein größeres Ganzes schreiben können wohlgebildet vom Anfang bis zum Ende, dann könnte sich auch die Geschichte niemals endgiltig von mir loslösen und ich dürfte ruhig und mit offenen Augen als Blutsverwandter einer gesunden Geschichte ihrer Vorlesung zuhören, so aber läuft jedes Stückchen der Geschichte heimatlos herum und treibt mich in die entgegengesetzte Richtung. (KAF, 9:177)

> (The unordered sentences of this story with gaps you could put your hand through; one sentence sounds high, another sounds low just as it comes; one sentence rubs against the next, like your tongue rubbing against a hollow or false tooth; one sentence comes marching up with such a coarse beginning that the whole story is thrown into ill-tempered astonishment. . . . I explain this to myself as the result of having too little time and peace to raise the entire potential of my talent to the surface of my being. This is why the only things ever to emerge are broken-off beginnings, such as the broken-off beginnings throughout the entire automobile story. If I were ever able to create a larger whole, well formed from beginning to end, I would never be able to detach the story from

> myself completely and I could listen calmly and with open eyes to its recitation, as a blood relative of a healthy story; as things stand, however, every little piece of the story runs around without a home and drives me off in the opposite direction.)

When we read this story, which Kafka wrote in September 1911 (*Reisetagebücher* KAF, 12:75–78) after seeing a car accident in Paris together with Max Brod, we cannot wholly disagree with Kafka's verdict. In a way we are reminded of a film clip by Charlie Chaplin, with people coming and gesticulating, vehicles moving around and filling the square, and finally a crowd waiting for further developments. The sentences comment on the situation ironically in a rather erratic sequence, following the confusion on the square. The laboriously detailed description creates a staccato effect or resembles a film going into reverse from time to time. This impression is intensified when a policeman enters the scene and starts to take down details from the witnesses. His pedantic accuracy corresponds to the kind of behavior we know from silent movies and reaches a peak at the end, when he runs into trouble with his report:

> Er hat nämlich den Bogen an einer Stelle zu beschreiben angefangen, wo er aus irgend einem Grunde nicht hätte anfangen dürfen. . . . Er muß den Bogen immerfort wieder umdrehn, um den schlechten Prot.[okoll]anfang zu glauben. Da er aber von diesem schlechten Anfang bald abgelassen und auch anderswo zu schreiben angefangen hat, kann er, wenn eine Spalte zu Ende ist, ohne großes Auseinanderfalten und Untersuchen unmöglich wissen, wo er richtigerweise fortzusetzen hat. Die Ruhe die dadurch die Angel.[egenheit] gewinnt, läßt sich mit jener frühern durch die Bet.[eiligten] allein erreichten gar nicht vergleichen. (KAF, 12:78)

> (You see, he had started to write on a part of the page where, for some reason, he ought not to have begun. . . . He has to turn the sheet of paper round several times in order to believe the bad beginning of the report. As he quickly abandons this bad start and begins writing somewhere else, it is impossible for him to know, without much unfolding of paper and searching, where the report should continue once he has reached the bottom of a column. The calm imparted to the incident through this procedure simply cannot compare with the calm previously achieved by the parties involved alone.)

The narrator describes the event from the position of an observer. His manner of reporting recalls the role of the witness in the famous "street scene" Brecht used to teach his actors how to give an objective, unemotional description of an accident when the narrator claims: "Es handelt sich nun zuerst darum zu erklären, wie es zu dem Unfall gekommen" (KAF, 12:75) ("What matters in the first instance is to explain how the accident came about"). This witness misses no opportunity to describe as fully as possible all the movements and discussions he is able to observe. We are dealing here with a witness who reports extensively on an episode and thus becomes a real, if somewhat long-winded narrator. Not until we get near the end of the text does the policeman begin recording the witness statements without much investigation of his own, at which point the unconscious and "unverständige Hoffnung aller Anwesenden auf eine sofortige sachliche Beendigung der ganzen Angel[egenheit] durch den Pol[izisten] ging in eine Freude an den Einzelheiten der Prot[okoll] aufn[ahme] über" (KAF, 12:78) ("unreasonable hope of all present that the whole matter would be brought to a rapid and objective conclusion gave way to delight in the details recorded in the officially recorded statements").

The reader who is familiar with Kafka's type of narrative progression (or lack of it) and the difficulties involved, will intuitively read this passage as an indirect self comment, exemplified in the actual presentation, which comes to a stop while the policeman is still struggling with his various beginnings in an attempt to find the right place to continue. In spite of the transposition of place and time and an apparently dissimilar situation, there can be little doubt that Kafka is using the figure of the policeman to satirize his own problems with this text. Intensified by its orchestration as a public event, the whole scene becomes very awkward and results in the incomparable calm of the crowd as the policeman struggles with the different beginnings in an effort to arrive at the last entry. It seems that the feelings provoked in Kafka by Brod's reading "meine kleine Automobilgeschichte" were particularly linked to his dissatisfaction at the "abreißenden Anfänge" (KAF, 9:177) ("broken-off beginnings"). In addition he criticizes a lack of fluency and the disparate directions the many beginnings take throughout the story. The holes in the argumentation emerge from a lack of decent workmanship, in contrast to his ideal of continuous narration without gaps.[4] Although a writer's criticism of his own work may not be reliable, what we are witnessing here is Kafka's lifelong struggle for coherence, evident in the countless attempts to bring off the kind of narratives he had in mind. His own observation that his account lacked fluency convinced him that what he had written was not designed for reading, as he writes to Max Brod in 1922: "Dieses Heft, das ich Dir nach Deiner Novelle zu geben gewagt hatte, obwohl ich weiß, daß es doch nur da ist zum Geschrieben-, nicht zum Gelesenwerden" (MB, 389) ("This notebook that I dared to give you after your novella, although I know that it is only there to be written, not to be read"). Nevertheless, despite this deeply felt skepticism, Kafka still thought of his writing as being like "die Fahne des Robinson auf dem höchsten Punkt der Insel" (MB, 386) ("Robinson [Crusoe's] flag on the highest point of the island").

At the end of 1909, while plagued by an inability to write, Kafka defined his difficulties thus:

> Alle Dinge nämlich, die mir einfallen, fallen [mir] nicht von der Wurzel aus ein, sondern erst irgendwo gegen ihre Mitte. Versuche sie dann jemand zu halten, versuche jemand ein Gras und sich an ihm zu halten, das erst in der Mitte des Stengels zu wachsen anfängt. Das können wohl einzelne, zum Beispiel japanische Gaukler, die auf einer Leiter klettern, die nicht auf dem Boden aufliegt, sondern auf den emporgehaltenen Sohlen eines halb Liegenden, und die nicht an der Wand lehnt, sondern nur in die Luft hinaufgeht. Ich kann es nicht, abgesehen davon, dass meiner Leiter nicht einmal jene Sohlen zur Verfügung stehen. (KAF, 9:15)[5]

> (You see, all the things that occur to me do so not from the root up but rather from somewhere about their middle. Let someone then attempt to hold them, let someone attempt to hold a blade of grass and support himself by holding on to it as it begins to grow, starting in the middle of its stalk. Some individuals can probably do this, like those Japanese acrobats for example who climb up a ladder that is standing not on the ground but on the raised soles of another acrobat who is lying half prostrate, and which is not leaning against a wall but simply goes up in the air. I can't do it, quite apart from the fact that my ladder doesn't even have such a pair of soles to stand on.)

A year later Kafka wrote: "Kein Wort, das ich schreibe, paßt zum andern. . . . Meine Zweifel stehn um jedes Wort im Kreis herum. . . . Wenn ich mich zum Schreibtisch setze, ist mir nicht wohler als einem, der mitten im Verkehr der Place de l'Opéra fällt und beide Beine bricht" (KAF, 9:103) ("Not one word I write matches the next. . . . My doubts stand in a circle around every word. . . . When I sit down at my desk I feel no better than someone who falls and breaks both legs in the middle of traffic on the Place de l'Opéra"). Kafka's comparisons are virtually unique in their vividness and degree of self-exposure. In the first example, he fears he lacks the artistic ability to meet the challenges presented by his calling as a writer. The second example expresses a crisis so intense that even his writing desk, that most precious object to which he often clung for dear life, makes him feel utterly exposed and vulnerable (see chapter 4 for Gerhard Neumann's discussion of the abandoned writing desk in "The Stoker"). He tries to explain why he is incapable of putting on paper things he had imagined before sitting down to write:

> Es liegt natürlich zum großen Teil daran, daß ich frei von Papier nur in der Zeit der Erhebung, die ich mehr fürchte als ersehne, wie sehr ich sie auch ersehne, Gutes erfinde, dass dann aber die Fülle so groß ist, dass ich verzichten muß, blindlings also nehme nur dem Zufall nach, aus der Strömung heraus, griffweise, so dass die Erwerbung beim überlegten Niederschreiben nichts ist im Vergleich zur Fülle, in der sie lebte, unfähig ist, diese Fülle herbeizubringen und daher schlecht und störend ist, weil sie nutzlos lockt. (KAF, 9:195)

> (Of course this mainly stems from the fact that away from paper I only invent good things during a time of exaltation ["Erhebung"], something I fear more than I long for, however much I may long for it, but then the abundance is so great that I have to become selective and let some things pass, snatching things blindly, as chance dictates, out of the current, in handfuls, so that when it comes to writing down in a moment of reflection what I have managed to capture in this way, it is nothing compared with the abundance in which it lived, the writing process is incapable of conjuring up that abundance and is therefore bad and disturbing, because it entices to no avail.)

The passage illustrates vividly why Kafka was unable to capture in writing the richness of things he had imagined *before* beginning to write. It can be contrasted with other, successful moments when the imaginative conception of an *Einfall* ("inspiration," literally the "falling in" of a creative idea) and its material transformation into ink on the page coincided completely.

Given the difficulties Kafka had in finding the right beginning from which to unroll a whole story, we may ask quite properly whether Kafka can be called an *Erzähler* ("story-teller") in the ordinary German sense of the word. The incoherent argumentation and the lack of logic, which we also find in "The Judgment," resist straightforward, sequential representation. At the beginning of *The Trial* too we observe a protagonist who stumbles over his arguments, muddles them in his own mind, turns them around, and puts them in doubt. In many sketches, Kafka begins a narrative sequence, but then the flow of narration becomes hesitant or gets blocked entirely. He complains about the difficulties of finding the right starting point that will offer him a guarantee of getting into the story:

> Anfang jeder Novelle zunächst lächerlich. Es scheint hoffnungslos, daß dieser neue noch unfertige überall empfindliche Organismus in der fertigen Organisation der Welt sich wird erhalten können, die wie jede fertige Organisation danach strebt sich abzuschließen. Allerdings vergisst man hierbei, dass die Novelle, falls sie berechtigt ist, ihre fertige Organisation in sich trägt, auch wenn sie sich noch nicht ganz entfaltet hat; darum ist die Verzweiflung in dieser Hinsicht vor dem Anfang einer Novelle unberechtigt . . . (KAF, 11:65)
>
> (The beginning of every novella is laughable in the first instance. There seems to be no hope that this new, unfinished organism, vulnerable at every point, will be able to survive in the already finished organisation of the world which, like every complete organization, strives to become self-enclosed and to exclude other things. Admittedly one forgets, as one thinks along these lines, that the novella, if it is justified, carries its own already finished organization within itself, even if this has not yet unfolded completely; thus this kind of despair before the beginning of a novella is unjustified.)

When Kafka really did find a beginning, he could become dominated by the unhappy sense of a "fortwährenden Anfangs, das Fehlen der Täuschung darüber, dass alles nur ein Anfang und nicht einmal ein Anfang ist" (KAF, 11:187) ("permanent, continuous beginning, the absence of the illusion that everything is just a beginning and not even that"), so that he was able neither to progress any further nor to find a way of ending the story.[6]

Kafka regarded Dickens with envy as a writer who seemingly "eine Geschichte von ihrem Anfang an in sich erlebt vom fernen Punkt bis zu der heranfahrenden Lokomotive aus Stahl, Kohle und Dampf . . . von ihr gejagt wird und aus eigenem Schwung vor ihr läuft wohin sie nur stößt und wohin man sie lockt" (KAF, 9:33) ("experiences a story within himself from its very beginning, from that point in the distance up to the approaching train made of steel, coal and steam . . . is pursued by the story and runs ahead of it under his own impetus in whichever direction it pushes him and wherever he entices it to follow him")—whereas he himself experienced all the troubles described above when trying to find a thread that would at least help him to get a story moving.

If we look at two of Kafka's earliest texts, the first from 1906, the draft of a response to Max Brod's article on aesthetics "Man darf nicht sagen" (One may not say) and the other the beginning of a planned novel, the so-called Raban story, which in some respects is a predecessor of the "Metamorphosis," we can see some characteristic features of his writing that are connected to the problem of "vorwärts zu kommen" (KAF, 11:187) ("moving ahead").[7] The first of these texts is just three pages long and deals with the term "ästhetische Apperception" ("aesthetic apperception"). In it Kafka offers a kind of philosophical reflection, but the discussion of the term is challenging and inconsistent. There is something of a lawyer's and a philosopher's discursive practices in play here. The author of the text promises a rational procedure but never arrives at a clarifying solution; rather, he persuades the reader that it is not possible to arrive at such a solution. Here we can readily recognize many of the elements found in such short narratives as "Gib's auf!" ("Give Up!") and other writings: tiredness, loss of orientation, and an unsuccessful struggle, while logical reasoning becomes more and more difficult and contradictory and ends in unresolved conflict. The reader, who has followed the argumentation eagerly in the hope of learning more about this important concept, is left at the end facing both its "uncertainty" and the impression of its lack of fit with practical life. As so often is the case in Kafka's stories, the line of argument is inverted and the conclusion is missing.

The next text Kafka wrote in the same year is familiar to many readers, namely the opening sequence of "Hochzeitsvorbereitungen auf dem Lande" ("Wedding Preparations in the Country"), of which various drafts exist.[8] There are differences in the descriptions, some simplifications, and some enhancements between version one and two. Both start in an easy manner with an everyday situation, as a man steps out of his door into the street:

> Als Eduard Raban, durch den Flurgang kommend, in die Öffnung des Tores trat, sah er, daß es regnete. Es regnete wenig.
>
> Auf dem Trottoir gleich vor ihm gab es viele Menschen in verschiedenartigem Schritt. Manchmal trat einer vor und durchquerte die

Fahrbahn. Ein kleines Mädchen hielt in den vorgestreckten Händen ein müdes Hündchen. Zwei Herren machten einander Mitteilungen. Der eine hielt die Hände mit der innern Fläche nach oben und bewegte sie gleichmäßig, als halte er eine Last in Schwebe. Da erblickte man eine Dame, deren Hut viel beladen war mit Bändern, Spangen und Blumen. Und es eilte ein junger Mensch mit dünnem Stock vorüber, die linke Hand, als wäre sie gelähmt, platt auf der Brust. Ab und zu kamen Männer, welche rauchten und kleine aufrechte längliche Wolken vor sich her trugen. Drei Herren—zwei hielten leichte Überröcke auf dem geknickten Unterarm—giengen oft von der Häusermauer zum Rande des Trottoirs vor, betrachteten das, was sich dort ereignete und zogen dann sprechend sich wieder zurück. . . .

Raban fühlte sich müde. . . . Man arbeitet so übertrieben im Amt, dass man dann sogar zu müde ist, um seine Ferien zu genießen. . . . Und solange Du "man" sagst an Stelle von "ich", ist es nichts und man kann diese Geschichte aufsagen, sobald Du aber Dir eingestehst daß Du selbst es bist, dann wirst Du förmlich durchbohrt und bist entsetzt. (KAF, 5:15)[9]

(When Eduard Raban, after coming through the hall, stepped into the opening of the entrance onto the street he saw that it was raining. It was raining lightly.

On the pavement directly in front of him he saw people walking in a variety of ways. Sometimes someone would step forward and cross the street. A little girl held a tired little dog out in front of her on outstretched arms. Two gentlemen were giving information to each other. One of them held out his hands with the palms upwards, moving them evenly, as if he were balancing a load. Then one saw a lady whose hat was heavily laden with ribbons, brooches and flowers. And a young man with a thin stick hurried past, holding his hand flat against his chest, as if it were lamed. Now and again men would come who were smoking and carried small, thinnish, vertical clouds of smoke before them. Three gentlemen, two of them carrying light coats over bent arms, would frequently go from the wall across to the edge of the pavement, look at what was going on there, and then step back to the wall again, still talking. . . .

Raban felt tired. One works so excessively at the office that one is too tired even to enjoy one's holidays. . . . And as long as you say "one" rather than "I," it's nothing and one can tell this story, but as soon as you admit that this is about you, then it cuts you to the very quick and you are horrified.)

It is a typical Kafka scene—like something taken from a painting by Georges Seurat. The first part of the fragment is written in the third-person perspective, with events being observed by an omniscient narrator who reports in the past tense. Then the point of view changes, and in certain passages we hear Raban arguing with himself in the present tense about his undertakings. Later the author changes the perspective yet again and reverts to the authorial point of view. However hilarious many of the scenes may look, we are soon confronted with the protagonist's problems, difficulties we are also familiar with from the author's life. The switch to the first-person perspective thus is not merely a technical choice but indicates that the protagonist is the author's alter ego, expressing moods and analyzing situations and decisions that Kafka himself was struggling with. The crucial moment lies in the switch from the impersonal pronoun "one" to the personal pronoun "I," a change which opens up a gulf between the detached recital of a story and the experience of being cut to the quick by its significance. James Rolleston (1979, 404) has called Raban a "transparent substitute" for the author (a connection confirmed by Kafka's free play with the letters of his own name). There is certainly much autobiographical material in these drafts, expressed in a rather direct and subjective form, whereas Kafka later tried to find less immediate ways of expressing his inner concerns. Thus, Raban conjures up in his mind a picture of himself lying securely in bed in the shape of a huge stag beetle while the empty shell of his bourgeois persona is to be sent out into the world on unsteady legs. The image will return in the figure of the transformed Gregor in the "Metamorphosis" but with the fundamental difference that in the later story the dream is no longer a dream and the reader is confronted with an unacceptable premise he is nevertheless forced to accept, not least because the point of view is shifted into the protagonist Gregor, a narrative move that brings the figure close to the reader while at the same time alienating the reader from empirical reality.

We find specific elements of Kafka's art in this fragmentary novel about Raban. Kafka's language is plain and unpretentious, and the narrator presents figures and settings visually and theatrically. Raban has to cope with so many movements, so many sharply observed people crossing his path, and so many visual curiosities that he soon gets tired. There is also Kafka's characteristic way of opening the narrative—inviting the reader to follow the narrator into a seemingly harmless, innocent looking world, which soon turns out to be confusing and difficult to deal with despite the simple language and all the seemingly humorous deviations that prolong the protagonist's promenade almost ad infinitum.[10] If readers simply follow the narrator's authorial perspective, they might be misled by the colorful street scene and only discover the first suggestion of a disconnection between form and content when Raban reveals what he is thinking. A crucial point here is Kafka's combination of the pronouns "man" (one), "du" (you), and "ich" (I) in the reflection at the end of the paragraph that turns the passage into a metatext that conveys the narrator's own options regarding the choice between different ways of describing things via the protagonist's revelations about his state of mind.

Another typical element, the "impossibility of narration," seems to be implicit in Kafka's texts from early on, both in the struggle for explanations and sometimes in the fragmentary character of the texts. The attentive reader will be brought to reconsider his or her reading strategy and ask whether Kafka's texts offer more resistance than other texts and therefore whether they demand to be read in different ways. Is it enough to describe Kafka's narrators as unreliable narrators, or is the problem located in the approach to subject matter? Does it originate, for example, in the typical "Schaukel-Diskurse als sprunghafte Widerspruchsentwicklung" ("see-sawing discourses as a way of developing contradictions by discontinuous progression") with which Kafka was familiar from the Jewish narrative tradition (BrM, 154), whereby the meaning changes according to shifts of perspective, as in the famous discussion between Josef K. and the prison chaplain in *The Trial?*[11] The "Negierung der Erzählbarkeit" ("negation of narratability") in Kafka's work is the starting point of Peter Höfle's argument. He characterizes the specific form of Kafka's narratives as "aufbauende Zerstörung" ("constructive destruction"), an expression taken from Kafka's notebooks in spring 1918 (KAF, 6:222). In Höfle's view (1998, 159), Kafka's entire oeuvre embodies a "Poetik des Mangels" ("poetics of deficiency").

In the two texts from 1906, we find two important indications for both the deviant discursive progression highlighted by Höfle and the relation between the narrator's perspective and the exposure of the narrative as such or, to put it another way, between the shifting loyalties of the narrator and the communicative effect of the text. When reading *The Trial* and other narratives by Kafka, early readers experienced difficulty in getting hold of the content and the argument because the narration appeared to lack consistency and logical stringency. The peculiarities of Kafka's narration are largely responsible for the ways his works have been read—or misread—over the years because his strange stories and uncommon motifs made the strongest impression on his early readers, prompting them to compare his stories to others they were already familiar with, such as the fantastical tales of E. T. A. Hoffmann. After all, what do we do when we have difficulties with understanding a text? We often refer to something similar in order to get some help for the interpretation. This kind of normalization can be carried out on different levels.

If we look at the beginning of some of the published texts, a novel and some stories, we can take the first chapter of *Der Verschollene* (*The Man who Disappeared*) as an invitation from Kafka to read the novel in the tradition of the great novels of self-formation from the classical and realistic periods in Europe. A suitable model for Karl's story might also be sought in the novel of travel (see Gerhard Neumann's discussion in chapter 4). In both types of novel a young person is sent out into the world to gain experience, but with the aim of bringing him home again, matured by the challenges and adventures he had to deal with, and ready to settle down to an ordinary life as a useful member of society. Kafka seems at first to open his novel with the same procedure, but the reader soon discovers complications that neither the young protagonist nor the reader knows how to tackle or to integrate in their fields of experience. Even if Karl Roßmann seems initially to be guided by a benevolent Providence when he gains admission to the fine house of his rich uncle, where he is provided with riding and piano lessons and an English teacher so that he can have as "brilliant" a career as his uncle, the reader senses from early on the dangers in the situation Karl is sliding into.

In this way Kafka designs a pattern and invites the reader to follow it, while at the same time building in warning signals that an experienced reader will spot immediately. Through these expressions, signs, and words, the narrator establishes an unobtrusive but important degree of distance between the narrator and the protagonist. Thus, the narrator may either lead the naive reader to see the fictional world through the eyes of the protagonist and feel alienated along with him, or he may make the more experienced reader suspicious and wary of looking at the world in this way.

Beside this network of motifs and patterns that help the reader to navigate through the texts, Kafka uses other means, which have a contrary effect. He organizes a game of ambiguities, contradictions and traps that force the reader into strenuous mental gymnastics in an effort to establish some logical order.[12] The reader follows the narrator and his syntactic model: conjunctions like "if," "though," "but," and "however" invite him to make rational pirouettes, while causal and consecutive clauses give the impression of logical argumentation, although such an argument is not actually present. Other expressions like "perhaps," "in a way," "rather," "in a sense," "seemingly," "nearly," "at first glance," and "in reality" relativize the logic of progression, as in the opening lines of a key narrative from his last period of writing, "Der Bau" ("The Burrow"):

> Ich habe den Bau eingerichtet und er scheint wohlgelungen. Von außen ist eigentlich nur ein großes Loch sichtbar, dieses führt aber in Wirklichkeit nirgends hin, schon nach ein paar Schritten stößt man auf natürliches festes Gestein. (KAF, 8: 165)

> (I have established my burrow, and it seems to be a success. From the outside all that is visible is a large hole, but in fact it leads nowhere; after just a few steps you hit hard, natural rock.) (KSS, 162)

In the first half of the opening sentence, the first-person narrator, a mole-like creature, talks about the result of his labors, but the second half concludes only that the burrow *seems* to be well made. At first the hole mentioned in the second sentence is taken by the reader to be the entrance, but it turns out to be merely a mock opening leading straight into a wall of rock. That the narrator's logic does not match the reader's expectations is made clear when the narrator applies the adjective "natural" to a system that does not immediately strike one as the most natural. But the reader is likely to stop fighting against the narrator's strange logic quite quickly and to listen instead to the narrator who is the architect of this building/burrow as he explains the distinctiveness of his burrow/construction (detecting perhaps in the ambiguity of the term "Bau"—meaning both burrow and construction—that this strange enterprise may allude to the narrative itself).[13]

A contrasting example is the opening of "Ein Landarzt" ("A Country Doctor"), which begins with an admission: "Ich war in großer Verlegenheit" (KAF, 1:200) ("I was in great difficulty"). From this not very promising start, which goes on to enumerate all manner of hindrances preventing the doctor from responding to a call to visit a patient, the story suddenly starts to accelerate, trapping the doctor on his carriage and whisking him away "wie Holz in die Strömung" (KAF, 1:201–2) ("like wood in a current"), finally leaving the reader in great difficulties as he too struggles to understand the nightmarish story.

We surely can agree with Beicken when he says that Kafka "takes over the gesture of traditional narration without fulfilling the promise of familiar contents. What he narrates is always alien in character" (1979,

37). The difference between the traditional form of narration and Kafka's can be ascribed to certain factors on different levels. He certainly did not write in accordance with the ruling literary conventions of his time, neither stylistically nor with regard to expectations of meaningfulness or logical progression. As many critics have demonstrated, this had an impact both on his narrative technique and on the reception of his works. Beda Allemann found that Kafka's works do not have a conventional narrative structure—typically, an opening situation, complication, development and resolution, all arranged in chronological order (see Introduction, note 1). Not only does the action usually stagnate in Kafka's stories almost immediately but the narrated world is not situated in the empirical world and seems to be detached from time as we know it. This is what Kafka might have meant when he spoke of "Stillstand im Fortschritt" ("stasis in progress") or "stehender Sturmlauf" ("charging on the spot") (see Andringa 2008, 331).

Klaus Ramm (1971, 1979), on the basis of earlier investigations by Beißner, Walser, Allemann, and others, has made important observations that may help us to understand why Kafka often did not succeed in his efforts to carry a narrative through from beginning to end. Kafka himself may have been aware of more hidden obstructions than those he mentions. Ramm was interested in the problem of narrative organization in Kafka's narratives. He saw the main difficulty in the non-congruence of traditional narrative terminology with Kafka's mode of narrative progression. Instead of following a particular path, Kafka's protagonists are ceaselessly thinking of alternatives, which are incorporated in the action in hypothetical or subjunctive form (cf. Kremer 2008, 344). "On the Gallery" and "Before the Law" are two striking examples of a form of narration that takes the form of a reflection that is progressively deepened and yet arrives at no goal, a pattern of thinking that we have met as a central characteristic of Kafka's writing from the very beginning.[14] No wonder it was extraordinarily difficult to guide a protagonist through all these hypothetical alternatives, relativizations, and constrictions toward a solution. When an experiment of this kind failed because "the plenitude of what was imagined" could not be got down on paper, Kafka had simply to dismiss his figures. Such a complicated method does not aim at a synthesis or conclusion but rather produces a sequence or series of sequences in which construction is followed by deconstruction.

In his study on the art of portraiture, Peter von Matt tries to capture this phenomenon of Kafka's very special kind of writing. He argues that the fury of the writing spirit transforms Kafka into "ein Textwesen" ("a textual entity") who ignores all kinds of obligations and laws: "Even within an evolving text a preceding sentence has no power over its successor, the event currently being described is not determined by the event that has just been described; saying A does not involve the obligation to say B, and saying B does not involve the obligation to have said A first. References to a reality or an idea are only necessary in as much as they facilitate the gesture of emancipation from any such obligation on the part of the writer to refer to things outside the text" (1983, 16). Other critics have been struck by the same peculiarity. Umberto Eco, for example, describes the phenomenon as "the autonomous movement of a text" (1984, 13), while Neumann outlines the movements of "reversal and deviation" in Kafka's "slipping paradoxes."[15]

Perhaps one of the most outstanding examples of this kind of procedure is to be found in "The Judgment," where almost every statement is inverted in the course of the action. In spite of this lack of narrative consequence (seen from a traditional point of view), Kafka is filled with an exuberant feeling of happiness or even ecstasy, which he usually expresses through his feelings of exaltation, euphoria, sovereignty, and domination. These feelings find its equivalents on the level of narrated events through the suspension of gravity (as in "The Bucket Rider," "A Hunger Artist," "Investigations of a Dog"). In "The Metamorphosis" and in "The Burrow" we find examples of a similar kind of happiness, such as the "Schwingen" ("swinging/vibration") experienced by Gregor as he hangs from the ceiling. At such moments he feels free and no longer bound by the laws of gravity, even if he has lost the outer attributes of a human being:

> Besonders oben auf der Decke hing er gern; es war ganz anders, als das Liegen auf dem Fußboden; man atmete freier; ein leichtes Schwingen ging durch den Körper; und in der fast glücklichen Zerstreutheit, in der sich Gregor dort oben befand, konnte es geschehen, dass er zu seiner eigenen Überraschung sich losließ und auf den Boden klatschte. (KAF, 1:126–27)

> (He especially liked hanging from the ceiling; it was completely different from lying on the floor; one could breathe more freely; a faint swinging sensation went through the body; and in the almost happy absent-mindedness which Gregor felt up there, it could happen to his own surprise that he let go and plopped onto the floor). (KSS, 23)

In "The Burrow" too we find a description that recalls Kafka's images of happiness on those few occasions when all the obstacles to writing were eliminated. The first-person narrator expects to find the greatest possible happiness in a specially constructed room in his burrow once the whole work is finished (something that is never in fact realized and indeed may not ultimately be achievable):

> In diesem Hohlraum hatte ich mir immer, und wohl kaum mit Unrecht, den schönsten Aufenthaltsort vorgestellt, den es für mich geben konnte. Auf dieser Rundung hängen, hinauf sich ziehen, hinabzugleiten, sich überschlagen und wieder Boden unter den Füßen haben. (KAF, 8:192)

> (I had always imagined this hollow space, probably not without some justice, as the most wonderful abode I could ever have. To hang from this dome, to pull yourself up, to slide down, to turn a somersault, and once again to feel the ground under your feet.) (KSS, 179–80)

In all these examples we find the above-mentioned overlap between the narrator's and the protagonist's feelings that the editor of the critical edition, Malcolm Pasley, noticed when working with Kafka's manuscripts. The close link between the author and the writing process, the interpenetration of the writing situation and the situations being narrated, results in the recording of processes in which the movement of writing (literally the movement of the pen across the page), narrative progression, and the unfolding of events correspond to one another so that the text as a whole absorbs the flow of narration with all its obstacles and recalcitrant reflections. This illustrates what Kafka meant when he said, in numerous variations, that his entire life was dictated by his relation to literature and the writing of literature. It is the *process of writing* that matters more to him than the final outcome—although of course he was always disappointed if that process could not be unfolded and pursued to a fitting conclusion. In this writing process lay for Kafka the most intimate connection between living and writing. As he writes, life is transformed into literature and literature into life.[16] Only as a writer did he feel fully alive, albeit at the cost of radical separation from what the majority of non-writers would recognize as life truly lived.

In his letters and diaries, Kafka almost invariably uses the term *writing* ("mein Schreiben") for the activity on which his life depended. He does not distinguish between his fictional and non-fictional writing in this respect (he turned back to his diary, for example, when the fictional vein dried up), and the reason seems to be that all forms of writing had the virtue of keeping the activity of putting words on paper going in the hope of not missing that crucial moment when the flow of a story might emerge, involuntarily, from the movement of his pen.[17]

It is important to remember that not all of Kafka's literary works fall under the category of "narratives." His longer works are definitely narratives, and so are many of his novellas or longer short stories. But it seems important to draw a categorical line between these texts and some of the shorter pieces of prose, "die kleinen Winkelzüge" ("minor maneuvers") as Kafka called them (see Kurz 1995, 345), which are not really narratives but rather short descriptions or reflections. These are often strikingly visual and can have a strong element of tentative, sometimes unsuccessful or inconclusive reasoning, as in "Die Bäume" ("The Trees") from *Betrachtung* (*Contemplation*), Kafka's first published book of prose. As Neumann has argued convincingly (1968, 728), this whole text is concentrated on and built around deviation—no action takes place other than in the mind contemplating some tree trunks in the snow, no conflict, no resolution. There is instability, but the instability is concentrated in the movement of thought and perception. Each mental movement undoes the previous perception so that by the end we are left totally unsettled. If we think of the first text mentioned above on apperception, "Man darf nicht sagen," it seems that these two texts permit an interesting comparison. The text about apperception started in logical reasoning but moved toward narrative as the reasoning faltered, whereas "Die Bäume" starts with perception and moves toward an increasingly reflective mode of discourse as it becomes unclear what is actually seen—or not seen.

Such deviations, which are not narratives per se, are sometimes integrated in the narrative flow of the longer texts. More often than not, they seem to hinder the flow, at least temporarily. Although part of the narrative progression, they seem to turn and redirect it, moving it toward some kind of paradox. In this way the deviant movements on the micro-level seem vital for the structure on the macro-level, alienating the text from normal narrative progression and perhaps even from the concept of narrative itself.

As we have seen, Kafka tried repeatedly to describe the difficulties he felt when struggling to grasp a topic and find an adequate form for it. At the end of January 1921, while staying at a sanatorium in Matliary, vainly trying to build up some strength after the debilitating onset of tuberculosis, he tried to write to Max Brod to explain some of the difficulties he had with his conception of life, but the letter swelled up both in volume and in complexity. Finally he tried to explain his difficulties figuratively to his friend in the following passage:

> Es ist aber eben das Musterbild eines schlechten Schriftstellers, dem das Mitzuteilende wie eine schwere Seeschlange in den Armen liegt, wohin er tastet, nach rechts, nach links immer nimmt es kein Ende, und selbst was er umfasst, kann er nicht ertragen. (MB, 313).[18]
>
> (It is the paradigm of a bad writer, who carries what he has to convey in his arms like a heavy sea-snake; in whichever direction he reaches out, whether to the right or the left, it never comes to an end, and he cannot even support the part he is holding in his arms.)

There are many drafts by Kafka that start like this at some point in the middle of a story rather than at the beginning. As James Rolleston has noted, "Kafka's stories begin in the middle; or rather, near the end, as the very specific situational details seize hold of the hero's mind (sometimes his body too) and propel him forward" (1979, 3). As Anniken Greve points out in her analysis of the "Metamorphosis" in chapter 2 of this volume, even this story that otherwise satisfies the definitions of a narrative, does not start at the very beginning. The reader gets no indication of how the metamorphosis came about, how the changes started, and what exactly happened to Gregor as he was assuming his new, verminous shape. Of course, here we can point to the convention that the narrator may start at any point he wants to and thus throw the reader in medias res, but that is not the kind of problem we are discussing at this point.

All of Kafka's protagonists have a history behind them when they appear on the scene, whether one looks at Karl Roßmann, whose embarrassing past is pulled apart by his uncle in front of the authorities in New York, or K. in *The Castle* who (like Josef K. in this respect) is not regarded as trustworthy by the reader because his past is unknown and unverifiable. But we are familiar with this technique from analytical drama and from many other texts as well, especially from all kinds of detective stories where the past has to be unfolded once the action has begun and as things happen in the present time. As readers we are willing to read on and find out, as we do at the beginning of *The Trial,* only to discover after some time that this text, in spite of many similarities, does not fulfill the norms of the genre it initially seemed to belong to. Thus, pretending to follow a specific pattern seems to facilitate the beginning of a new text for Kafka even when he does not actually intend to continue along the same lines.

The last two examples I wish to consider are taken from Kafka's last years of writing. After the onset of his tuberculosis in 1917, a series of narratives mark the beginning of a new period of creativity for Kafka. From 1918 onward, he wrote, for example, a number of very short stories or sketches based on Greek myths, such as "Prometheus," "Poseidon," and "Das Schweigen der Sirenen" ("The Silence of the Sirens").[19] By taking these pre-existing stories as his point of departure, Kafka seems to have avoided the frustrations of beginning and not finding an end. He can simply leap into the middle of the story, twist it in another direction, and mystify the reader by estranging its content. Another such case is a little story about the Tower of Babel, written in September 1920 and published by Brod in 1931 under the title "Das Stadtwappen" ("The City Coat of Arms").[20]

The motif of the Tower of Babel accompanied Kafka throughout his life (see Binder 1975, 241). Kafka's well-known comment "Wir graben den Schacht von Babel" (KAF, 8:95) ("We are digging the Shaft of Babel") dates from the same time as the story, and here again we can see him using the image in a quite unfamiliar way, for instead of referring to the new structure as a kind of skyscraper, he inverts the dimension of the tower, sending it beneath the surface of the earth.

If we compare Kafka's story with the original myth in the Book of Genesis, we can see the difference between the two narratives immediately. The people of Babylon decided their city should have a tower so immense that it would reach into the heavens. The tower was built not for the worship and praise of God but for the glory of man: "And they said, Go to, let us build us a city and a tower, whose top may reach unto heaven; and let us make us a name, lest we be scattered abroad upon the face of the whole earth" (Gen. 11:4, King James Version). God, seeing what the people were doing, confounded their languages and scattered the people across the earth.

Kafka starts the narrative "somewhere in the middle," pointing out that all is well when the construction of the tower begins, at which time interpreters and workers are already at work. Thus, the building activity starts after the confusion of language, reversing the biblical order of cause and effect. What matters is only to construct a tower that reaches into heaven, and to achieve this goal it is considered wise to build as slowly as possible because technical progress that they hoped to achieve within one hundred years would make it easier to accomplish the building. On the other hand, it is unclear to the builders whether the next generation would like the building or would prefer to destroy it and start again. These doubts undermined the project and the morale of the building workers who neglected the tower and concentrated instead on building a nice town to live in. This in turn gives rise to jealousy and quarrels among the workers, which further hinders work on the tower. While the second and third generations continue the work with even greater skill, the senselessness of the undertaking becomes obvious. But it is too late to give up because people in the city are now too involved with one another. From this point onward, the city is filled with longing for the prophesied day when a "Riesenfaust" (giant fist) will smash the whole city. Which is why, according to the conclusion of Kafka's story, the city has a hammer in its coat of arms.

If one compares Kafka's version to the original myth, the most obvious change is the lack of a larger, framing narrative, since the pact between God and mankind has been omitted. God is never mentioned by Kafka, the building of the tower has nothing to do with disobedience or hubris, and no reason is given for the confusion of tongues. The focus is not on the accomplishment of the tower, but on changes from an early stage that obstruct progress. Ultimately, the only apparent purpose of the story is to "explain" Prague's coat of arms, albeit with one crucial difference. Just as Kafka exchanged the torch in the hand of the Statue of Liberty for a sword in *The Man Who Disappeared,* Kafka changed the meaning of the fist with the sword in the Prague coat of arms, turning it into an image of the desire for destruction rather than for protection. Thus the original story loses its meaning entirely in the new version, while the new story changes the meaning on every level to produce an antithesis. Although the narrator constructs a new pseudo-logic, he deconstructs it at the same time: the senselessness of the project is acknowledged by all, but the work goes on while everybody waits for its destruction. Instead of God's punishment, the people damn themselves to a Sisyphean prolongation of their undertaking. The story seems to illustrate Kafka's aphorism that in life generally there is a goal, but no way (KAF, 7:146). It may also (and consistently) express Kafka's view of his own creative work.

The manuscripts written after 1920 consist of numerous recordings of small events, impressions, or thoughts, but they also contain a good number of promising stories in which we as readers are left regretting the fact that we seem to be deprived of the solution, which sometimes appears to lie just round the corner. The evidence of the manuscripts shows that Kafka was still struggling "in immer neuen Ansätzen den Einstieg in das Erzählen zu finden" (KAF, 8:251) ("to find a way into narration by attempting one new approach after another"). In 1921 he states that he wants to use small components from his "autobiographical investigations" (KAF, 8:10) to build a "house," but he still fears that he lacks the strength to complete the construction.[21]

The last story I wish to discuss was not, as Binder assumed (1975, 239–41), written at the same time as the other stories, which were based on pre-existing narratives, but was actually composed in the autumn of 1923 when Kafka was living in Berlin, away from Prague and his family for the first time in his life.[22] This finding, one of the results of the critical edition of Kafka's works, puts the text, entitled "Heimkehr" ("Homecoming") by Brod, into a new context. His difficult economic situation and the spread of his tuberculosis made Kafka think more and more of the necessity of returning to Prague. The little story alludes almost certainly to the parable of the prodigal son from the gospel of St. Luke, but it differs significantly from its predecessor, possibly because of the ambivalent feelings Kafka had with regard to his return to his hometown.[23]

In the biblical parable we hear of a man who has two sons. The younger demands his share of the inheritance and goes off to a distant country, where he wastes everything and finally has to take work as a swineherd. There he comes to his senses and decides to return home and throw him self on his father's mercy, thinking that even if his father does disown him, being one of his servants would be better than feeding pigs. But when he returns home, his father greets him with open arms and celebrates his return. The older brother resents his father's favored treatment of the younger brother, but the father responds that he must be glad, for his brother who once was dead is alive again, was lost and now is found. In the original story we can recognize the narrative schema of "someone telling somebody on some occasion that something happened." Kafka, however, makes some surprising and radical changes that throw this scheme into disorder:

> Ich bin zurückgekehrt, ich habe den Flur durchschritten und blicke mich um. Es ist meines Vaters alter Hof. Die Pfütze in der Mitte. Altes unbrauchbares Gerät in einander verfahren verstellt den Weg zur Bodentreppe. Die Katze lauert auf dem Geländer. . . . Ich bin angekommen. Wer wird mich empfangen? Wer wartet hinter der Tür der Küche? . . . Ist Dir heimlich? Fühlst Du Dich zuhause? Ich weiß es nicht, ich bin sehr unsicher. (KAF, 8:162)

> (I have returned. I have crossed the entrance and look around me. It is my father's old farmyard. The puddle in the middle. A tangled jumble of useless equipment blocks the way to the stairs leading up to the loft. The

> cat lies in wait on the balustrade. . . . I have arrived. Who will receive me? Who is waiting behind the kitchen door? . . . Do you feel safe and secure? Do you feel at home? I don't know, I'm very unsure.)

The crucial change lies in the shift from an authorial third-person story to a first-person narrative told in the present tense and in direct speech. All the preceding events of the biblical story are absent, and if we do not assume that the story of the prodigal son is the underlying model for this one, we have to admit that we are confronted with a person we know nothing about. We see the lurking cat and the disorder of the neglected farm through his eyes, and it is not long before the narrator addresses me, the reader, asking if I feel at home. Who answers? I (the reader) or the man who has just arrived? We deduce that the latter does, for he explains that it is his father's house, although he does not feel connected to anything. He does not dare to knock on the door. He tries to listen from a distance to what is going on in the kitchen but can hear nothing and carries on waiting so as to respect the secret of those sitting in the kitchen. "Je länger man vor der Tür zögert, desto fremder wird man. Wie wäre es wenn jetzt jemand die Tür öffnete und mich etwas fragte. Wäre ich dann nicht selbst wie einer der das Geheimnis wahren will" (KAF, 8:163) ("The longer one hesitates outside the door, the more of a stranger one becomes. How would it be if someone were now to open the door and ask me something? Wouldn't I then be like someone who wants to keep a secret?").

The story ends with an unbridgeable distance between the returning man and his family, who may be sitting in the kitchen. They do not know about his arrival, while he adopts the posture of someone who is hesitating, someone who is just as reluctant as they are to reveal his secret. No reunion with his father takes place; indeed, who knows if the father is even alive? There is no joy at seeing one another again, no reconciliation, not even an effort on the part of the returning man to overcome his timidity to knock at the door and reveal his presence. If the opening sentences look like the preparation for the last steps to complete the return, the closing sentences show that the reunion does not take place. Uncertainty and ambivalence take over: every observation is relativized, what seemed to be secure becomes uncertain, home becomes an alien place. We as readers enter the story via a typically Kafkaesque route, by following the protagonist and arriving at the same state of mind as he is in when it is over. We feel as uncertain as he does, we do not know if we have reached the end or if some act of courage might change the situation or the door might open or whether everything might end in great disappointment.

Similarly, between the beginning and the end of the story about the tower or shaft of Babel, we find Kafka's well-known words: "Es gibt nur ein Ziel, keinen Weg. Was wir Weg nennen, ist Zögern" (KAF, 7:146) ("There is only a goal, but no path. What we call a path is hesitation"). Again, the story shows exactly this pattern of movement, taking one step forward and two steps back, before it finally stagnates at some point, unsure if it is at the end.

Notes

1. Unless otherwise indicated, translations are by Ronald Speirs.

2. Zimmermann discusses, for example, six defective twists in the plot or incredible suspensions that contradict all narrative logic (2004, 65–72).

3. See Rolf Selbmann's analysis (2002, 36–58).

4. As a parallel we can see Karl Roßmann's thoughts in "The Stoker" by listening to Schubal's words: "Sie bemerkten freilich nicht, daß selbst diese schöne Rede Löcher hatte" (KAF, 2:29) ("Admittedly they did not notice that even this fine speech had holes in it").

5. Written in November or December 1909 after seeing a group of Japanese acrobats at the Theater Variété of Prague.

6. See Guntermann's excellent study (1991; esp. pp. 148–90) of narrativity, self-reflexivity, and Kafka's problems with writing.

7. The earliest existing story is from December 1902, enclosed in a letter to Oskar Pollak. See Höfle (1998, 169).

8. There are two versions of this fragment; the later one dates from 1910. Between 1904 and 1906, and again from 1909 to 1910, Kafka wrote these short, often fragmentary, narratives, which were subsequently published in *Beschreibung eines Kampfes* (*Description of a Struggle*). In 1909 he started writing about his journeys (*Reiseberichte*), and from 1910 onward he wrote his diary.

9. *Hochzeitsvorbereitungen auf dem Lande* (*Wedding Preparations in the Country*), "Fassung A" (KAF, 5:14–37).

10. See also the *Blumfeld* fragment, which Kafka started writing in 1915 after abandoning his work on *The Trial,* for marvelous examples of movement, stasis, and the expansion and contraction of narrative time. Kafka notes on January 18, 1915, "Unfähig zu längerer koncentrierter Arbeit. . . . Trotzdem eine neue Geschichte angefangen die alten fürchtete ich mich zu verderben. Nun stehen vor mir 4 oder 5 Geschichten aufgerichtet wie die Pferde vor dem Cirkusdirektor Schumann bei Beginn der Produktion" (KAF, 11:70–71) ("Incapable of a longer period of sustained concentration. . . . Despite this, I have begun a new story, I was afraid to spoil the old ones. Now 4 or 5 stories are standing up on their hind legs in front of me like horses in front of the circus director Schumann at the beginning of a performance").

11. Peter U. Beicken (1979, 43) argues that Kafka reveals the deficient vision of a main character or focalizer through the dialectical interplay of contradictions between the protagonist's and the narrator's perspectives ("the perspective of experience" and the "perspective of observation").

12. The assumption that the reader is often led along a course parallel to that of the protagonist and his attempts to orient himself is still made by critics today; see, for example, Schmidt (2007, 228).

13. In her excellent study on Kafka's textgenesis, Annette Schütterle analyzes Kafka's *Oktavhefte* (*Journals*) from the period 1916–1917 and beyond as "a process of writing that takes the form of a system of partial construction" (2002, 140) as described in Kafka's story "Building the Great Wall of China."

14. Cf. Friedrich Schmidt's profound analysis of the legend of the doorkeeper for a thorough critical presentation of the history of research (2007). Cf. also chapter 8 for Jakob Lothe's analysis of the narrative beginning of "In der Strafkolonie."

15. Scheffel's narrative analysis (1999/2000) is based on Gerhard Neumann's basic finding (1968).

16. A few quotations indicate this important topic: "nur der Wellengang des Schreibens bestimmt mich. . . . Meine Lebensweise ist nur auf das Schreiben hin eingerichtet" (F, 66) ("Only the wave-like movement of writing determines my life. . . . My way of life is entirely organized for the purpose of writing"); "dass Schreiben meine einzige innere Daseinsmöglichkeit ist" (F, 367) ("That writing is the only inner possibility of existence for me"); "Alles, was sich nicht auf Literatur bezieht, hasse ich" (DW, 140) ("I hate everything that is not related to literature"); "Ich habe kein literarisches Interesse, sondern bestehe aus Literatur" (F, 444) ("I don't have literary interests, I consist entirely of literature"); "Mein ganzes Wesen ist auf Literatur gerichtet" (F, 456) ("My entire being is directed towards literature").

17. Kafka was certainly not alone in having this problem. Many great novelists experienced difficulties in writing, and at the beginning of the twentieth century we find a great number of writers suffering not just from writer's block but also from the crisis of language—the disjunction of signifier and signified—that became acute around that time.

18. In his next letter from the beginning of February, Kafka apologizes that his long letter might not have arrived, but if so, this would not matter, since nothing was lost because "so wie er kein Ende hatte, hatte er auch keine Mitte, nur Anfang, nur Anfang. Ich könnte gleich wieder von neuem anfangen" (MB, 314) ("Just as it had no ending, it had no middle, only a beginning, only a beginning. I could start from the beginning again immediately").

19. In a study from 1985, Hans Dieter Zimmermann analyzed these and other short narratives by Kafka on a modified structural basis and in comparison with Robert Walser's prose. He showed the specific way in which the two authors construct a narrative, paying particular attention to Kafka's use of a pre-existing pattern as a starting point and his deviation from it, as in the examples mentioned earlier. Also many other critics have pointed out this specific procedure (cf. Neumann 1968, 702–44).

20. Like most of the stories in Kafka's manuscripts, this story was given no title by Kafka.

21. Here we are reminded of the Babel metaphor as an impossible undertaking.

22. For the evidence of the manuscripts, see KKANIIA, 134–42).

23. There are several fragmentary texts from this period dealing with the theme of return: "Es ist meine alte Heimatstadt und ich bin wieder in sie zurückgekehrt" (KKANII, 562) ("It is my old home town and I have returned to it") and "Es ist meine alte Heimatstadt und ich irre langsam, stockend durch ihre Gassen" (KAF, 8:154) ("It is my old home town and I stray slowly, hesitantly, through its streets").

Works Cited

Andringa, Els. 2008. Die Facette der Interpretationsansätze. In *Kafka-Handbuch: Leben—Werk—Wirkung,* ed. Bettina von Jagow and Oliver Jahraus, 317–35. Göttingen: Vandenhoeck & Ruprecht.

Beicken, Peter U. 1979. Erzählweise. In *Kafka-Handbuch,* ed. Hartmut Binder. Vol. 2. *Das Werk und seine Wirkung,* 36–48. Stuttgart: Metzler.

Binder, Hartmut. 1975. *Kafka-Kommentar zu sämtlichen Erzählungen.* Munich: Winkler.

———, ed. 1979. *Kafka-Handbuch.* Vol. 2, *Das Werk und seine Wirkung.* Stuttgart: Metzler.

Guntermann, Georg. 1991. *Vom Fremdwerden der Dinge beim Schreiben: Kafkas Tagebücher als literarische Physiognomie des Autors.* Tübingen: Niemeyer.

Heller, Erich/Beug Joachim. 1977, ed. *Franz Kafka. Der Dichter über sein Werk*: München: Deutscher Taschenbuch Verlag (DW).

Höfle, Peter. 1998. *Von der Unfähigkeit, historisch zu werden: Die Form der Erzählung und Kafkas Erzählform.* Munich: Wilhelm Fink.

Jagow, Bettina, and Oliver Jahraus, eds. 2008. *Kafka-Handbuch: Leben—Werk—Wirkung.* Göttingen: Vandenhoeck & Ruprecht.

Jahraus, Oliver, and Stefan Neuhaus, eds. 2002. *Kafkas "Urteil" und die Literaturtheorie: Zehn Modellanalysen.* Stuttgart: Reclam.

Kafka, Franz. 1995. *Erzählungen.* Ed. Michael Müller. Stuttgart: Reclam.

Koelb, Clayton. 2006. Critical editions II: Will the real Franz Kafka please stand up? In *A companion to the works of Franz Kafka,* ed. James Rolleston, 27–31. New York: Camden House.

Kremer, Detlef. 2008. Kafka und die Hermeneutikkritik. In *Kafka-Handbuch: Leben—Werk—Wirkung,* ed. Bettina von Jagow and Oliver Jahraus, 336–52. Göttingen: Vandenhoeck & Ruprecht.

Kurz, Gerhard. 1995. Nachwort. In Franz Kafka: *Erzählungen,* ed. Michael Müller, 342–66. Stuttgart: Reclam.

Matt, Peter von. 1983. *. . . fertig ist das Angesicht: Zur Literaturgeschichte des menschlichen Gesichts.* Munich: Hanser.

Neumann, Gerhard. 1968. Umkehr und Ablenkung: Franz Kafkas "Gleitendes Paradox." *DVjS* 42:702–44.

Ramm, Klaus. 1971. *Reduktion als Erzählprinzip bei Kafka.* Frankfurt: Athenaeum.

———. 1979. Handlungsführung und Gedankenführung. In *Kafka-Handbuch,* ed. Hartmut Binder. Vol. 2, *Das Werk und seine Wirkung,* 93–107. Stuttgart: Metzler.

Rolleston, James. 1979. Die Romane, Ansätze der Frühzeit. In *Kafka-Handbuch,* ed. Hartmut Binder. Vol. 2, *Das Werk und seine Wirkung*, 402–7. Stuttgart: Metzler.

———, ed. 2006. *A companion to the works of Franz Kafka*. New York: Camden House.

Scheffel, M. 1999/2000. Ins Endlose angelegt: Franz Kafkas Romanprojekt *Der Verschollene* aus narratologischer Sicht. *Runa,* 279–95.

Schmidt, Friedrich. 2007. *Text und Interpretation: Zur Deutungsproblematik bei Franz Kafka; Dargestellt in einer kritischen Analyse der Türhüterlegende.* Würzburg: Königshausen & Neumann.

Schütterle, Annette. 2002. *Franz Kafkas Oktavhefte: Ein Schreibprozeß als "System des Teilbaues."* Freiburg: Rombach Cultura.

Selbmann, Rolf. 2002. Kafka als Hermeneutiker: *Das Urteil* im Zirkel der Interpretationen. In *Kafkas "Urteil" und die Literaturtheorie. Zehn Modellanalysen,* ed. Oliver Jahrhaus and Stefan Neuhaus, 36–58. Stuttgart: Reclam.

Zimmermann, Hans Dieter. 1985. *Der babylonische Dolmetscher: Zu Franz Kafka und Robert Walser.* Frankfurt: Suhrkamp.

———. 2004. *Kafka für Fortgeschrittene.* Munich: Beck.

8

THE NARRATIVE BEGINNING OF KAFKA'S "IN DER STRAFKOLONIE"

Jakob Lothe

The beginning of a narrative is closely related to its title, which in one sense is both its beginning and its ending. Since a narrative's title is what we read first, it shapes our reading of the narrative beginning—and of the whole text. Moreover, once we have read the narrative and asked what it means, what its thematic significance is, we may discover that a good title—and Kafka's titles are often good—approximates a radically condensed version not only of the narrative text but also of a possible interpretation of that text.[1]

Yet although the title of a fictional text is closely linked to its narrative beginning, a title's narrative dimension can be more or less clear, and also more or less significant. Here too it makes a difference whether we have read the text or not: if we know the story, the title's narrative potential is activated in ways we cannot possibly appreciate on our first reading. An illustrative example is the first sentence of Kafka's *Der Proceß* (*The Trial*): "Jemand musste Josef K. verleumdet haben, denn ohne dass er etwas Böses getan hätte, wurde er eines Morgens verhaftet" (KKAP, 7) ("Someone must have been telling lies about Josef K. for without having done anything wrong he was arrested one morning" [Kafka 1988, 17]). Repeating and thus stressing the title of chapter 1, "Verhaftung" ("Arrest"), the verb form "verhaftet" ("arrested") indicates that the process against Josef K. has already started. Positioned just before the last comma, "hätte" is a key word in this sentence. The subjunctive form of the verb signals that although K. was not aware of having done anything wrong, perhaps he still might have done something precipitating his arrest. Thus "hätte" makes the literary text ambiguous in a way that creates suspense.[2] This kind of ambiguity, in evidence later in the text too, is not only linked to Josef K. as a main character but also associated with the third-person narrator and with the implied author.[3] Although the narrator informs us that Josef K. was arrested, his use of the subjunctive form "hätte" suggests that it remains open whether this was with good reason or on thin evidence. Perhaps the narrator does not know the reason for his arrest; perhaps nobody does; perhaps there is no simple reason. Moreover, as Ronald Speirs and Beatrice Sandberg have noted, the subjunctive form makes the narrative perspective approach Josef K.'s experiential perspective: "We are not reading the story of a man who is arrested despite the *fact* that he is innocent, but rather the story of a man who *maintains* that he has been wrongfully arrested" (1997, 68; original emphases). With a view to the novel's title, the essential point to make here is that already in the opening sentence Josef K. is implicated in a process whose starting-point and cause are apparently unknown to him, and from which, as we may suspect on a first reading and as we know on a second, he will never escape. The title represents, in condensed form, the frustratingly circular plot and thwarted plot progression in which Josef K. is not only engaged but also trapped.

There is a striking similarity between the beginning of *Der Proceß* and that of "In der Strafkolonie" ("In the Penal Colony"). Kafka wrote this long short story in the autumn of 1914, just after the outbreak of the First World War. On August 13, he had started *Der Proceß,* but because of the problems of beginning and developing this text, he took a two-week holiday "um den Roman vorwärtszutreiben" ("in order to press on with the novel").[4] This writing strategy failed (as did that of first writing the novel's first and last chapters), and in fact *Der Proceß* was never finished. However, during the holiday Kafka managed to write "In der Strafkolonie." In order to indicate the affinity of the beginnings of these two texts, I briefly note how the passive construction "wurde . . . verhaftet"—the words at the end of the first sentence of *Der Proceß*—further increases the uncertainty associated with "hätte." Since in a presumably civilized society (the word "Rechtsstaat" is used on page 11 of *Der Proceß*) one is not arrested unless one has done or is suspected of having done something wrong, and since any arrest prompts the question of who ordered it, our attention as readers is drawn to the issue of power and to the agent representing that power. This agent, a kind of court, remains enigmatic throughout. In "In der Strafkolonie" too there is a similar agent, or rather there are two, represented by the conflicting values and legal systems of "der alte Kommandant" ("the old commander") and "der neue Kommandant" ("the new commander"). If the court's distance from the accused in *Der Proceß* is counteracted by its all-pervasive presence in the narrative discourse, the officer in the short story repeatedly refers to the absent old and new commanders in the penal colony—and thus implicitly to the systems of power and law enforcement associated with them.[5] In "In der Strafkolonie" too, the main characters are already engaged in an ongoing legal process when the narrative discourse begins.

In his seminal study of beginnings, Edward W. Said finds that although beginnings appear to mark a distinct break with that which precedes them (e.g., a story's title), they may seem curiously predetermined:

> Where, or when, or what is a beginning? If I have begun to write, for example, and a line has started its way across the page, is that all that has taken place? Clearly not. For in the act of asking a question about the meaning of a beginning, I seem to have discerned vague outlines of significance where very little had been suspected. Claude Lévi-Strauss suggests that the mind's logic is such that "the principle underlying a classification can never be postulated in advance. It can only be discovered *a posteriori*." Moreover, language, which seems to be man's most influential instrument of classification, is, according to Lévi-Strauss, "an unreflecting totalization [of] . . . human reason which has its reason and of which man knows nothing." (Said 1975, 29; Lévi-Strauss 1966, 58, 252)

Even though Said agrees that to identify a point as a starting-point is to classify it after the fact, he certainly does not find the study of beginnings a critically useless exercise. That a beginning is hard to pinpoint, that we can hardly intellectually conceive of such an idea, does not in itself make the questions prompted by the problem of beginnings uninteresting or irrelevant to literary studies. On the contrary, a number of issues actualized by the problem of narrative beginnings are, as Kafka's fictional texts demonstrate, not just important in themselves but also closely associated with other constituent elements of the complex mechanics of narrative.

One essential reason why beginnings appear arbitrary and peculiarly ungraspable is suggested by the way in which language operates. The beginning of a text is *there,* observable on the page, and yet it is not there since the first linguistic sign or the first linguistic utterance is preceded by something about which we are ignorant, something located before or beyond the text. Although there is a sense in which all narratives start *in medias res,* Brian Richardson is right to note that "modernist texts . . . typically begin with a plunge into the middle of an action of deceptive casualness" (2008, 4). This is an important point, as is the accompanying observation that in modernist fiction "the artifice of the textual beginning is . . . contrasted to the unbounded plenum of events it partially circumscribes" (Richardson 2008, 5).

By linking narrative and event Richardson implicitly highlights what I consider as an original and extreme variant of narrative beginnings, "Kafka's technique of absolute beginnings" (Ramm 1979, 95; my translation). In a thoughtful essay on processes of action and thought in Kafka's fiction, Klaus Ramm finds that, for Kafka, the challenge of beginning to narrate is imbued with an existential dimension in that it reveals the author's doubt about new beginnings in his own life—ultimately even his "Zögern vor der Geburt" (KKAT, 888) ("hesitation before birth") evoked in his diary entry for January 24, 1922. Ramm elaborates, "With the first words the characters emerge, wake up, are ready to travel . . . the beginning of the narrative corresponds to its thematic movement [and] the characters are without any precondition pushed into the narrative" (1979, 95; my translation). One could counter that such an observation applies to many narratives, not least modernist ones; and one could also contend, as did Maurice Blanchot—one of the finest of Kafka's early critics—that the protagonists of his stories have in a way already died.[6] Still, Ramm's description of Kafka's beginnings has much to recommend it, since the narrative into which the characters are thrown may seem to begin near the end. Moreover, as Ramm implies, the complexity of Kafka's narrative beginnings is further enhanced once we attempt to relate the question of the beginning of the literary text to the beginning of the action and to the first event within this text. Writing of a "contamination of text and action" (1979, 95), Ramm argues that the "iterative quality" of beginnings in Kafka's fiction expresses his "peculiar conception of time, of history generally" (97; my translation).

Ramm's perceptive observation is linked to several points of the following discussion. Succinctly put, my argument is that the first paragraph of "In der Strafkolonie" is possessed of a combination of narrative features that, almost immediately assuming the form of what James Phelan (2005, 19–20) calls tensions (unsettled relationships among author, narrator, and audience based on disparities of knowledge, understanding, or values) and/or instabilities (unstable relationships among the characters), further the text's movement in one direction rather than another. As should be clear already, my focus will be on issues of narrative, and one premise for my discussion is that the narrative features of a fictional text's beginning are highly significant structurally, thematically, and ideologically. In mentioning this premise I draw attention to the problem of reading and rereading a narrative beginning. Two dissimilar critical dispositions are at work here. On the one hand, we may want to study a beginning as a "pure" beginning, thus attempting to read and interpret it without paying attention to the text's middle and end. On the other hand, as my use of the verb "attempt" reveals, in practical criticism this turns out to be impossible. Nor is it desirable: there is actually very little to say about a beginning if we do not relate it to the following parts of the narrative, and of course the significance of a beginning is in large part determined by the narrative's middle and by its ending.[7]

"In der Strafkolonie" begins thus:

> "Es ist ein eigentümlicher Apparat," sagte der Offizier zu dem Forschungsreisenden und überblickte mit einem gewissermassen bewundernden Blick den ihm doch wohlbekannten Apparat. Der Reisende schien nur aus Höflichkeit der Einladung des Kommandanten gefolgt zu sein, der ihn aufgefordert hatte, der Exekution eines Soldaten beizuwohnen, der wegen Ungehorsam und Beleidigung des Vorgesetzten verurteilt worden war. Das Interesse für diese Exekution war wohl auch in der Strafkolonie nicht sehr gross. Wenigstens war hier in dem tiefen, sandigen, von kahlen Abhängen ringsum abgeschlossenen kleinen Tal ausser dem Offizier und dem Reisenden nur der Verurteilte, ein stumpfsinniger, breitmäuliger Mensch mit verwahrlostem Haar und Gesicht und ein Soldat zugegen, der die schwere Kette hielt, in welche die kleinen Ketten ausliefen, mit denen der Verurteilte an den Fuss- und Handknöcheln sowie am Hals gefesselt war und die auch untereinander durch Verbindungsketten zusammenhingen. Übrigens sah der Verurteilte so hündisch ergeben aus, dass es den Anschein hatte, als könnte man ihn frei auf den Abhängen herumlaufen lassen und müsse bei Beginn der Exekution nur pfeifen, damit er käme. (KKAD, 203–4)
>
> ("It is a peculiar piece of machinery," said the officer to the traveler and with a look that contained some admiration surveyed the machine that was after all so familiar to him. It was apparently only from politeness that the traveler had accepted the invitation of the commandant, who had requested his presence at the execution of a soldier condemned to death for disobeying and insulting his superior officer. The interest in this execution, even in the penal colony, did not seem to be very great.

> At any rate, apart from the officer and the traveler, here in the deep, sandy little valley enclosed on all sides by bare slopes there were only the condemned man—a stupid fellow with a big mouth and unkempt hair and face—and a soldier who held the heavy chain into which the small chains ran with which the condemned man was bound at the wrists, ankles, and throat and which were further linked together by connecting chains. In fact, the condemned man looked so doggishly submissive that it seemed you could let him run around freely on the slopes and would only have to whistle at the start of the execution for him to come.) (KSS, 35–36)

This is a strange first paragraph, engrossing and yet difficult to understand. Even though it is not the whole beginning, it is surely an important part of it, and it will be the focus of my critical attention here. We first note an interesting detail: the word "Beginn" which in German is used synonymously with "Anfang" in a manner broadly corresponding to "beginning" and "opening" in English, is actually mentioned at the end of the paragraph. The use of "Beginn" here is symptomatic of the way in which the beginning is simultaneously accentuated and problematized. One function of the word is to confirm what we have been told already, thus suggesting that we (the characters as well as the reader) are at the beginning of a course of action presumably revolving around the execution itself. At the same time, however, the phrase "Beginn der Exekution" indicates that what begins here is neither the narrative account of the crime nor, as in *Der Proceß,* of the arrest. Rather, "Beginn" is closely linked to the last stage of a trial—the implementation of what is presumably the death sentence.

In order to structure the following discussion, I use James Phelan's account of four different aspects of a narrative beginning: exposition, launch, initiation, and entrance. Although Phelan's understanding of narrative is more explicitly rhetorical than my formal-historical approach, I find his concepts and the way he uses them helpful and critically productive (see James Phelan's discussion in the introduction and in chapter 1).

By *exposition* Phelan means "everything, including the front matter, that provides information about the narrative, the characters (listings of traits, past history, and so on), the setting (time and place), and events of the narrative" (2007, 17). In this particular text, the most important element of the front matter is clearly the title. Relating the title of "In der Strafkolonie" to the short story's first paragraph, we first note the correspondence between the preposition "in" and the location of the narrative. By using "in" rather than, for instance, "nach" ("to"), Kafka signals that the story's focus is on what happens here, in this particular place. There is a close link between the "in" of the title and the *in medias res* beginning that follows. When we start reading, we are already on location in two senses. By force of homology, we are both present as imaginary observers at a distant location and present as readers, at this very moment and place, within the "penal colony" that the author's narration, with our collaboration, is building out of words. Moreover, we are in a place it is difficult to escape from, both for the characters in the story and for the readers who are its imaginary co-creators, and where, as we have noted already, the first paragraph seems to mark the ending of a course of action rather than its beginning.[8]

The key word of the title in German is a composite noun, made from combining the two nouns "Strafe" ("penalty or punishment") and "Kolonie" ("colony"). Both of these nouns are semantically loaded and have numerous connotations associated with them. The number, range, and interpretive immediacy of these will of course vary from reader to reader. My point here is that our response to the words "Strafe" and "Kolonie" contributes to our attempt, even as we start reading, to understand the formation of a new noun consisting of these two. Reading the first paragraph, our knowledge of the title helps us to rapidly understand that the events recounted in the narrative take place in a colony in which an act of punishment is to be carried out and that the two elements are closely related. And yet there is something strange about the relationship between the word "Strafkolonie" and the following sentences. The associations we get when reading the title do not seem wholly reconcilable with the information provided in the short story's opening: "Strafkolonie" makes us think of the historical practice of deportation, but nowhere in Kafka's story is the word "deportation" mentioned. This does not mean that the word is unimportant, however. Rather, due to the strong associative field of "Strafkolonie" and "deportation" in many readers' minds, a more dynamic element—the act or practice of being deported—is added to, or superimposed on, the stasis of being "in der Strafkolonie." The interpretive relevance of this association is qualified, though not canceled, in the following narrative.

In a detailed study entitled *Die Deportation des Menschen* ("The deportation of man"), Walter Müller-Seidel situates Kafka's story in its historical and cultural European context. Although, as he reminds us, punishment by deportation was an invention of Roman law, the practice of deportation became more widespread once European powers started to establish colonies in the wake of the discoveries of the Americas and other (from a European perspective) remote regions. A supplement to or variation of banishment, deportation was often considered as a substitute for the death penalty; thus there is a sense in which, for the reader possessed of this knowledge, the condemned man (who may or may not have been deported to the penal colony) will be punished twice. On a second reading of the beginning, we know that the language spoken in the penal colony is French. France did not abolish deportation as an element of the nation's criminal law until 1945. Linked to this colonial power's use of deportation, moreover, is the famous Dreyfus affair—a historical event likely to be known by many readers of Kafka's story.

Even though the importance of the Dreyfus affair may be exaggerated in a discussion of the narrative beginning of "In der Strafkolonie," it provides an interesting example of a strong intertextual echo already in the story's title.[9] Two aspects are particularly striking. First, there is the blend of issues—historical, political, religious—associated with the affair itself.[10] Centered on the relationship between crime and punishment, the Dreyfus affair revolved, as does Kafka's story, around the use and possible abuse of power. Second, there is the significance of location. Dreyfus was deported to Devil's Island, off the coast of French Guiana. One of the best known and most infamous of all penal colonies, the French colony in Devil's Island was in use from 1852 to 1946. The point I want to make here is not that Kafka wants the reader to think of Devil's Island as he or she starts reading "In der Strafkolonie." In common with many other authors, including Joseph Conrad, Kafka tended to shy away from linking his fictional locations to places in the real world. The only one mentioned in the story is Europe, since we are told that the traveler is a European. What is important about the penal colony is, first, that it is not limited to one place only and, second, that it is far removed from Europe. If the former element enables Kafka to cast his narrative in more general terms, thus furthering its suggestiveness and continuing resonance in the world today, the latter serves to establish a link among various activities involving spatial distance—punishment, colonization, and, in the case of the traveler (*der Forschungsreisende*), research. By associating the traveler's mission with the first two activities, Kafka uses the title to suggest the dubious nature of that mission. To draw attention to the story's suggestiveness and lack of geographical specificity, however, is not to argue that, seen from the perspective of readerly dynamics, the association of the Dreyfus affair and Devil's Island is unimportant. Rather, reminding us of the subtle ways in which Kafka's fiction is both related to and inspired by historical events, the intertextual echo of the Dreyfus affair serves to extend the thematic range of the story's beginning.[11]

While it is significant that the word "Beginn" is mentioned toward the end of the paragraph, it is also important that the key word of the title is repeated in the text's third sentence. The word "Strafkolonie" is thematically productive here: repeating and thus calling renewed attention to the title, it colors the information provided about the event, the characters, and the narrative's time and place. The specification of "Strafe" as execution—the short story's main event—is part of the exposition, but the element of tension suggested by the combination of "Strafe" and "Kolonie" blends into the narrative's launch which I will discuss shortly. By "*launch,*" Phelan means "the revelation of the first set of global instabilities or tensions in the narrative" (2007, 18).

The short story's four characters are all introduced in the first paragraph: "der Offizier," "der Forschungsreisende," "der Verurteilte," and "der Soldat." What brings them together is the implementation of the punishment. Thus "Strafe" is actualized once again. Moreover, as in the case of the interlinking of "Strafe" and "Kolonie," exposition of the characters almost immediately blends into launch.

When it comes to the exposition of time and place, we note that the time seems to be unspecified yet modern, and as indicated already, the place is somewhere far from Europe. The beginning is possessed of a relatively imprecise temporal marker associated with the officer and particularly his relationship with the machine. Already at this early stage, before the officer explains the details of the apparatus to the traveler, we sense that this "Apparat" is a product of modernity, of European industrialization. As Hans Dieter Zimmermann has noted, the officer is a European "above all in his admiration for technique, this European invention, which in the apparatus has reached a degree of perfection: in the apparatus which has no purpose but to torture the condemned man for twelve hours and then to kill him" (Zimmermann 1994, 159; my translation). That our attempt to specify the time of the story involves the adjective "European" illustrates the narrative's interplay of temporal and spatial elements: it proves difficult to delineate one element without referring to or at least implying the other. The historical process of European modernity is linked to European imperialism and European colonization of other continents.[12] The officer's identity as a European whose uncomfortable uniform is at least a reminder of his distant *Heimat* ("homeland") establishes a link to *der Forschungsreisende* from Europe. The nationalities of the condemned man and the soldier, however, are not specified. The traveler seems troubled by being in an intermediate position between these parties, and his sense of inescapable entrapment is suggested right from the start.

For Phelan, the launch "marks the boundary between the beginning and the middle" (2007, 18). Broadly agreeing with Phelan's identification of this significant aspect of a narrative beginning, I argue that elements pointing in the direction of such a launch are observable in the first paragraph of Kafka's story. One possible location of the launch is the moment when the officer announces the sentence: "Unser Urteil klingt nicht streng. Dem Verurteilten wird das Gebot, das er übertreten hat, mit der Egge auf den Leib geschrieben" (KKAD, 210) ("Our judgment does not sound severe. The harrow will write the commandment he has violated on the condemned man's body" [KSS, 39]). At this moment the revelation of the global instability is complete and the reader is likely to ask, will this sentence be carried out and how will the traveler respond to the implementation of the sentence? It could be countered that the paragraph under consideration is too short to allow for the narrative direction and subsequent progression associated with the launch. However, in this short story narrative movement and progression remain curiously illogical, unpredictable and suspended, and the tensions I identify seem to me global in the sense of informing not only the narrative beginning but also the textual movement from beginning through middle to ending. The first paragraph lays important groundwork for the launch by emphasizing that each of the four characters has a different relation to the "Apparat," a difference that also influences their attitude and relation to one another.

By identifying and discussing the tensions pointing toward the narrative launch, I want to comment on the narrator, and his role in what Phelan calls the "initiation"—"the initial rhetorical transactions among implied author and narrator, on the one hand, and flesh-and-blood and authorial audience on the other" (2007, 18). As in *Der Proceß* and *Das Schloß* (*The Castle*), Kafka uses a third-person narrator. This narrator describes the setting, introduces the characters, and reports the action (and, significantly, the lack of action). Moreover, the narrator repeatedly, though not wholly consistently, links his perspective to that of the traveler, telling us about the latter's thoughts, doubts, and impressions of the three other characters. Just as important, however, is what Kafka does *not* make his narrator do. As we note right from the beginning, the narrator does not provide much background information. More importantly, we cannot help noticing how reluctant the narrator is to position himself in relation to, and to distance himself from, the event he reports. The two key factors here are, first, the narrator's limited knowledge and, second, his inability—or unwillingness—to respond morally to the event of the execution. Revealing the narrator's human qualities, these factors are constituent aspects of Kafka's original variant on third-person narration. Interestingly, what may be a personal weakness of the narrator is also the narrator's strength. As Zimmermann rightly points out, the narrator juxtaposes two perspectives: the officer's and the traveler's. And yet the narrator's attitudinal perspective approximates that of the traveler. An early indication of this attitudinal affinity comes toward the end of the paragraph, when the narrator describes the condemned man in a manner that is not only biased but condescending. That the traveler is a *Forschungsreisende* evidently does not exempt him from racial and cultural prejudice; nor is the narrator free of such prejudice.

If the story's narration is rhetorically effective and thematically productive, it also signals that the implied author views the narrator's and the traveler's positions as ethically dubious. It is the interaction of these positions (implied author's, narrator's, traveler's, and authorial audience's) that constitutes the initiation. I am not claiming that as authorial audience we are in a position to ascertain the implied author's value system at the end of the story's first paragraph. But it does signal that the implied author's ethical stance is at odds with that of the officer, and that it is not unproblematically identifiable with that of the traveler or the narrator, either.

Phelan relates one more aspect of the narrative beginning to our activity as authorial audience. This fourth facet is "entrance": "the flesh-and-blood reader's multileveled . . . movement from outside the text to a specific location in the authorial audience at the end of the launch. When the entrance is complete, the authorial audience has typically made numerous significant interpretive, ethical, and even aesthetic judgments, and these judgments influence what is arguably the most important element of the entrance: the authorial audience's hypothesis . . . about the direction and purpose of the whole narrative, what I will call its configuration" (Phelan 2007, 19). The narrative beginning of "In der Strafkolonie" is hardly an entrance as Phelan understands it; it is too short, and comes too early, to enable the authorial audience to form a coherent hypothesis about the short story's configuration. While the instabilities and tensions we have noted simultaneously point toward and complicate the launch, however, these tensions also further a provisional hypothesis about configuration. One such hypothesis could be that this narrative will dramatize the execution of the condemned man. Yet although tentative ideas of configuration are being formed, or starting to be formed, Kafka appears to halt narrative progression almost as soon as he has made his narrator initiate it. There is a sense of *Windstille* ("wind calm") in this narrative beginning—an impression of stasis and deadlock, and equally, a sense of complication and deferment of narrative progression.[13] There is a hesitation, *Zögern,* in the narrator's (and behind him, Kafka's) attitude to the story he is starting to tell.

One consequence of this narrative feature is that the transition from the text's narrative beginning to its turning point—the traveler's refusal to grant the officer's request and the latter's decision to put himself in the other party's shoes—is unusually abrupt. Again, I am not arguing that this peripety, rhetorically effective in forcing us to revise our hypothesis about the narrative's configuration, is prefigured in the opening paragraph. Still, already in the first sentence the officer's attitude to the machine is presented as very peculiar: "'Es ist ein eigentümlicher Apparat,' sagte der Offizier zu dem Forschungsreisenden und überblickte mit einem gewissermassen bewundernden Blick den ihm doch wohlbekannten Apparat." The adjective "eigentümlich," not easily translated into English, accurately describes the sentence. The word suggests that the machine is not just "peculiar" (probably the best English word if we must choose just one) but also "original" and "curiously fascinating." This first sentence seems to make a simple statement, and yet this statement is doubly qualified—first by the officer's use of an unexpected adjective before "Apparat" and then by his "bewundernden Blick." It is remarkable how accurately the officer's negotiations, which approximate to a redefinition of progression as bifurcation and eventually result in a senseless mutilation of himself, are presented in embryo in the story's first paragraph. The statement is also qualified by a narrator who not only reports the officer's strange observation on the apparatus but also comments on his strange, and partly unresolved, attitude to it. The oddity of the officer's observation is reinforced in a narrative comment that not only confirms but tentatively questions the text's first sentence. As the qualification embedded in the narrator's remark reveals a limitation of narrative knowledge, the ending of the first sentence prepares the reader for the use of "schien" ("seemed") at the beginning of the following one; thus, a pattern of narrative uncertainty, though not necessarily unreliability, is ingrained in the formation of that very narrative.[14]

One important function of the tensions is to create suspense—a suspicion on the first reading, blending into expectation on the second—that the constellation of these four different characters may provoke a conflict, probably violent, whose outcome is uncertain. Lurking underneath the narrative discourse of this opening paragraph are issues of power, authority, and dominance. As we have seen, some of these issues are suggested by, and activated through, the intertextual field of the story's title. They are also prompted by the ways in which the first paragraph's tensions are negotiated later in the narrative. Contributing significantly to the story's curiously hesitant yet dramatic plot progression, these narrative negotiations are linked to the characters' actions, involvement, and development. As regards the condemned man and the soldier guarding him, we are more forcibly struck by the affinity of their positions than by the opposition between them. This kind of resemblance (which becomes particularly striking at the very end of the story when the condemned man and the soldier unsuccessfully try to enter the traveler's boat) is signaled by the reference to both of them as soldiers in the first paragraph. One thematic effect is to illustrate the contingency of the system and the use of the machine. It seems a matter of chance which of the two is condemned to death; the other one might also easily have done something that, given the penal colony's strange and unpredictable legal system, could have resulted in the death sentence. The arbitrariness of crime, arrest, and punishment calls the beginning of *Der Proceß* strikingly to mind. As readers we wonder to what kind of "Rechtsstaat" the penal colony could possibly belong.

The peculiar affinity of the soldier and the condemned man is strengthened by the traveler's stance: his attitude toward them is virtually as hostile as that of the officer. Kafka's narrative presentation of these two main characters, including the ways in which they differ from each other and resemble each other, is a significant aspect of the story's thematic import and interpretive suggestiveness. If the soldier and the condemned man strangely resemble each other, so do the officer and the traveler. Constituent elements of their peculiar relationship are hinted at already in the first paragraph, both in the paragraph as a whole (including the title) and in key words such as "bewundernden" ("admiring") and "schien" ("seemed"). Inspired by these two words' thematic significance, I relate the introductory presentation of the officer and the traveler to the following action in which they are engaged.

The officer looks at the machine "mit einem gewissermassen bewundernden Blick" ("with a look that, to a certain extent, expressed admiration"). By telling us not only that the officer admires the machine but also that his admiration is somehow qualified, the third-person narrator suggests, right at the beginning of the narrative, that the officer's attitude to the machine—and thus to his own activity as an officer in the penal colony—is problematically ambiguous. Referring reverently to the old commander who constructed the machine, he presents himself as an ardent supporter of the machine, the penal system, and the practice of torturing victims for twelve hours before they are eventually killed. At the beginning of the story, the officer seems as eager to defend the continued use of this practice as he is keen that this particular execution succeeds. Yet he is also keen to give his account of the machine and its operations to the traveler; it is almost as though he needs to persuade his visitor that the method of punishment is justifiable in order to convince himself that it is. There is an important connection between the doubt suggested by "gewissermassen" ("to a certain extent") in the first paragraph and the officer's observation some pages later that "Der Grundsatz, nach dem ich entscheide, ist: Die Schuld ist immer zweifellos") (KKAD, 212) ("The principle according to which I decide is: 'Guilt is always beyond all doubt'" [KSS, 40]). Insisting that guilt is always "zweifellos," the officer may secretly doubt that it is. He calls it a "principle," but actually it is more like a working assumption or legal fiction. Reminding us that a large portion of the text is made up of the officer's act of narration, Richard T. Gray observes that "when we as readers exit the fictional world of the past invoked by the Officer . . . and enter the real time of the Explorer's experiences in the penal colony, the events that transpire, in particular the operation of the penal machine, run absolutely counter to the fictions invoked in the Officer's narrative" (2006, 217). Perhaps, in spite of his claims to the contrary, he needs to support the old commander and his views in order to counter the influence exerted on him by the new commander and the ladies associated with him. These ladies, the officer tells the traveler, are opposed to the death penalty; yet when he later unbuttons his uniform before putting himself under the harrow of the machine, "fielen ihm zunächst die zwei Damentaschentücher, die er hinter den Kragen gezwängt hatte, in die Hände" (KKAD, 240) ("the two lady's handkerchiefs that he had squeezed under the back of his collar immediately fell into his hands" [KSS, 55]). John Zilcosky finds that the officer "longs masochistically to become like his victim" (2003, 118). Yet as Zilcosky also notes, masochism is not the only issue here; it is blended with elements of sadism and other aspects of the officer's psyche related to, and shaped by, the complex historical developments of punishment, deportation, and colonialism.

If the officer asserts that guilt is "zweifellos," and if his unresolved understanding of guilt and punishment is signaled by his ambivalent attitude to the machine he admires, the traveler is also fascinated by the apparatus of torture from which he claims to distance himself. In one sense his interest in the machine is as ethically dubious as the officer's defense of its continued use. Even though he expresses his doubts about the proceedings, he does not interfere to stop or change them. In fact he is, in Alexander Honold's apposite phrase, a "teilnehmender Beobachter" (2008, 491) ("participating observer"). The sudden appearance of the traveler in the penal colony contributes essentially to the story's *in medias res* beginning. On a second reading, we understand better why the officer wants the traveler to attend the execution, and then we can also appreciate the dramatic irony resulting from our knowledge that the victim, contrary to the officer's intention at the outset of the story, will be himself. Concomitantly, once the execution has occurred and the traveler abruptly leaves the colony, the story ends.

On arrival the traveler is immediately plunged into a murderous situation from which it is impossible to emerge ethically unscathed. This impossibility establishes an important link between the traveler and the reader, who also pays a visit to the colony during the act of reading the story and who may also be simultaneously fascinated and repulsed by the machine. To make this point is not to argue that we are asked to identify with the traveler. But it is to suggest that since our attitudinal distance from the traveler is less marked than that from the officer, we are forced to reconsider our attitudinal affiliation with him as the narrative progresses. The word "schien" suggests, as does the sentence of which it is a part, the curious ambiguity of the traveler's position. The third-person narrator does not seem to know why the traveler accepts the officer's invitation, yet this kind of narrative uncertainty proves thematically productive and remarkably accurate.

With the important exception of his violent act of repelling the soldier and the condemned man when they try to enter his boat as he is leaving the colony, the traveler's behavior is characteristically reluctant: "Der Reisende überlegte: Es ist immer bedenklich, in fremde Verhältnisse entscheidend einzugreifen. . . . er reise nur mit der Absicht zu sehen und keineswegs etwa, um fremde Gerichtsverfassungen zu ändern" (KKAD, 222) ("The traveler reflected: It is always a sensitive matter to interfere decisively in other people's affairs . . . he was traveling with the sole purpose of observing and by no means altering other people's legal institutions" [KSS, 46]). If, as the traveler asserts, he has come to the colony just to observe, then in one sense the narrative progresses to its ending because that is exactly what he does. And yet, as "schien" may also suggest, he is actually more interested, and more deeply involved, than his insistence on "sehen" leads the reader to expect. The paradoxical culpability of his position becomes conspicuous two sentences later in the narrative: "Die Ungerechtigkeit des Verfahrens und die Unmenschlichkeit der Exekution war zweifellos" (KKAD, 222) ("The injustice of the procedure and the inhumanity of the execution were beyond all doubt" [KSS, 46]). If the officer's emphatic employment of the word "zweifellos" signals his lurking doubt about the procedure he defends, the traveler's use of the same word similarly suggests a growing doubt about the applicability of European law in the penal colony. Revealing his European prejudice and sense of superiority, even and not least as a researcher,[15] it aligns his position with that of colonialism and its systematic use of violence against the natives of the conquered territories around the world.

In *Imperial Eyes,* Mary Louise Pratt coins the concept of the "contact zone," "the space of colonial encounters, the space in which peoples geographically and historically separated come into contact with each other and establish ongoing relations, usually involving conditions of coercion, radical inequality, and intractable conflict" (1992, 6). During his brief stay in the penal colony, the traveler is situated in one such contact zone, and once in it his attitude and behavior are colored by its conditions. His characteristic reluctance as a "seeing-man" (Pratt 1992, 7) is related to another of Pratt's key terms, "anti-conquest": "strategies of representation whereby European bourgeois subjects seek to secure their innocence in the same moment as they assert European hegemony" (7). Even though this kind of resemblance does not necessarily make the traveler a typical representative of European colonialism, it strengthens the colonial aspect apparent in the story's title. It also strengthens the link between the traveler and the European (or Western) reader: with a view to the processes of European colonialism and imperialism (including its use of penal colonies), there is a disconcerting sense in which the reader is also a bystander. In his *Evil and Human Agency* (2006), Arne Johan Vetlesen discusses the distinction that Raul Hilberg (1992) makes between perpetrator, victim, and bystander. We must of course be wary of linking such character designations—which Hilberg and Vetlesen construct from thorough discussions of acts that historical people performed, or failed to perform, during the Holocaust and other instances of genocide—to fictional characters in a short story. Still, I conclude by suggesting that in Kafka's story both the narrators and the main characters are complex fictional representations of all three categories, and all of them are introduced, and even to some extent developed and refined, in the narrative beginning. Engaged in systematic and repeated acts of torture and murder, the officer is a perpetrator; since the punishment of the condemned man is absurdly disproportionate to the offense he has committed, he is presented as a victim. Even though both of these categories are destabilized, however, it is the role of the bystander that is most insistently explored by Kafka. Starting in the first paragraph, the narrative discourse of "In der Strafkolonie" demonstrates that this category is less neutral, and ethically more dubious, than the bystander himself tends to think. "Der Forschungsreisende" regards himself as a bystander, yet his passivity is a form of participation that makes him complicit in the action; moreover, at the end of the narrative he acts violently in his own self-interest.

Concluding, I return to the third-person narrator, whose function is crucially important yet difficult to accurately describe. Not just reporting the story, the narrator includes—and is thus capable of including—references to the characters' thoughts and reflections, for instance those of the traveler discussed above. Yet there is also, as his use of "schien" in the first paragraph indicates, a lot that the narrator does not know. As we have seen, though, this kind of narrative uncertainty proves thematically productive and remarkably accurate. In an essay on Kafka's story "Der Bau" ("The Burrow"), J. M. Coetzee writes of the "complex and indeed baffling . . . relations between the *time of narration* (the moving *now* of the narrator's utterance) and the *time of the narrative* (referential time)" (1981, 557; emphasis in the original).[16] A similar point can be made about "In der Strafkolonie": as the qualifications and elements of doubt observable already in the first paragraph suggest, the narrator is removed from, yet also dangerously close to, the events he reports and the characters he describes. This relation is temporal, yet it is also spatial. It is "dangerous" because there is a sense in which the narrator, though he takes care to distance himself from the traveler, also becomes a kind of bystander (and one who draws the reader into like complicity) whose ethical position is perhaps also dubious. Indeed, one significant achievement of this story is to suggest that, confronted with and reporting the story's events and the historical processes which, as fiction, they represent, no available perspective is ethically unproblematic. This concluding point, too, applies to the reader, who, after having read the short story, is prompted to reread and reflect on its title and narrative beginning—and on his or her preparedness to read on.

Notes

1. For further discussion see Rabinowitz (1987, esp. 58–65).
2. As we can see, this aspect of the sentence's meaning is lost in the English

translation. For a comparison of the beginning of *Der Proceß* and that of Orson Welles's *The Trial,* see Lothe (2002). A detailed study of Kafka's language is Kobs (1970).

3. Even though, in contrast to a first-person narrator, a third-person narrator is not active as an identifiable character in the plot, he or she (or it) is an integral part of the fiction, serving as the author's narrative instrument and yet sometimes revealing limited knowledge and expressing views distinct from those of the implied author. For further discussion see Lothe (2000, 20–25). James Phelan defines the implied author as "the streamlined version of the real author responsible for the construction of the text" (2005, 5), and I would add that in constructing the text the implied author creates an image of himself that readers are able to discern. A helpful discussion of the concept is Shen (forthcoming).

4. Kafka (1995, 28); cf. Kurz (1995, 348). If no references are given, translations from the German are my own.

5. An excellent study of repetition in narrative fiction is Miller (1982); see also Miller (1998, esp. 57–60).

6. Quoted by James Rolleston (2006, 3); cf. Blanchot's essay "Kafka et la littérature" (1949). In the introduction to his *Companion to the Works of Franz Kafka,* Rolleston comments perceptively on the issue of beginnings in Kafka. For short discussions of the beginnings of Kafka's "Die Verwandlung" ("The Metamorphosis") and *Das Schloß* (*The Castle*), see Lothe (2004, 2008). See also the chapters by Anniken Greve and Beatrice Sandberg in this volume.

7. Since the following discussion presupposes the reader's knowledge of the basic events and characters of the short story, I provide the following summary or "story" (i.e., "the content plane of narrative as opposed to its expression plane or discourse," [Prince 1991, 91]): Visiting an unnamed penal colony, a European traveler is invited by an officer to attend the execution of a condemned man who is guarded by a soldier. Designed by the earlier commandant of the colony, the execution device is an elaborate torture machine that carves the sentence the man has violated on his skin before letting him die after twelve hours. Praising the machine, the officer asks the traveler to speak to the current commandant on behalf of the machine's continued use. As he refuses to do so, the officer puts himself under the harrow of the machine. However, its needles malfunction and quickly stab him to death. The traveler then leaves the colony, repelling the soldier and the condemned man as they try to board his boat.

8. Alexander Honold finds that the colonial situation of violence and punishment "has always begun before it can be exposed as narrative at all" (2008, 484).

9. On this point I register a minor dissent from Richard T. Gray, who in a thoughtful interpretation of the short story argues that Müller-Seidel, as a leading representative of "the faction of literalist interpreters . . . insists that Kafka's text is grounded primarily in 'contemporary history,' not in 'metaphysics, a theology of redemption, or other such themes'" (2006, 215). For me, the distinction between literalist and figurative interpreters—represented by, for instance, Müller-Seidel's (1986) historical and contextual approach on the one hand and Wilhelm Emrich's (1965) and Ingeborg Henel's (1973) allegorical approaches on the other—is less clear-cut than it appears to be for Gray. "In der Strafkolonie" provides the textual basis for widely divergent interpretations, and one main reason why is that, as Gray observes,

"of all the texts published by Kafka during his lifetime, it is perhaps the most fractured, disjunctive, and inconclusive" (2006, 216).

10. A great political scandal that divided France at the turn of the twentieth century and that was widely discussed across Europe, the Dreyfus affair concerned the conviction for treason in 1894 of Captain Alfred Dreyfus, a young French artillery officer of Jewish descent. Sentenced to life imprisonment for allegedly having passed on French military secrets to the German embassy in Paris, Dreyfus was deported to the penal colony in Île du Diable (Devil's Island) in French Guiana; several years later, due to vehement protests by Émile Zola and others, he was exonerated and reinstated as an officer. At the time when Kafka wrote his story in 1914, Dreyfus was serving as a major in the French army.

11. The rich and varied intertextual field in which the story is situated, and to which it is related, is mapped by Müller-Seidel (1986) and Klaus Wagenbach (Kafka 1995). Seen from a literary perspective, one intertext interestingly related to and in some ways extending that of the Dreyfus affair is Dostoevsky's *Notes from the Underground* (1864).

12. It is also linked to the outbreak of the First World War. As Zimmermann notes (2004, 87), there is little reason to doubt that Kafka's experience of the beginning of the war played a part in his writing of "In der Strafkolonie." A thoughtful discussion of the beginning of the Second World War is Philippe Carrard's "September 1939" (2008).

13. This point was made by Stanley Corngold in conversation (see chapter 9 of this volume). For helpful suggestions and comments on earlier drafts of this chapter, I also thank Jeremy Hawthorn, James Phelan, and Beatrice Sandberg. I am particularly grateful to Ronald Speirs, whose constructive criticisms and wise advice enabled me to recast and extend an earlier version of the essay.

14. Honold also finds the first sentence of the short story unusually suggestive (2008, 477). Curiously encapsulating the story's thematics and evoking its threatening atmosphere, the first sentence is, I suggest, an extension of the title as much as the first sentence of the narrative discourse.

15. Müller-Seidel thinks that Kafka's fictional traveler is modeled after Robert Heindl. A German jurist, Heindl was commissioned by the German Colonial Ministry to investigate deportation practices in New Caledonia and other European penal colonies. See Müller-Seidel (1986, 80–87, 108–10) and Zilcosky (2003, 230). See also Mladek (1994).

16. There are notable similarities between the beginning of "In der Strafkolonie" and that of Coetzee's *Waiting for the Barbarians* (1980). For a brief discussion of the beginning of Coetzee's novel, see Lothe (2008).

Works Cited

Blanchot, Maurice. 1949. Kafka et la littérature. In *La part du feu,* 9–19. Paris: Gallimard.

Carrard, Philippe. 2008. September 1939: Beginnings, historical narrative, and the outbreak of World War II. In *Narrative beginnings: Theories and practices,* ed. Brian Richardson, 63–78. Lincoln: Univ. of Nebraska Press.

Coetzee, J. M. 1981. Time, tense and aspect in Kafka's "The burrow." *Modern Language Notes* 96, no. 3 (April): 556–79.

Emrich, Wilhelm. 1965. *Franz Kafka.* 5th ed. Frankfurt am Main: Athenäum.

Gray, Richard T. 2006. Disjunctive signs: Semiotics, aesthetics, and failed mediation in "In der Strafkolonie." In *A companion to the works of Franz Kafka,* ed. James Rolleston, 213–45. Rochester, NY: Camden House.

Henel, Ingeborg. 1973. Kafkas "In der Strafkolonie": Form, Sinn und Stellung der Erzählung im Gesamtwerk. In *Untersuchungen zur Literatur als Geschichte: Festschrift für Benno von Wiese,* ed. Vincent J. Günther, Helmut Koopmann, and Joachim E. Krause, 480–504. Berlin: Erich Schmidt.

Hilberg, Raul. 1992. *Perpetrators, victims, bystanders: The Jewish catastrophe 1933–1945.* New York: Harper Collins.

Honold, Alexander. 2008. "In der Strafkolonie." In *Kafka-Handbuch: Leben—Werk—Wirkung,* ed. Bettina von Jagow and Oliver Jahraus, 477–503. Göttingen: Vandenhoeck & Ruprecht.

Kafka, Franz. 1988. *The Trial.* Trans. by Douglas Scott and Chris Walker. London: Picador.

———. 1995. *In der Strafkolonie: Eine Geschichte aus dem Jahre 1914.* Ed. Klaus Wagenbach. Berlin: Verlag Klaus Wagenbach.

Kobs, Jörgen. 1970. *Kafka: Untersuchungen zu Bewusstsein und Sprache seiner Gestalten.* Ed. Ursula Brech. Bad Homburg: Athenäum Verlag.

Kurz, Gerhard. 1995. Nachwort to *Erzählungen,* by Franz Kafka. Ed. Michael Müller, 343–66. Stuttgart: Reclam.

Lévi-Strauss, Claude. 1966. *The savage mind.* Chicago: Univ. of Chicago Press.

Lothe, Jakob. 2000. *Narrative in fiction and film: An introduction.* Oxford: Oxford Univ. Press.

———. 2002. Das Problem des Anfangs: Kafkas *Der Proceß* und Orson Welles' *The Trial.* In *Franz Kafka: Zur ethischen und ästhetischen Rechtfertigung,* ed. Beatrice Sandberg and Jakob Lothe, 213–31. Freiburg: Rombach Verlag.

———. 2004. Short fiction as estrangement: From Franz Kafka to Tarjei Vesaas and Kjell Askildsen. In *European and Nordic modernisms,* ed. Mats Jansson, Jakob Lothe, and Hannu Riikonen, 97–115. Norwich: Norvik Press.

———. 2008. Space, time, narrative: From Thomas Hardy to Franz Kafka and J. M. Coetzee. In *Literary landscapes: From modernism to postcolonialism,* ed. Attie de Lange, Gail Fincham, Jeremy Hawthorn, and Jakob Lothe, 1–18. New York: Palgrave Macmillan.

Miller, J. Hillis. 1982. *Fiction and repetition: Seven English novels.* Oxford: Blackwell.

———. 1998. *Reading narrative.* Norman: Univ. of Oklahoma Press.

Mladek, Klaus. 1994. "Ein eigentümlicher Apparat": Franz Kafkas "In der Strafkolonie." Sonderband, *Text + Kritik: Zeitschrift für Literatur* 7 (94): 115–42.

Müller-Seidel, Walter. 1986. *Die Deportation des Menschen: Kafkas Erzählung "In der Strafkolonie" im europäischen Kontext.* Stuttgart: Metzler.

Phelan, James. 2005. *Living to tell about it: A rhetoric and ethics of character narration.* Ithaca, NY: Cornell Univ. Press.

———. 2007. *Experiencing fiction: Judgments, progressions, and the rhetorical theory of narrative.* Columbus: Ohio State Univ. Press.

Pratt, Mary Louise. 1992. *Imperial eyes: Travel writing and transculturation.* London: Routledge.

Prince, Gerald. 1991. *Dictionary of narratology.* Aldershot: Scholar Press.

Rabinowitz, Peter J. 1987. *Before novels: Narrative conventions and the politics of interpretation.* Columbus: Ohio State Univ. Press.

Ramm, Klaus. 1979. Handlungsführung und Gedankenführung. In *Kafka-Handbuch,* ed. Hartmut Binder. Band 2. *Das Werk und seine Wirkung,* 93–107. Stuttgart: Alfred Kröner Verlag.

Richardson, Brian. 2008. Introduction: Narrative beginnings. In *Narrative beginnings: Theories and practices,* ed. Brian Richardson, 1–10. Lincoln: Univ. of Nebraska Press.

Rolleston, James. 2006. Introduction: Kafka begins. In *A companion to the works of Franz Kafka,* ed. James Rolleston, 1–19. Rochester, NY: Camden House.

Said, Edward W. 1975. *Beginnings: Intention and method.* Baltimore: Johns Hopkins Univ. Press.

Shen, Dan. Forthcoming. What is the implied author? *Style* 45 (2011).

Speirs, Ronald, and Beatrice Sandberg. 1997. *Franz Kafka.* London: Macmillan.

Vetlesen, Arne Johan. 2006. *Evil and human agency: Understanding collective evildoing.* Cambridge: Cambridge Univ. Press.

Zilcosky, John. 2003. *Kafka's travels: Exoticism, postcolonialism, and the traffic of writing.* New York: Palgrave Macmillan.

Zimmermann, Hans Dieter. 1994. "In der Strafkolonie": Die Täter und die Tätigen. In *Franz Kafka: Romane und Erzählungen,* ed. Michael Müller, 158–72. Stuttgart: Reclam.

———. 2004. *Kafka für Fortgeschrittene.* Munich: Verlag Beck.

9

MUSICAL INDIRECTIONS IN KAFKA'S "FORSCHUNGEN EINES HUNDES"

Stanley Corngold

Constrained—and fascinated—by the narrative of Kafka's "Forschungen eines Hundes" ("Researches of a Dog"), I will proceed by indirections, in the hope "by indirections [to] find directions out." And so readers may be glad to see a précis of the argument in advance.[1]

As a young dog, the narrator is overwhelmed by the music accompanying the sudden appearance of a group of dancing dogs. This shock brings about a great change in his life, forcing him—for a time—to focus all his attention on these dogs and their music. Instead of consistently pursuing this reflection, however, he suddenly turns in another direction: he begins to investigate the source of "nourishment" for dogs, now claiming that this is the more fundamental question. His change of direction appears to be driven by an impulse of self-protection, a need to flee the thoughts thrown up by music's power to dissolve the boundaries of the ego and, indeed, the self at whatever depth.

There is a homology between the dog's intellectual life and Kafka's: just as the dog deviates from his concern with music toward his concern with nourishment, so Kafka's organism represses his reflective response to music in order to concentrate on writing—a repression that prompts Kafka to refer afterwards to his absolute unmusicality. Only late in life, with the story "Josefine, die Sängerin oder das Volk der Mäuse" ("Josefine, the Singer or the Mouse People") does Kafka attempt to bring his repressed reflection into the half-light of literature.

The dog's original deviation is central to the story, corresponding to Kafka's own great thesis on his writing life as a deviation, a falling off, from an authentic origin. The story takes its shape, rhythm, or flow from tensions both proleptic and analeptic, carrying the reader along on a forward loop of thought, then backward, then forward again. The reader is impelled toward the end in the hope, shared with the narrator, of discovering something crucial about a lost or never-understood origin that might be called "traumatic knowledge."[2]

I

"Wie sich mein Leben verändert hat und wie es sich doch nicht verändert hat im Grunde!" (KKANII, 485) ("How my life has changed, and how, at heart, it has not!" [KSS, 132]). The opening sentence of "Researches of a Dog" contains rich but contrary narrative signals, which at once retard and advance the narrative, yet the final effect is to advance it in an interesting way. The opening thesis produces interest through its sense and thrust: the reader is eager to know in what way the narrator's life has changed, especially as the claim is asserted with such gusto, promising a vigorous and engaging story. But Kafka's signature tendency toward "stehender Sturmlauf" (KSS, 259–60), toward marking double time in place ("immobile assault" [D1, 157]), quickly produces a skeptic arrest through antithesis: My life has changed, and my life has not changed. The skepticism of this arrest is of the ancient kind, as in Sextus Empiricus's celebrated citation of Pyrrhonism, that is, "the ability that sets up antitheses among appearances and judgments. . . . By such skepticism, on account of the 'equal weight' which characterizes opposing states of affairs and arguments, we arrive first at 'suspension of judgment' and second at 'freedom from disturbance'" (Long, 75).

This "suspension" would bring the narrative to an end, in what Kafka calls a "Windstille" (KKANII, 72), a wind calm. But this story must advance, and it does so, propelled forward by the end signal "im Grunde" ("at heart," "basically"), which in wonderfully concise form announces the voice of a philosopher. The phrase "im Grunde," spoken by a mind questioning its first vigorous affirmation, breaks up this standstill *by going further.* It is a mind that cannot rest. The story advances on the wings of a flight from antithesis. By Kafka's own account, from his diary entry of November 20, 1911,

> Sicher ist mein Widerwillen gegen Antithesen. . . . Sie erzeugen zwar Gründlichkeit, Fülle, Lückenlosigkeit aber nur so wie eine Figur im Lebensrad; unsern kleinen Einfall haben wir im Kreis herumgejagt. So verschieden sie sein können, so nuancenlos sind sie, wie von Wasser aufgeschwemmt wachsen sie einem unter der Hand, mit der anfänglichen Aussicht ins Grenzenlose und mit einer endlichen mittlern immer gleichen Größe. Sie rollen sich ein,sind nicht auszudehnen, geben keinen Anhaltspunkt. (KSS, 259)

> (My antipathy to antitheses is certain. . . . Admittedly, they generate thoroughness, fullness, completeness, but only like a figure on the "wheel of life" [a toy with a revolving wheel]; we have chased our little idea around the circle. As different as they can be, they also lack nuance; they grow under one's hand as if bloated by water, beginning with a prospect onto boundlessness and always ending up the same medium size. They curl up, they cannot be straightened, they offer no leads.) (KSS, 196)

There is more than one kinetic aspect to the opening sentence of "Researches of a Dog": there are also the expectations aroused by (1) the imperial first-person, (2) the double focus on the imputed *past* event of "Veränderungen" ("Wie sich mein Leben verändert hat") and the *present* of reflective consideration ("und sich doch nicht verändert hat"), and (3) the tone of exclamation. These signals define the unfolding text as at once objective report and intimate memoir. It unfolds as an account of the chief episodes of the narrator's past life as a cynic philosopher—presented, however, in a charged, subjective focus—a form not rare in Kafka's work, as in "Ein Bericht für eine Akademie" ("A Report to an Academy"). The time conjured by the first person in the first sentence is the *present* of the consciousness that remembers, thinks, feels, as quite explicitly in the following sentence, "Wenn ich jetzt zurückdenke . . . " ("If I now think back . . . "). As the thinking subject begins to construct its opening narrative, it conjures the *past* time of remembered events, "die Zeiten mir zurückrufe, da ich noch inmitten der Hundeschaft lebte" ("the times [of which I 'summon up remembrance'] when I was still living in the midst of dogdom"). But, as the sentence advances, we watch it perform a loop forward, from the past of remembered events to the present of active remembering, thinking, and feeling:

> *finde ich . . . leicht,* daß hier seit jeher etwas nicht stimmte, . . . eine kleine Bruchstelle vorhanden war, der bloße Anblick eines mir lieben Mithun-

> des . . . mich verlegen, erschrocken, hilflos, ja mich verzweifelt machte (KKANII, 485; emphasis added)
>
> (*I soon find* that something was not quite right from the very beginning . . . , that a little fracture was in place, [. . . that] the mere sight of another dog, someone dear to me . . . filled me with embarrassment, fright, helplessness, even despair). (KSS, 132; emphasis added)

With the words "seit jeher" ("from the very beginning"), the loop defines the temporal continuum of the narrative. And so this report, which we have also called a memoir, continually associates the times of the present of a narrating consciousness with the past of remembered events in ways that shape the narrative's temporal rhythm.

We have called the text a memoir because it conveys the felt presence of a personal voice, tone, or mood telling the tale, and we have called it a report because, as the title indicates, it amounts to a summary of research accomplished, the kind of text that one might submit to a committee to justify a research grant. And indeed this objective, reportorial dimension is strengthened by the objectivity of the title's diction. "Forschungen eines Hundes" is a title less likely to be given to his text by the reporter or memoirist than by an administrator to which it had been submitted.[3] And so we have from the start the trace of an overarching consciousness reading or registering this memoir. For, just as the narrator throughout the tale will reveal almost no trace whatsoever of the existence of a consciousness higher than that of the dog—in a word, no trace of a human consciousness—we cannot imagine the dog narrator himself, or then again, a dog administrator, or even a dog readership to whom this report was to be submitted, titling it the researches of "a dog"—of whom else would the product be?[4] Rousseau did not title his confessions *Confessions d'un homme.* Goethe did not title his autobiography *Dichtung und Wahrheit im Dasein eines Menschen.* This trace-presence in the title of "Forschungen eines Hundes"—the tailings of a higher, a human consciousness—alert us to the narrative duplicity that informs the entire memoir-report, an ontological duplicity mirroring the duplicity of genres. It is the omnipresence of the unremarked, invisible human order.[5] The narrative, as readers of the story know, portrays a pursuit of the edible in the face of the unutterable.

A brief return to Rousseau's *Confessions* will illustrate a basic feature of this narrative situation: this is the famous distinction between (1) the location and the tone of voice of the narrator remembering and commenting and (2) the location and the tone of voice, so to speak, of the stages of past research he reports. This often remarked upon doubleness of narrative, which sometimes leaps out and is sometimes kept hidden in Kafka's story, is analyzed by Rousseau in his letters to M. Malesherbes apropos of his writing his *Confessions.*

Rousseau explains that his story will portray not a history of events (it is not a report) but a history of the *états d'âme* that he felt along the way: this dimension we have called the memoir-element. Thereafter—and this is very interesting—according to Rousseau's account of these moods, these *états d'âme* will be "doubled" (*dédoublé*) by the mood of Rousseau's interpretation of them. If genuine autobiographical language begins, for Rousseau, with an act of recollection of the self as a past affective state, this recollection must then abandon itself to what he calls its "description" and above all to the mood that accompanies this description. Rousseau writes, "In delivering myself over at once to the memory of a past impression (*de l'impression receue* [*sic*]) and to the feeling of the moment, I would doubly paint my state of mind, namely, at the moment in which the event occurred and the moment in which I described it" (1959, 1:1154).

Consider this interlacement of affects at the beginning of "Forschungen." The narrator writes, after reporting his malaise in the company of dogs, about the return of more serene and settled moments: "Wie hätte ich auch ohne diese Erholungspausen das Alter erreichen können, dessen ich mich jetzt erfreue" (KKANII, 485) ("Without these periods of rest and recovery, how could I ever have reached the age I now enjoy" [KSS, 132])—an example of the loop of affects modulating one another. Rousseau teaches us to regard this latter moment of pleasure as involved in the pleasure of the peace he knew in the past. Present pleasure adjusts the tone of the narrative of the past, the narrative of the formation of "einen kalten, zurückhaltenden, ängstlichen, rechnerischen, aber alles in allem genommen doch regelrechten Hund" (KKANII, 485) ("a cold, reserved, timid, calculating dog, but, all in all, a regular one" [KSS, 132]). The factor of such attunement, let it be noted, appears in Nietzsche's writings on Wagner as the tempo of affect.[6] And thinking now of Walter Benjamin's reflections on history, we discover here, in a phrase, the phenomenon of dialectical affect.[7]

The narrative is charged from the start with the passion for origins of a *libido sciendi.* I earlier cited the sentence "finde ich . . . leicht, daß hier seit jeher etwas nicht stimmte" (KKANII, 485) ("I soon find that something was not quite right from the very beginning" [KSS, 132]). This activity of remembering, thinking, feeling plunges us back again to "the very beginning" and as such is the signature of a narrative haunted by origins. The "Grund" ("heart," "basis") sought by the narrative is the absolute origin of the drive toward "research," of which this narrative itself is the crown. Threading through the succession of empirical moments in the protagonist's life of research is an insistently regressive pursuit of clues as to the origin *of this very narrative.* The story is not an end product but is itself an expression of a drive toward beginnings. And this—the dog's drive to understand—must be attributed to Kafka's drive to understand something of the greatest importance for him: the place of music, and, indeed, the place of his resistance to music at the origin of his own writing.

II

The narrator's crucial formative experience is his encounter with the "musical dogs." Something of the importance of this moment is conveyed by the higher mimicry of subject matter and narrative ductus that informs the telling. And now, *this* narrative—the one you are reading—will resort to a higher mimicry of its own in assuming the voice of Professor Michael Levine, who has written about this passage with such an uncanny appositeness to the present argument that you, reader, cannot be better served than to have *his* words (with small interpolations of my own). The following brief discussion has four authors: Kafka, the narrator, Michael Levine, and (in a chiefly secretarial fashion) Stanley Corngold—a rare instance of cooperation in this dog-eat-dog world.[8]

The dog finds himself in "dem leeren Raum" (KKANII, 490) ("that empty space" [KSS, 134]) from which seven strange dogs conjure music. Coming from nowhere, this music is suddenly everywhere, for "alles war Musik" (KKANII, 490) ("everything was music" [KSS, 134]). Indeed, the brevity of the three-word sentence "Everything was music" seems to register not only the abruptness of the change but the narrator's own startled sense of transport, the sense of being somewhere utterly remote from the place he now occupies. Like the hallowed atmosphere in which the dog suddenly finds himself—both as *past* agent and *present* narrator—the music that fills this place is indescribable. It is music that pours into the ears and floods the body, moving it to dance. And dance indeed is just what is performed by the seven dogs that the narrator goes on to describe—the cadences and intricate turns of his own description seemingly patterned on the reciprocal "Wendungen" ("attitudes"), "Verbindungen" ("combinations"), and "verschlungene Figuren" ("intertwined figures") of the dance, only to find footing, at the close, in the beat that the "others, great masters," so steadily maintained:

> Das Heben und Niedersetzen ihrer Füße, bestimmte Wendungen des Kopfes, ihr Laufen und ihr Ruhen, die Stellungen die sie zueinander einnahmen, die reigenmäßigen Verbindungen, die sie mit einander eingingen, indem etwa einer die Vorderpfoten auf des andern Rücken stützte und sie sich dann so ordneten, daß der erste aufrecht die Last aller andern trug oder indem sie mit ihren nah am Boden hinschleichenden Körpern verschlungene Figuren bildeten und niemals sich irrten; nicht einmal der letzte, der noch ein wenig unsicher war, nicht immer gleich den Anschluß an die andern fand, gewissermaßen im Anschlagen der Melodie manchmal schwankte, aber doch unsicher war nur im Vergleich mit der großartigen Sicherheit der andern und selbst bei viel größerer, ja bei vollkommener Unsicherheit nichts hätte verderben können, wo die andern, große Meister, den Takt unerschütterlich hielten. (KKANII, 490–91)

> (The way they raised and set down their feet, certain turns of the heads, their running and their resting, the attitudes they assumed toward one another, the combinations they formed with one another like a round dance, as when, for example, one braced his front paws on the other's back and then they all positioned themselves so that the first dog, erect, bore the weight of all the others, or as when, their bodies slinking close to the ground, they formed intertwined figures and never made a mistake—not even the last one, who was a little unsure of himself, did not always immediately hook up with the others, staggered a little, as it were, when the melody struck up, but was unsure only by comparison with the magnificent certainty of the others, and even had he been much more unsure, indeed utterly unsure, he would have ruined nothing, since the others, great masters, were keeping time so steadily.) (KSS, 134–35)

And, as though the scene were too much for the little dog to take in—and even after all this passage of time, too much for the mature narrator to remember—the description abruptly breaks off at this point. Objecting to his own account, the narrator promptly adds:

> Aber man sah sie ja kaum, man sah sie ja alle kaum. Sie waren hervorgetreten, man hatte sie innerlich begrüßt als Hunde, sehr beirrt war man zwar von dem Lärm, der sie begleitete, aber es waren doch Hunde, Hunde

> wie ich und Du, man beobachtete sie gewohnheitsmäßig, wie Hunde, denen man auf dem Weg begegnet, man wollte sich ihnen nähern, Grüße tauschen, sie waren auch ganz nah, Hunde, zwar viel älter als ich . . . aber doch auch . . . recht vertraut vielmehr, viele von solcher oder ähnlicher Art kannte ich . . . (KKANII, 428–29)
>
> (But it is too much to say that you actually saw them, you hardly saw any of them. They had appeared, you welcomed them silently as dogs; true, the clamor that accompanied them was very confusing, but in the end they were dogs, dogs like you and me; you observed them in the usual way, like dogs that you meet on the street; you wanted to go up to them, exchange greetings, for they were also very close—dogs, certainly much older than me . . . but . . . really rather familiar; I knew many of such a breed. . . .) (KSS, 135)

This sobering series of reflections, which are here cited only in part, moves gradually from the impersonal pronoun "man" [translated above as "you," SC] to the first person "I." The function of these reflections is to distance the narrator from his initial report, to detach the dazzled spectator he once was from the spectacle whirling before his eyes, and to affirm the separate identity of protagonist and narrator. Such separations, however, cannot be maintained as soon as the irrepressible music wells up again. As it does so, the narrative "I" disappears and is replaced once again by a series of impersonal pronouns:

> während man noch in solchen Überlegungen befangen war, nahm allmählich die Musik überhand, faßte einen förmlich, zog einen hinweg von diesen wirklichen kleinen Hunden und ganz wider Willen, sich sträubend mit allen Kräften, heulend als würde einem Schmerz bereitet, durfte man sich mit nichts anderem beschäftigen, als mit der von allen Seiten, von der Höhe, von der Tiefe, von überall her kommenden, den Zuhörer in die Mitte nehmenden, überschüttenden, erdrückenden, über seiner Vernichtung noch, in solcher Nähe, daß es schon Ferne war, kaum hörbar noch Fanfaren blasenden Musik. (KKANII, 429)
>
> (But while you were still caught up in such reflections, the music gradually took over, practically seized hold of you, swept you away from these real little dogs, and quite against your will, resisting with all your might, howling as if pain were being inflicted, you could attend to nothing but this music that came from all sides, from the heights, from the depths,

> from everywhere, pulling the listener into its midst, pouring over him, crushing him, and even after annihilating him, still blaring its fanfares at such close range that they turned remote and barely audible.) (KSS, 135)

As this and other passages make clear, everything in the text is a question of rhythm, of tempo—not only that of the dance and the music to which it is set but that of the narration itself.[9] Just as the telling seems at times to become immersed in (and engulfed by) the story told, so too does the narrative "Ich" have a tendency to dissolve into an impersonal "man," only to resurface and reconsolidate itself time and again. Such moments of dissolution are often associated with a loss of conscious control, with a sometimes anxious, sometimes ecstatic feeling of being swept away. [Here we might recall Kafka's aperçu of the man with his arms raised: "Der Verzückte und der Ertrinkende—beide heben die Arme. Der erste bezeugt Eintracht, der zweite Widerstreit mit den Elementen" (KKANII, 53) ("The man in ecstasy, and the man drowning: both throw up their arms. The first does it to signify harmony; the second to signify strife with the elements") (DF, 77), SC]. This loss of control is seemingly the case in the passage cited above—"seemingly" because what is so remarkable about it is the contrast between its descriptive precision and the overwhelming nature of the experience described. The narrative precision suggests not only the sharpness of the narrator's memory as he tells the story many years after the fact but his surprising presence of mind at the time of the actual occurrence—at a time, that is, when he is said to have been crushed, overwhelmed, and nearly annihilated. It appears then that even in the midst of extreme dissolution, something of the "I" remains. [We again recall Kafka's distinction between two kinds of self-loss—one negative, one positive: "Nicht Selbstabschüttelung sondern Selbstaufzehrung" (KKANII, 77) ("Not shaking off the self but consuming the self") (DF, 87), the latter evidently suggesting its survival as a shadow of itself, SC]. The "I" endures but only as an infinitely small point . . . (Levine 2005, 1–4).

Exeat, with my gratitude, Michael Levine. I now resume in my own voice, turning, first, to Kafka's own memorial account of his early relation to music.

III[10]

On January 3, 1912, Kafka noted in his *Diaries:*

> In mir kann ganz gut eine Koncentration auf das Schreiben hin erkannt werden. Als es in meinem Organismus klar geworden war, daß das Schreiben die ergiebigste Richtung meines Wesens sei, drängte sich alles hin und ließ alle Fähigkeiten leer stehn, die sich auf die Freuden des Geschlechtes, des Essens, des Trinkens, des philosophischen Nachdenkens der Musik zu allererst richteten. Ich magerte nach allen diesen Richtungen ab. (KSS, 341)

For years, readers of the standard American edition of the *Diaries* have been accustomed to seeing the key sentence translated by Joseph Kresh as follows:

> When it became clear in my organism that writing was the most productive direction for my being to take, everything rushed in that direction and left empty all those abilities which were directed toward the joys of sex, eating, drinking, philosophical reflection and above all music. I atrophied in all these directions. (D1, 211)

But there is a crucial, attention-grabbing detail in the German text that this translation elides. The Frankfurt manuscript edition reveals above that there is no comma between "philosophischen Nachdenkens" and "der Musik." In his polemic called "Sprachlehre" ("Grammar"), Karl Kraus began a tirade thus: "Of course, one would be unable to get the esteemed author to grasp that owing to the missing comma . . . ," a rhetorical and semantic disaster ensues (Kraus 2010, 154). I shall pursue the exact, symmetrically opposite tack in reading Kafka's diary entry. I shall not suppose that an author for whom—mutatis mutandis—my esteem is immense, never noticed, in a diary that he scrupulously kept, that he had omitted the comma that would safeguard him from a rhetorical and semantic disaster. This is especially true when the omitted comma produces an altogether different—and an altogether compelling—meaning.

This diary passage contrasts the implicit, unnamed, ascetic joy of writing—its dilettantism (about which "süßer wunderbarer Lohn" [Br, 384] ["sweet, wonderful reward" (KSS, 211)], Kafka would have a great deal to say in the following decade)—with several explicitly named joys, of which the strangest is the philosophical reflection performed by music, provoked by music, or addressed to music as its object. It is this considerable joy of thinking in the circle of music—by and about music—that *has to be renounced* in the name of writing. Writing exists as the specific renunciation of the joys of having sex, eating, drinking, and thinking philosophically about music or listening to the sort of reflection that music might be imagined to produce about itself, as is if this utterly and crucially unstable, unresolved character of music were a sort of siren song that Kafka had to resist at all costs if he were to write. The ontological question for Kafka would then be, not "why is there Something rather than Nothing?" but rather, in the words of the narrator of "Josefine, the Singer," "wie es sich mit dieser Musik eigentlich verhält" (KKAD, 350) ("what [is] this music . . . really all about?" [KSS, 95]). Writing exists as the resistance to such consideration, a refusal of a philosophy of music—as if to give oneself over to this principal reflection would be to cut oneself off from writing and be lost.

The issue, then, is not Kafka's fascination with silence as the absence of music but with silence as the specific outcome of a refusal to listen to a meditation on the nature of music, one that might come as a development of the peculiar fact about him: his unmusicality, his unmusicality as a problem—and, as a problem, something to resist or selectively not to resist—but in both instances harboring, in its very problematic character, an unwonted source of strength. Consider Kafka's letter to Milena of July 17, 1920: "Eine gewisse Stärke habe ich, will man sie kurz und unklar bezeichnen, so ist es mein Unmusikalisch-Sein" (BrM, 122) ("I do possess a certain strength that might be briefly and imprecisely described as being unmusical" [LM, 92]). You can hear in the word "imprecisely" the implicit requirement that unmusicality be "nachgedacht" ("thought through"). This strength is a function, too, of the *perfection* of Kafka's "being unmusical." In an earlier letter to Milena of June 14, 1920, Kafka insisted that he was "vollständig . . . unmusikalisch, in einer meiner Erfahrung nach überhaupt sonst nicht vorkommenden Vollständigkeit" (BrM, 65) ("completely unmusical, more completely than anyone I have ever known" [LM, 48]). This claim to a perfection of "Unmusikalisch-Sein" belongs in any synoptic view of Kafka together with another, earlier claim bearing on the perfection of his "Schriftstellersein," his "being (as) a writer." In the diary entry of February 19, 1911, he noted,

> Die besondere Art meiner Inspiration in der ich Glücklichster und Unglücklichster jetzt um 2 Uhr nachts schlafen gehe .... ist die, daß ich alles kann, nicht nur auf eine bestimmte Arbeit hin. Wenn ich wahllos einen Satz hinschreibe z.B. Er schaute aus dem Fenster so ist er schon vollkommen. (KSS, 30)

> (The special nature of my inspiration in which now, at two in the morn-

ing) . . . is this, that I can do everything, not only with respect to a particular piece of work. If I write a sentence at random, for example, "He looked out of the window," it is already perfect.) (KSS, 195)

In his famous Plana letter to Max Brod of July 5, 1922, however, the same ontological question runs decisively in the negative: "Aber wie ist es mit dem Schriftstellersein selbst?" (Br, 384) ("But how do things stand with this being a writer?" [KSS, 211]). The answer is that it is a killing sweetness and the prelude to a terrible death. "Schriftstellersein" and "Unmusikalisch-Sein" belong in a fluctuating relation that is not merely antithetical. In looking for models of their relation, one might consider the Dionysian/Apollonian pair in Nietzsche's *The Birth of Tragedy,* where these energies figure as antagonists but then also as siblings (they are complementary and have a common root) and then also as parent and offspring (each strives for primacy).

But whether we have here anything as productive as even a "Holzweg" will depend on the power of this errant path to draw evidence from the stories to itself. This is where "Forschungen eines Hundes" comes in, with its concern for the pursuit of the origin of music as a topic for philosophical reflection. Referring to that initial clamor, the dog reflects, in a first version of this story,

> Hätte ich nicht deutlich gesehn daß es Hunde waren und daß sie selbst diesen Lärm mitbrachten, trotzdem ich nicht erkennen konnte, wie sie ihn erzeugten—ich wäre sofort weggelaufen, so aber blieb ich. Damals wußte ich noch fast nichts von der nur dem Hundegeschlecht verliehenen schöpferischen Musikalität, sie war meiner sich erst entwickelnden Aufmerksamkeit entgangen, nur in Andeutungen hatte man mich darauf hinzuweisen versucht, umso überraschender, geradezu niederwerfend waren jene sieben großen Musikkünstler für mich. (KKANII, 427–28)

> (Had I not clearly seen that they were dogs and that they themselves brought this clamor with them—although I could not see how they produced it—I would have run away this minute, but as matters stood, I stayed. At that time I knew almost nothing about the creative musicality with which only the race of dogs is endowed; it was something that until now had escaped my powers of observation, which were only slowly developing; others had attempted to call my attention to it; all the more surprising, then, even shocking, were those seven great musical virtuosi.) (KSS, 134)

Thereafter, Kafka begins the story again at another place in his notebooks; and after the sentence that speaks of the creative musicality of dogs that had until then escaped the dog's powers of observation, he adds these lines:

> natürlicher Weise, hatte mich doch die Musik schon seit meiner Säuglingszeit umgeben, als ein mir selbstverständliches unentbehrliches Lebenselement, welches von meinem sonstigen Leben zu sondern nichts mich zwang; nur in Andeutungen, dem kindlichen Verstand entsprechend, hatte man mich darauf hinzuweisen versucht. (KKANII, 490)

> (naturally, ever since infancy, music had surrounded me as a self-evident, indispensable vital element, but nothing had compelled me to separate it from the rest of my life; others had attempted to call my attention to it.) (KSS, 134)

With the addition of this sentence, the passage revolves entirely around the action of a "Sonderung," a "separating off" of music; this means making music a fit subject of philosophical reflection. The narrator's first formative experience, as he tells us, is of the separation of music from the naturally given life-world. And, indeed, "Mit jenem Koncert aber begann es. . . . Ich lief umher, erzählte und fragte, klagte an und forschte und wollte jeden hinziehn zu dem Ort wo alles geschehen war" (KKANII, 435, 434) ("It was with that concert that everything began. . . . I ran around telling my story and asking questions, making accusations and doing research; I wanted to drag everyone to the spot where it had all happened" [KSS, 138]).

This drive to research is not organized, no direction is given to the heightened consciousness of the dog by the mere fact of this separation. The development of the trauma comes from his own nature, the "eingeborenes Wesen" ("innate nature") that continues to force the separation of music from the rest of life:

> Ich klage nicht darüber, es ist mein eingeborenes Wesen das hier wirkt und das sich gewiß, wenn das Koncert nicht gewesen wäre, eine andere Gelegenheit gefunden hätte, um durchzubrechen, nur daß es so bald geschah, tat mir früher manchmal leid. (KKANII, 435–36)

> (I am not complaining, what is at work here is my innate nature, which would surely have found another opportunity to emerge even without

> the concert, except that the fact of its happening so soon used to cause me a great deal of pain.) (KSS, 138)

The result of the dog's pursuing his research is the loss of "Kindheit" ("childhood") and its joys—"das glückselige Leben der jungen Hunde" ("the blissful life of young dogs")—though quite possibly, he thinks, it is a preparation for a much greater bliss when he is old: the discussion concerns the kinds and amounts of joy a body can bear (KKAN2, 436). The main thrust of this discussion, however, is not about joy. It concerns an epochal turning, fraught with "despair":

> Ich begann damals meine Untersuchungen mit den einfachsten Dingen, an Material fehlte es nicht, leider, der Überfluß ist es, der mich in dunklen Stunden verzweifeln läßt. Ich begann zu untersuchen wovon sich die Hundeschaft nährte. (KKANII, 435–36)

> (I began my investigations at that time with the simplest things; there was no lack of material, unfortunately; it is its very overabundance that, in the darkest hours, makes me despair. I began to investigate what dogdom took as nourishment.) (KSS, 138)

These sentences are not innocent; the explicit note of despair may be a displacement of a primary despondency, since the choice of direction implies a direction *not* taken. The missing direction, the path not taken is . . . music, the question of music (read "unmusicality"). But what path has been taken instead? What can the sense of "nourishment" be? I shall claim a connection between "nourishment" and the "fullness of writing," enlisting Gerhard Kurz's comment on a related moment in Kafka's other great, late, long, unfinished story "The Burrow": "Through this Eucharistic act of feeding and drinking, [this creature] defends itself against the crush of the provisions—in an allegorical sense, the crush of poetic inspiration" (KSS, 342). Research flees to writing, the opposite direction from reflecting on music, which is to say, from practicing "Musikwissenschaft" ("the science of music") (KKANII, 480).

Well and good, but how then does the constitution of music as a philosophical object stand in relation to the subject of his research—to nourishment—for which I have claimed an intuitive connection to writing? Music is not the object of this research; it is its provocation *ex negativo:* "It was," after all, "with that concert that everything began." The moment has the identical structure of the origin of the life of writing as given in the *Brief an den Vater* (*Letter to his Father*): "Mein Schreiben handelte von Dir . . . er [war] zwar von Dir erzwungen, aber [verlief] in der von mir bestimmten Richtung" (KKANII, 192) ("although [my writing] . . . was forced by you, it took its course in the direction determined by me") (KSS, 206); compare the father's force with the traumatic shock of sound. In "Forschungen eines Hundes," the direction leads away from a meditation on "what this music is really all about" and toward nourishment, bringing the concert and nourishment, music as a philosophical object and writing onto the same ontological plane.

In "Forschungen," Kafka had by no means finished posing the origin of music as a virtual topic for reflection. At this very point in his text we are discussing, he writes the following lines in the margin of his notebook before crossing them out: "wie viel Zeit mag vergangen sein, ehe das Hundegeschlecht erkannte, dass es inmitten einer Tonwelt lebte und vielleicht ist bis heute noch nicht genug Zeit vergangen, dies genau zu erkennen (KKANIIA, 391) ("How much time may have passed before dogdom recognized that it lived in the middle of a world of sound, and perhaps until today not enough time has passed for it to recognize this clearly").

To live in the middle of a world of sound but not to recognize it means never to find the Archimedean point of silence from which the "separation" between the apprehension of music and the failure of the apprehension of music (unmusicality) could be "clearly" accomplished.

At any rate, the sentence was crossed out as . . . could we say . . . a dangerous piling on too soon of that philosophical reflection on music that is the negative counterpart of writing?

But "Forschungen eines Hundes" does not abandon the matter. Just as the question of the claim of music was taken up at the beginning of the story—and, as we have shown, repudiated—it is again taken up at the very close, where it then enriches before abruptly ending the story, although not without leaving a nimbus of radiant insight.

The ending is immediately preceded by an extraordinary passage. At the conclusion of the dog-narrator's account of the agonies of his fasting, he conjures another musical dog:

> Ich merkte . . . daß der Hund aus der Tiefe der Brust zu einem Gesange anhob. . . . Und ich glaubte damals, etwas zu erkennen, was kein Hund je vor mir erfahren hat, wenigstens findet sich in der Überlieferung nicht die leiseste Andeutung dessen, und ich versenkte eilig in unendlicher Angst und Scham das Gesicht in der Blutlache vor mir. Ich glaubte nämlich zu erkennen, daß der Hund schon sang ohne es noch zu wissen, ja

mehr noch, daß die Melodie, von ihm getrennt, nach eigenem Gesetz durch die Lüfte schwebte und über ihn hinweg, als gehöre er nicht dazu, nach mir, nur nach mir hin zielte.

Heute leugne ich natürlich alle derartigen Erkenntnisse und schreibe sie meiner damaligen Überreiztheit zu, aber wenn es auch ein Irrtum war, so hat er doch eine gewisse Großartigkeit, ist die einzige wenn auch nur scheinbare Wirklichkeit, die ich aus der Hungerzeit in diese Welt herübergerettet habe und zeigt zumindest, wie weit bei völligem Außer-sich-sein wir gelangen können. Und ich war wirklich völlig außer mir. . . . Körperlich erholte ich mich übrigens in wenigen Stunden, geistig trage ich noch heute die Folgen. (KKANII, 479–80)

(I noticed that from the depths of his chest this dog was getting ready to sing. . . . And then I believe I perceived something that no dog had ever experienced before me; at any rate, cultural memory does not contain even the slightest hint of it; and in infinite anxiety and shame I hurriedly lowered my face in the puddle of blood in front of me. What I seemed to perceive was that the dog was already singing without his being aware of it—no, more than that: that the melody, detached from him, was floating through the air and then past him according to its own laws, as if he no longer had any part in it, floating at me, aimed only at me.

Today of course, I deny any such perceptions and attribute them to my overstimulation at the time, but even if it was an error, it nevertheless had a certain grandeur and is the sole reality, even if only an apparent reality, that I salvaged and brought back into this world from the time of my fast, and shows, at least, how far we can go when we are completely out of our senses. And I really was completely out of my senses. . . . As it happened, I recovered physically in a few hours; mentally, I bear the consequences even today.) (KSS, 159–60)

In this episode, ecstasy and error mingle in equal parts. (The error consists, very likely, of a profound misapprehension of the music produced by the hunting horns of the humans that the researcher cannot or will not see.) The Kafka scholar John Hargraves notes that here "music obliterates the insight that the dogs are not alone in the world" (KSS, 325). For us it is chiefly important that the episode prompts the narrator's meditation at the close:

Meine Forschungen aber erweiterte ich auf die Musik der Hunde. . . . Die Wissenschaft von der Musik ist . . . vielleicht noch umfangreicher als jene von der Nahrung, und jedenfalls fester begründet. Es ist das dadurch zu erklären, daß . . . es sich hier mehr um bloße Beobachtungen und Systematisierungen handelt, dort dagegen vor allem um praktische Folgerungen. Damit hängt zusammen, daß der Respekt vor der Musikwissenschaft größer ist als vor der Nahrungswissenschaft, die erstere aber niemals so tief ins Volk eindringen konnte wie die zweite. Auch ich stand der Musikwissenschaft, ehe ich die Stimme im Wald gehört hatte, fremder gegenüber als irgendeiner anderen. Zwar hatte mich schon das Erlebnis mit den Musikhunden auf sie hingewiesen, aber ich war damals noch zu jung. . . . Auch war *zwar die Musik bei jenen Hunden das zunächst Auffallendste gewesen, aber wichtiger als die Musik schien mir ihr verschwiegenes Hundewesen,* für ihre schreckliche Musik fand ich vielleicht überhaupt keine Ähnlichkeit anderswo, ich konnte sie eher vernachlässigen, aber ihr Wesen begegnete mir von damals an in allen Hunden überall. *In das Wesen der Hunde einzudringen, schienen mir aber Forschungen über die Nahrung am geeignetsten und ohne Umweg zum Ziele führend.* (KKANII, 480–81; emphasis added)

(I widened my researches to include the music of the dogs. . . . The science of music is . . . perhaps even wider in scope than that of food and in any case more firmly grounded. . . . In music, it is more a matter of pure observations and systematizations; there, [in the field of nutrition] . . . it is above all one of practical consequences. Connected to this is the fact that the science of music enjoys greater respect than the science of nutrition, but the former could never affect the people so deeply as the latter. Before I had heard the voice in the woods, my relation to the science of music was also more remote than to any other science. It is true that my experience with the music dogs had already drawn my attention to it, but at that time I was still too young. . . . Furthermore, while in the case of the air dogs, music had been the first thing to strike me, *their secretive nature seemed to me more important than the music;* their terrible music was probably like nothing else in the world, and so I could neglect it more readily, but from that time on it was their nature that I encountered in all dogs everywhere. *To penetrate into the nature of dogs, however, research into nutrition seemed to me most suitable and to lead unerringly to the goal.*) (KSS, 160; emphasis added)

We have now learned something crucial. If research into nutrition means immersion in writing, then the project of writing, too, is in error from the start since this research into nutrition (read "writing") is bent on nothing more nor less than "penetrating into the nature of dogs." It involves from the start, for good or for ill, something comparable to a cognitive program promising ethical insight, for moral, practical education. Everything goes back to the dancing dogs' shamelessness and taciturnity. But how can this human, this ethical side of things be wrong, an error construed as an impurity? In an extraordinary letter to Felice, written September 30–October 1, 1917, during the very last days of their courtship, Kafka formulated the goal of real writing as the one goal that matters, the goal "einem höchsten Gericht zu entsprechen" ("to answer to a Highest Court"). Yet it might also subserve a baser practice as "sehr gegensätzlich" ("quite to the contrary"), it contents itself with a philosophical survey of mankind, striving, as Kafka writes, "die ganze Menschen- und Tiergemeinschaft zu überblicken, ihre grundlegenden Vorlieben, Wünsche, sittlichen Ideale zu erkennen, sie auf einfache Vorschriften zurückzuführen" ("to know the entire human and animal community, to recognize their fundamental preferences, desires, and moral ideals, to reduce them to simple rules [or laws]"). This entire effort—this psychological or anthropological study—is undertaken with another aim in mind, which Kafka surprisingly motivates as follows:

> daß ich durchaus allen wohlgefällig würde, und zwar (hier kommt der Sprung) so wohlgefällig, daß ich, ohne die allgemeine Liebe zu verlieren, schließlich, als der einzige Sünder, der nicht gebraten wird, die mir innewohnenden Gemeinheiten offen, vor allen Augen, ausführen dürfte. (KKAB2, 333)

> (so that this way I should become thoroughly pleasing to all, and, to be sure, [here comes the jump] so pleasing, that, without sacrificing this general love, I might finally, as the sole sinner who will not be roasted, parade the meanness that dwells in me, openly, before all eyes.) (LF, 545; translation modified)

We are dealing with a perversion of writing that suggests its vanity in the ordinary sense of the word, for this "nourishment" is not something that properly comes in from other people or goes out to other people. This text stands in a family relation with another text that highlights the same tension between a "pure" and an anthropological writing. This is the extended aperçu known as the wish on Laurentian Hill. Describing his wish as a young man to write—let us say—"purely," Kafka concludes,

> Aber er konnte gar nicht so wünschen, denn sein Wunsch war kein

> Wunsch, er war nur eine Verteidigung, eine Verbürgerlichung des Nichts, ein Hauch von Munterkeit, den er dem Nichts geben wollte, in das er zwar damals kaum die ersten bewußten Schritte tat, das er aber schon als sein Element fühlte. Es war damals eine Art Abschied, den er von der Scheinwelt der Jugend nahm; sie hatte ihn übrigens niemals unmittelbar getäuscht, sondern nur durch die Reden aller Autoritäten ringsherum täuschen lassen. So hatte sich die Notwendigkeit des "Wunsches" ergeben. (KSS, 855)

> (But he could not wish in this fashion at all; for his wish was not a wish, it was only a defense of nothingness, a granting of protection and civil rights to nothingness, a breath of cheer that he wanted to lend to nothingness, into which at that time he had scarcely taken only his first few conscious steps but which he already felt as his element. At that time it [the writing destiny] was a sort of farewell that he took from the illusive world of youth; it had, incidentally, never directly deceived him but only caused him to be deceived by the utterances of all the authorities around him. The necessity of his "wish" had come about as a result.) (KSS, 207)

Here, the enterprise of beginning to write is motivated by a compulsory leave-taking from a world in which, the speaker alleges, he had been deceived. Writing begins enmeshed in the original sin of the son's complaint that an injustice has been committed against himself.[11]

In opposition to the science of music, the science of nourishment pursued by the dog is impure. But can we not learn what might be different from this enmeshment in impurity, this eternal deflection from the right way? We heard the dog declare that "to penetrate into the nature of dogs, research into nutrition seemed to me most suitable and to lead unerringly to the goal." He continues and herewith concludes his report:

> Vielleicht hatte ich darin Unrecht. Ein Grenzgebiet der beiden Wissenschaften lenkte allerdings schon damals meinen Verdacht auf sich. Es ist die Lehre von dem die Nahrung herabrufenden Gesang. Wieder ist es hier für mich sehr störend, daß ich auch in die Musikwissenschaft niemals ernstlich eingedrungen bin. . . . *Der tiefere Grund meiner wissenschaftlichen Unfähigkeit scheint mir ein Instinkt und wahrlich kein schlechter Instinkt zu sein. Wenn ich bramarbasieren wollte, könnte ich sagen, daß gerade dieser Instinkt meine wissenschaftlichen Fähigkeiten zerstört hat, denn es wäre doch eine zumindest sehr merkwürdige Erscheinung, daß ich, der ich in den gewöhnlichen täglichen Lebensdingen, die gewiß nicht die einfachsten sind, einen erträglichen*

> *Verstand zeige und vor allem, wenn auch nicht die Wissenschaft, so doch die Gelehrten sehr gut verstehe, . . . von vornherein unfähig gewesen sein sollte, die Pfote auch nur zur ersten Stufe der Wissenschaft zu erheben. Es war der Instinkt, der mich vielleicht gerade um der Wissenschaft willen, aber einer anderen Wissenschaft als sie heute geübt wird, einer allerletzten Wissenschaft, die Freiheit höher schätzen ließ als alles andere. Die Freiheit! Freilich, die Freiheit, wie sie heute möglich ist, ist ein kümmerliches Gewächs. Aber immerhin Freiheit, immerhin ein Besitz.* (KKANII, 481-82).

> Perhaps I was wrong on that count. Of course, there is some overlap between the two sciences that even then aroused my suspicions. I mean the doctrine of the song that calls down food from above. Here again I am severely handicapped by the fact that I have never seriously penetrated into the science of music. . . . *The deeper reason for my incapacity . . . seems to me to be an instinct, and to tell the truth, it is not a bad instinct. If I wanted to brag, I would say that precisely this instinct has destroyed my scientific skill, for it would certainly be a very remarkable phenomenon, to say the least, if I, who display a passable intelligence in the ordinary business of daily life, which is certainly not so simple, and above all who, even though I do not understand science, nevertheless understand scientists very well . . . were from the very beginning unable to raise my paw even to the first rung of science. It was my instinct that, perhaps precisely for the sake of science but a different science than is practiced today, an ultimate science, led me to value freedom above everything else. Freedom! Of course, the freedom that is possible today—a stunted growth. But nevertheless freedom, nevertheless a possession.*) (KSS, 160–61)

Pure writing equals a certain freedom, and also the perfect absence of sound: stillness.

We alluded earlier to the question of music in Kafka's "Josefine" of 1924. Observe that the very "joy," the philosophical reflection on music, of which Kafka was deprived in 1912 and which is named but resisted in 1922, will make its appearance here. This topic, when it resurges in Kafka's late work, would then have the character of a return of the repressed in a mode in which it could be tolerated, a fusion of the *even* pleasure of writing and the *odd* pleasure of a reflection on the nature of music.

Such a return would point to the gaiety, the subtle good humor that glances off the pages of his late work. Think of the movement of reconciliation that is especially vivid in *Das Schloß* (*The Castle*), Kafka's bliss in joining two alien worlds—*Schriftstellersein* ("the being of the writer") and *Beamtenwesen* ("the being of the bureaucrat"). What a happy thing to make the hell of bureaucracy redound to the benefit of his fiction. This is the only happiness Kafka could know: linking, fusing together in literature contesting parts of the structure of his desire—"die ungeheure Welt, die ich im Kopfe habe" (KSS, 562) ("the enormous world that I have in my head") (D1, 288).

Kafka's last proposals, in the passage from "Forschungen eines Hundes" to "Josefine," advance toward a reconciliation of his *Schriftsteller-sein* and his *Unmusikalisch-Sein* by a return to a meditation on music. But that immersion does not occur without resistance. "Forschungen eines Hundes" raises the topic only to conclude with the narrator's explicit refusal to do "the science of music," to reflect systematically on music, musicality (and, in principle) unmusicality; just as in "Josefine," we realize, the philosophy of music is alienated as a topic by the narrator's only questionable interest in it. In "Forschungen," the narrator speaks not on behalf of a pure reflection on music but instead on behalf of a freedom that is nurtured by its refusal—the unheard-of freedom that he terms "an ultimate science." We might call this moment the invocation of "pure literature," literature degree zero, and hence something more than the beautiful, enigmatic, but, alas, hybrid thing that "Josefine" is—"hybrid," because it is unremittingly ethical and anthropological in its bias.

IV

It might be fruitful to review our line of argument, extracted from its many turnings. "Forschungen eines Hundes" is driven by a task, one that continues to maintain a hold on the narrator as he reflects: he means to recover the origin of his drive to do research, which principally focuses on "the science of nourishment." But this focus is achieved only by dint of a fatal turning away from a musical concert, whose substance is his more authentic concern. The dog's development is marred by his suppression of a philosophical reflection on music, musicality, and unmusicality. Yet at the end he alleges that this movement, this very turning away, is an impetus toward "freedom," the promise of freedom, which I connect, now in Kafka's case, with the goal of "pure writing."[12]

The dog's claim does not jibe with what we have been told in the story or in Kafka's account of the emergence of his writing (*his* exercises in "the science of nourishment"). Accounts in his confessional work cloak this emergence in bad faith—a flight from a philosophical material that mattered; they are allegories of shock. A trace of that turning presumably survives as a fault in Kafka's writing, which can therefore never be pure: like the dog's research, his writing is informed by a barely suppressed consciousness of indwelling errancy. In the dog's own words, which are suited to his author, dogdom has deviated from "das wahre Wort" (KKANII, 456) ("the true word" [KSS, 148]).

Hence, something like the ethical, psychological fault at the outset of Kafka's decision continues to manifest itself as a strain in his writing, a strain that he abjures—an ethical, psychological, "anthropological" competence that is ultimately there only for show. Likewise with the dog, it is not music but rather the "nature of dogs" (KSS, 160) that, following his "innate nature" (KSS, 138), made him *run from* the study of an original traumatic event. Hence, all the knowledge the dog can acquire through his research is not of the urgent kind, not "traumatic knowledge" but a dusky knowledge of the error of his flight.

Kafka, it would appear, needed to (but did not) come to grips with a first cataclysmic separation; he was then captivated by a dream of pure writing, but, in the language of the Laurentian Hill aperçu, he could never dream this dream properly (KSS, 207). Henceforth, writing was an evasion of a primary task, his dream of freedom a fugitive, his "science" a deviation from the start.

This fear haunted him; his only relief was the memory of what once seemed an exalted state. His ecstasy in writing "Das Urteil" ("The Judgment") was the great warrant for the rightness of indulging an instinct for this other freedom, but he lived in the shadow of its loss.

Postscript

Professor Ronald Speirs, one of the editors of this volume, who generously shaped the opening of this essay (see note 1), has again made a remarkable contribution. I will quote in full a letter from him, which I consider apposite to my argument; his remarks widen my argument's frame. On January 18, 2010, Professor Speirs wrote,

> I would raise a question apropos your closing remark about *Das Urteil* ("The Judgment"). The question is connected with that story or, more precisely, with a letter to Milena referring to it. In that letter (August 28, 1920), Kafka wrote: "Die Übersetzung des Schlußsatzes ist sehr gut. In jener Geschichte hängt jeder Satz, jedes Wort, jede—wenn's erlaubt ist—Musik mit der 'Angst' zusammen, damals brach die Wunde zum ersten-

mal auf in einer langen Nacht . . . " (BrM, 235) ("The translation of the concluding sentence is very good. Every sentence, every word, every—if I may say so—music in that story is connected with the 'fear.' It was then, during one long night, that the wound broke open for the first time . . . ") (LM, 173–74).

The main point here is that Kafka connects writing not with unmusicality but with music. This is at odds with other cited passages in the letters to Milena, where he relates writing to unmusicality. My own way of dealing with this apparent contradiction is to regard *Das Urteil* as representing a quite exceptional experience of writing in his oeuvre. All his own recollections of the process of writing that story describe experiences of self-opening and self-abandonment in which the narrator moves along "wie in einem Gewässer" (KSS, 460) ("as . . . through a body of water" [KSS, 197]), as if he were both the fetus being delivered in the story and the duct through which it was delivered. This strikes me as rather like the dog's initial response to the music produced by the other dogs, of being overwhelmed and transported, especially in the passage where he hears the music before it has even entered the dog-performer, as if it were a disembodied force finding embodiment and expression in this chance agent. If the link is correct, *Das Urteil* would represent a rare, possibly unique example of the kind of writing that was not blighted by the reflections on morality, purpose, justification, nourishment or even "music" itself but rather something close to the *Poésie pure* he dreamt of ("die Erzählung ist mehr gedichtmässig als episch") (Br, 149) ("the story is more poetic than narrative" [L, 126]), in which all parts were connected by necessity, nothing joined up mechanically with the aid of factitious arrangements ["Konstruktionen" (KSS, 597]).

So is the dog that refuses the call of the music, closing himself off from its power in order to pursue other things, that part of Kafka with which the musician in him was in conflict, the self-aware, self-critical, analytic and reflective part (that eventually composes the scaffolding of the aphorisms to build a systematic tower out of experiences that actually resist such treatment and want to find a more proper outlet in the rare music of *Das Urteil*)?

Professor Speirs's view of the unique quality of "Das Urteil" is surely correct. I also argued this point in my book *Lambent Traces:*

On the night of September 22, 1912, Franz Kafka wrote his story "The Judgment," which came out of him "wie eine regelrechte Geburt" (KSS,

491) ("like a regular birth") (D1, 278). This act of creation struck him as an unmistakable sign of his literary destiny. Thereafter, the search of many of his characters for the Law, for a home, for artistic fulfillment can be understood as a figure for Kafka's own search to reproduce the ecstasy of a single night. [Corngold 2004a, 2].

The originality of Professor Speirs's comment consists in his connecting that ecstasy to the dog's experience of music so that all of Kafka's writing after "Das Urteil" would seem like a deflection, calling for punishment. This is an idea implied in Kafka's "In der Strafkolonie" ("In the Penal Colony"), when his main character asks of the culprit, "Er kennt sein eignes Urteil nicht?" (DL, 211) ("He doesn't know his own judgment?" [KSS, 40]). Professor Speirs is incisive in linking that deflection to Kafka's work on a sort of aphoristic Tower of Babel, an idea supported by the dog's describing "die Musikwissenschaft" (KKANII, 480) ("the science of music" [KSS, 160])—and not "die Musik" itself—as a place "wo es sich . . . mehr um bloße [also, nicht praktische] Beobachtungen und Systematisierungen handelt" (KKANII, 480) ([where] . . . it is more a matter of pure observations and systematizations" [KSS, 160]). These are directions that the reader of this volume may be interested in following.

Notes

1. A lengthy comment on this paper by Professor Ronald Speirs of Birmingham University was of inestimable help in formulating this précis of my argument.

2. See Geoffrey Hartman's excellent essay "On Traumatic Knowledge and Literary Studies" (1995, 537–63). See also the chapter by Gerhard Neumann in this volume for another analysis of the effects on Kafka's narratives of an inaccessible originary experience that both demands and evades narration.

3. A title assigned by Brod, true, but a title that we will consider to be a part of the story that has come down to us.

4. Note that this other order is (negatively) marked at the outset even through its absence: it is in the laws that dogs obey although "the rules [. . .] are not those of dogdom, indeed, are more truly opposed to it" (KSS, 133).

5. The narrative is a sequence of propositions, accompanied by a continual vertical reference, in both a concrete and a figurative sense: the dogs, the dogs' bodies, are themselves often turned upward toward the virtual source of their nourishment. The figurative sense of this verticality—figurative, because it is invisible—is this: the entire narrative is oriented toward the (unreadable) narrative of another law: the laws of the human world, to which this dog has no access. And so, not unlike *The Trial,* we have here a story of two worlds of law.

6. In notes unpublished in his lifetime, Nietzsche wrote of the decadence of Wagner's music as evident in "das Tempo des Affekts." See Nietzsche.

7. My phrase alludes, through modification, to the leading idea in Walter Benjamin's incomplete *Arcades Project* (1999, 462).

8. The degree of fraternity involved here exceeds anything to be encountered in dogdom at the best of times; on closer scrutiny we find the following footnote in Professor Levine's text: "As Corngold notes in his unpublished essay, 'Kafka and the Philosophy of Music; or, Des Kommas Fehl Hilft,' again and again, in Kafka's poetics, the dreamt-of poem is figured as a bodily birth.' I am grateful to Professor Corngold for sharing his very rich and provocative reading of Researches with me" (Levine 2005, 18). So I have returned—or, in fact, snatched—this favor.

9. For a similar account of the centrality of movement in other examples of Kafka's narration, see also chapter 10 in this volume.

10. An earlier version of part 3 of this chapter was published in Corngold (2004b, 4–16).

11. Kafka wrote, "Die Erbsünde, das alte Unrecht, das der Mensch begangen hat, besteht in dem Vorwurf, den der Mensch macht . . . daß ihm ein Unrecht geschehen ist, daß an ihm die Erbsünde begangen wurde" (KSS, 856) ("Original sin, the old injustice committed by man, consists in the complaint unceasingly made by man that he has been the victim of an injustice, the victim of original sin" [Benjamin 1955, 114]). Benjamin ingeniously sees the complaint as also directed by the son against the father for the sin of having produced an heir!

12. It was alleged by Dora Diamant that Kafka, in Berlin during the winter of late 1923, urged her to burn all his extant manuscripts, since they had been written under the spell of his Prague family, which was the very essence of unfreedom; only writing produced in a condition of freedom might one day be worth saving (Murray 2004, 371–72).

Works Cited

Benjamin, Walter. 1955. *Illuminations.* Trans. Harry Zohn. New York: Harcourt, Brace & World.

———. 1999. *Arcades Project.* Trans. Howard Eiland and Kevin McLaughlin, prepared on the basis of the German volume edited by Rolf Tiedemann. Cambridge, MA: Harvard Univ. Press.

Corngold, Stanley. 2004a. *Franz Kafka: Lambent Traces.* Princeton, NJ: Princeton Univ. Press.

———. 2004b. Kafka and the philosophy of music; or, Des Kommas Fehl Hilft. *Journal of the Kafka Society of America* 28 (1–2): 4–16.

Hartman, Geoffrey. 1995. On traumatic knowledge and literary studies. *New Literary History* 26 (3): 537–63.

Nietzsche, Friedrich. http:www.nietzschesource.org/texts/eKGWB/NF-1888,15

Kraus, Karl. 2010. "Sprachlehre," Karl Kraus: *Gedichte und Aufsätze zur deutschen Sprache.* Bremen: Europäischer Hochschulverlag.

Levine, Michael G. 2005. The place of the mouth in the canine corpus: Kafka's Investigations of a Dog. Paper presented at the annual meeting of the Modern Language Association, Washington, DC.

Long, A. A. 1986. "Outlines of Pyrrhonism," *Hellenistic Philosophy: Stoics, Epicureans, Skeptics*, 2nd ed. Berkeley, CA: Univ. of California Press.

Murray, Nicholas. 2004. *Franz Kafka.* New Haven, CT: Yale Univ. Press.

Nietzsche Source, http://www.nietzschesource.org/texts/eKGWB/NF-1888,15.

Rousseau, Jean-Jacques. 1959. *Ebauches des Confessions, Oeuvres Complètes.* Paris: Gallimard.

10

THE DYNAMICS OF NARRATION IN *BETRACHTUNG*, "DAS URTEIL," AND KAFKA'S REFLECTIONS ON WRITING

Ronald Speirs

Movement has always been a staple of storytelling, especially in narratives involving adventures, conquests, or banishments, pursuits or escapes, encounters or withdrawals, ascents or descents, finding or losing the way, or myriad combinations of such elements. It has also been associated with the experience and procedures of writing, as in the figure of Pegasus, who flies between the Muses and the poets, or the *motus animi continuus* that refuses to let Thomas Mann's Gustav von Aschenbach rest, or the scribbling pen from which emerge the journeys undertaken by Uncle Toby and the many other figures of wit and fancy who populate Sterne's *Tristram Shandy*. That Kafka had his own distinctive ways of presenting movement in his stories, ways that seem to promise some insight into his perplexing imaginings, has not escaped his commentators, though the topic deserves to be pursued more extensively.[1] This essay will consider movement as a focus of narration, as a motive of narration, and as a mode of narration. I shall begin by examining *Betrachtung,* Kafka's first published collection of prose, in some detail, before going on to consider the topic in more general terms.

As the double meaning of the title suggests, *Betrachtung* (*Contemplation*)[2] is a set of very short narratives addressed both to the eye and to the mind, in which the reader is shown scenes from life and invited to reflect on them in company with the (mostly first-person) narrator. One has to say "scenes *from* life" because the descriptions seldom create the illusion of solidity that is the aim of the conventional realist author. We are presented rather with imagery that captures a shifting kaleidoscope of states of mind.[3] In some of them, impressions drawn from nature and society predominate, while in others the narrator's imagination is clearly creating a quite distinct world of its own, but in every instance the border is permeable or fluctuating. Together they create what Kafka would later describe as the "monstrous" (*ungeheuer*, also meaning "uncanny" or "enormous") world in his head that it was the task of writing to set free.[4] What interests me here are the contrasting patterns of movement within and between these different spheres of experience, those that are completed and those that are not, and what they might tell us about the imagination in which movement and stasis feature so prominently and so pervasively.

The abruptness of the transition from one sphere to another, for example, is clearly conveyed in "Der plötzliche Spaziergang" (KAF, 1:19) ("The Sudden Walk"). Here the narrator-protagonist envisages the possibility of stepping completely outside the circumscribed world of social conformity simply by donning his outdoor coat and announcing that he must go for a walk at an hour when, like the rest of the family, he would normally be getting ready for bed. The little story is told in a series of "if" clauses (most of them belonging to a single, long, breathless sentence with a rising rhythm) which are hypothetical in sense but so specific and vivid in their details that the description reads like an account of a past event (or various such incidents) now being retold as if the events were happening in the present. The use of the indicative rather than the subjunctive is calculated to make it seem plausible that what is conjectured can indeed be realized. The narrator's increasingly agitated suppositions, carried on a surge of emotion, culminate in a moment of release, indeed almost of apotheosis, in which the body he is speaking about is suddenly filled with a strange form of physical movement that matches the flow of his thought and feelings:

> Wenn man sich auf der Gasse wiederfindet, mit Gliedern, die diese schon unerwartete Freiheit, die man ihnen verschafft hat, mit besonderer Beweglichkeit beantworten, wenn man durch diesen einen Entschluß alle Entschlußfähigkeit in sich gesammelt fühlt, wenn man mit größerer als der gewöhnlichen Bedeutung erkennt, daß man ja mehr Kraft als Bedürfnis hat, die schnellste Veränderung leicht zu bewirken und zu ertragen, und wenn man so die langen Gassen hinläuft,—dann ist man für diesen Abend gänzlich aus seiner Familie ausgetreten, die ins Wesenlose abschwenkt, während man selbst, ganz fest, schwarz vor Umrissen-

> heit, hinten die Schenkel schlagend, sich zu seiner wahren Gestalt erhebt. (KAF, 1:19–20)
>
> (When you come to yourself again on the street, with limbs that respond with particular mobility to the quite unexpected freedom you have given them, when you feel that your whole ability to make decisions has been concentrated by this one decision, when you recognize with greater significance than usual that your strength to effect and endure even the most rapid change with ease is greater than your need to do so, and when you walk in this manner down the long streets—then, for that evening, you have stepped out of your family entirely, which slips off into insubstantiality, while you, firm, silhouetted in black, slapping your flanks behind you, rise up to assume your true shape.)

These last few phrases suggest that the unremarkable, petty-bourgeois protagonist is transformed at this moment of exaltation or elevation (*Erhebung* is a key term for Kafka) into the figure of a rider on a horse, or even a fusion of the two. This strange notion of human-animal hybridism re-appears elsewhere in *Betrachtung* in the "Wish to Become a Red Indian," and it was later to recur in the name of Roßmann, the protagonist of *The Man Who Disappeared,*[5] and later still in the figure of the new lawyer, Dr. Bucephalus, formerly the warhorse of Alexander the Great (but now a student of the law), whose equine origins are betrayed to the knowledgeable eye by the curious way he walks up a flight of steps.[6] In "The Sudden Walk," however, the suggestion is developed no further, as the narrator-protagonist (denoted only by the impersonal pronoun "man") is imagined as using his newfound resolve merely to call on a friend at this late hour and to ask after his health. Taken at face value, the story seems to be one of the most optimistic in the collection; it implies that equilibrium can be achieved between the different forces pulling on the self so that it would be possible to remain a member of society, albeit an eccentric one, while "rising up" (*sich erheben*) in one's hybrid "true shape" and drawing energy and confidence from an experience of the self that places it wholly outside the control of "insubstantial" (*wesenlos*) family life. On the other hand, the narrator may actually be deluding himself that his ability to make decisions will be strengthened and confirmed simply by visiting a friend, even at this late hour. For by making this visit he could equally well be withdrawing again into the security of familiar social relationships rather than facing the challenges presented by the new dimension of the self that has just opened up to him. Most of the other stories in the collection do not support the optimistic conclusion of "The Sudden Walk."

Indeed, the very next story, entitled "Entschlüsse" ("Decisions"), which begins by asserting that it must be possible to "raise oneself up" (*sich erheben*) out of a state of misery ("Aus einem elenden Zustand" [KAF, 1:20]) through the determined use of will-power, proceeds, via an admission of the predictable failure of any such undertaking, to the desire for withdrawal into a state of complete isolation and immobility. The story unfolds as a series of conjectures about what would follow from a given starting point. In this case the narrating self appears to be alone at the outset (rather than in the midst of a family), and his ambition is not to "step outside the family completely" but rather to move, both literally and emotionally, into contact with others:

> Ich reiße mich vom Sessel los, umlaufe den Tisch, mache Kopf und Hals beweglich, bringe Feuer in die Augen, spanne die Muskeln um sie herum. Arbeite jedem Gefühl entgegen, begrüße A. stürmisch, wenn er jetzt kommen wird, dulde B. freundlich in meinem Zimmer, ziehe bei C. alles, was gesagt wird, trotz Schmerz und Mühe mit langen Zügen in mich hinein. (KAF, 1:20)
>
> (I tear myself out of my armchair, run around the table, make head and neck mobile, put fire into my eyes, tensing the muscles around them. I make efforts to go out to meet every feeling halfway, if A. comes I greet him with stormy enthusiasm, I tolerate B. amicably in my room, and, when C. is present, I draw everything that is said into myself in long draughts, despite all the pain and effort.)

The narrator-protagonist cannot imagine himself making such a move successfully, however, as he is convinced that he is bound to make some mistake, that the whole enterprise will *stocken* ("come to a standstill"), compelling him to "go back around the circle." Faced with this dismal prospect, his preference is for immobility. He decides that he should "als schwere Masse sich verhalten" ("behave as a heavy mass") and, even if he were to feel himself being *fortgeblasen* ("blown away"), he should not allow himself to be tempted into taking even "a single unnecessary step" or to engage in any emotional contact with others. In short, his aim is "was vom Leben als Gespenst noch übrig ist, mit eigener Hand niederdrücken, d.h., die letzte grabmäßige Ruhe noch vermehren und nichts außer ihr mehr bestehen lassen" (KAF, 1:20) ("to suppress with my own hand all that remains of life as a ghost, to increase the ultimate, grave-like rest and permit nothing else to exist"). Here the optimistic belief that an "elevating," truer form of movement could be attained as an alternative to the static routines of social existence is challenged by the pessimistic view that even entry into social intercourse may not be achievable by an effort of the will because the self feels itself to be fundamentally inert and alienated from all other selves. The condition of being "miserable" or more precisely *elend* (with the etymological root sense of being "out of the land" or "exiled") seems to entail inescapable stasis and loneliness in the midst of life. An explanation for this bleak conviction is perhaps to be found in the description of everyday existence as "das Leben als Gespenst" ("life as a ghost"). Something similar was suggested in "The Sudden Walk" by the notion that the family would slip away "ins Wesenlose" ("into insubstantiality") at the moment of the self's elevation to a truer state of being. If, at bottom, the self perceives life in society to be spectral, no more than a dead simulacrum of life, then it is no wonder that the self cannot be forced by the will to enter successfully into social interaction.

Taking these two stories together, the rational will appears to be ineffective and condemned to relapse into stasis, whereas the "Entschlußfähigkeit" ("capacity to make decisions") that seems to be concentrated by a sudden, apparently irrational impulse can lead to the release of an unfamiliar kind of dynamism. It is possible, however, that the sensation of concentrated *Entschlußfähigkeit* is merely epiphenomenal, the reflection in consciousness of an impulse that neither originates nor operates in the conscious part of the self.[7] Just as the rising gallop of the self's "true shape" was not allowed to have the last word in "The Sudden Walk," so the resolve of the self in "Decisions" to withdraw into utter, insensate immobility is subject to ironic relativization by the very last sentence of the story: "Eine charakteristische Bewegung eines solchen Zustandes ist das Hinfahren des kleinen Fingers über die Augenbrauen" (KAF, 1:20) ("A characteristic movement of such a condition is the passing of the little finger over the eyebrows"). No matter how socially alienated and static the mind of the narrator may perceive the self to be, this bodily gesture tells a rather different story. The tiny movement of the little finger suggests both that the protagonist's behavior is still constrained by social awareness, as he modestly conceals from others his intense feelings of despair and anomie, and that the body is still subject to dynamic impulses, no matter how "ghostly" the conscious mind may declare a life in the company of others to be. The attempt to attain complete immobility thus appears to be no more than the equally pointless obverse of inauthentic social interaction, a form of sulking, to put it harshly. Rest, it appears, is not to be found in this life, or at least not through any refusal to participate in life.

To the mind of the narrator of "Das Gassenfenster" (KAF, 1:29–30) ("The Window onto the Street"), the complete isolation and immobility allegedly desired by the protagonist of "Decisions" cannot even be *conceived* to be a sustainable mode of being. He imagines that anyone living alone (*verlassen* has the sense of "abandoned" or "desolate") would be bound to feel the need for human contact occasionally and an arm—any arm ("einen beliebigen Arm")—to hold on to. Even the most isolated of individuals, he insists, could not live for long without a window onto the street. Even if such a person is not actually seeking anything but simply goes to the window as a tired man whose eyes go up and down between the sky and the public, indeed even if he leans his head back a little because he simply "doesn't want to" look down at the street he will nevertheless be subject to an impersonal force that does not permit him to remain in static isolation: "so reißen ihn doch unten die Pferde mit in ihr Gefolge von Wagen und Lärm und damit endlich der menschlichen Eintracht zu" (KAF, 1:30) ("then, despite all his efforts, the horses down below will tear him into their retinue of carriages and din, and thus finally pull him towards oneness with humanity"). The protagonist's need for human support is prompted by awareness of the constant changes—movements—in his environment: "die Veränderungen der Tageszeit, der Witterung, der Berufsverhältnisse und dergleichen" (KAF, 1:29) ("changes in the time of day, the weather, working conditions and such like"). Surrounded by a restless world, his responsive gaze betrays his own restlessness. At the same time his tiredness suggests that it demands great effort to endure the conflicting pulls between a life of isolation on the one hand and the need for contact on the other, between the life of the public on the street and the view up toward the *Himmel* ("which could denote heaven or simply the sky"). The ironic twist at the end of this story consists in the fact that, whether because the isolated, hesitant individual feels the need for something to hold onto in a restless world or because he is simply exhausted by living with his internal tensions, he will ultimately be unable to resist the violent pull ("reißen") of the carriage horses towards oneness or harmony (*Eintracht*) with humanity. Given this individual's lack of oneness with even his own life (a condition he shares with Kafka),[8] however, it seems unlikely that the supposed *Eintracht* will prove to be anything more than a mirage.

By contrast, far from having to be "torn" into society willy-nilly by the irresistible pull of imagined human *Eintracht*, the narrator-protagonist of "Entlarvung eines Bauernfängers" (KAF, 1:17–19) ("The Unmasking of a Confidence Trickster") is determined to follow an invitation to join a social gathering (*Gesellschaft*)[9] in a "herrschaftlichen Hause" (KAF, 1:17) ("a well-to-do house"—the adjective *herrschaftlich* connotes membership of the ruling class). At the beginning of the story, however, it is already ten o'clock in the evening and he is still standing in the street outside the door of the house he wishes to enter. His progress into society has been delayed and is now blocked by a strange companion he first met soon after arriving in town and who, having re-appeared unexpectedly earlier that evening, has "dragged" the protagonist through the streets for the past two hours. During a long pause in which they face each other in silence, the narrator-protagonist of this story gradually comes to resemble the narrator of "The Window onto the Street" as more and more is revealed about his relation to the stranger/acquaintance. While insisting that he was invited to join the company upstairs and not to stand outside the door looking past the ears of his *Gegenüber* ("opponent/interlocutor"), the protagonist appears unable to move any farther—"als seien wir zu einem langen Aufenthalt auf diesem Fleck entschlossen" (KAF, 1:17) ("as if we had decided to stay on this spot for a long time"). As they stand there, seemingly joined by mutual resolve, the protagonist and the stranger are shrouded in a shared silence in which everything in the vicinity seems to participate:

> Dabei nahmen an diesem Schweigen gleich die Häuser ringsherum ihren Anteil, und das Dunkel über ihnen bis zu den Sternen. Und die Schritte unsichtbarer Spaziergänger, deren Wege zu erraten man nicht Lust hatte, der Wind, der immer wieder an die gegenüberliegende Straßenseite sich drückte, ein Grammophon, das gegen die geschlossenen Fenster irgendeines Zimmers sang,—sie ließen aus diesem Schweigen sich hören, als sei es ihr Eigentum seit jeher und für immer. (KAF, 1:17)
>
> (As we stood there, the houses around us and the darkness above them right up to the stars shared in this silence. And the steps of invisible pedestrians, whose ways one had no desire to guess, the wind that repeatedly pressed against the other side of the street, a gramophone that sang against the closed windows of some room or other—these things let themselves be heard from out of this silence, as if it always had been and forever would remain their property.)

As he stands facing this man, the protagonist's experience of the world as a dark place of profound silence in which every sound and sight speaks of the isolation of all things and all people, each in motion, resembles far too closely that of the man behind the "window onto the street" for us to accept readily his protestation that his proper place is in the company of those who are masters in society (an implication of the "herrschaftlichen Hause"). When his opponent/partner finally steps aside with a smile to permit him to proceed, the protagonist professes shame at his failure to have "recognized" the man for what he allegedly is, namely a confidence trickster. Shame, an important emotion in Kafka's work,[10] attests both to the social conditioning that outlaws certain actions and to the individual's attraction to those very things that have been declared taboo. In this instance, the feelings connoted by the dark silence on the street are likely to be part of the taboo area from which the protagonist tries to distance himself. He does so by claiming to feel ashamed of his failure to "recognize" this man as a confidence trickster rather than by admitting to the deeper shame of having been enveloped by an experience of alienation from the world so profound that it casts doubt on any notion of a harmonious life in society ("menschliche Eintracht"). Even as he insists that the man is nothing but a trickster, the protagonist confesses to having felt an instinctive affinity for such figures ever since he arrived in town:

> Ich verstand sie doch so gut, sie waren ja meine ersten städtischen Bekannten in den kleinen Wirtshäusern gewesen, und ich verdankte ihnen den ersten Anblick einer Unnachgiebigkeit, die ich mir jetzt so wenig von der Erde wegdenken konnte, daß ich sie schon in mir zu fühlen begann. (KAF, 1:18)

> (I understood them so well, they were after all my first acquaintances in the little pubs in the town, and I had them to thank for my first sight of a stubborn refusal to yield that I now felt so strongly to be part of the world that I was already beginning to feel it within myself.)

He confesses that the gaze of these figures is always convincing and that part of their technique of preventing people from reaching their goal is to offer instead "eine Wohnung in ihrer eigenen Brust" (a dwelling in their own breast). If one's feelings rebelled against such an approach, the figures would treat the resistance as an "Umarmung, in die sie sich warfen, das Gesicht voran" (KAF, 1:18) ("an embrace into which they would pitch themselves head first"). All of this testifies to the power of attraction the stranger exercises over the protagonist, illuminating both the source of his shame and his need to displace the feeling. Only by patronizing the man, by saying "Erkannt!" ("Found out!") and patting him on the shoulder, can the protagonist free himself from the confrontation and rush up the stairs to join the party, thereby rescuing his vision of a life devoted to upward movement in society. But as someone who recognizes that the loyal expressions on the faces of the waiting servants are "groundless," it is clear that he will never in fact be able to integrate himself securely into society. Having once been brought to a standstill in the dark silence reaching up to the stars, he is unlikely ever to forget that alienating experience of universal isolation and unconnected motion in the world.

That a life based on social success is not the prize envisaged by the protagonist in the "Unmasking of a Confidence Trickster" is confirmed by other stories in *Betrachtung.* In the reflection "Zum Nachdenken für Herrenreiter" (KAF, 1:28–29) ("Something for Jockeys to Think About"), for example, coming first in a horse race simply means a brief moment of exultation followed by a string of negative consequences that induce regret: the envy of one's opponents creates a painful contrast between the ride through the narrow railings to the winners' enclosure and the openness of the course glimpsed during the race; the friends who have backed the winner are more interested in their winnings than in him, while those who did not back him, for fear of losing, resent the fact that he won; the losers dismiss the winner's success and look forward to the next race, while the ladies find the winner ridiculous because he doesn't know how to handle the fuss that is made of him; to cap it all, at the end of the race it starts to rain. In other words, if life is regarded as a circular race to a finish line, the isolated individual will have progressed no further toward any worthwhile goal by the end of life's journey.

In "Der Nachhauseweg" (KAF, 1:25) ("The Journey Home"), events take a similarly dispiriting turn as the narrator recounts his changing feelings while walking home after an apparently successful day at work. At first, filled with pride in his achievements, he "marches" in step with the world around him: "Mein Tempo ist das Tempo dieser Gassenseite, dieser Gasse, dieses Viertels" ("My tempo is the tempo of this side of the street, of this street, this quarter"). Like some embodiment of Schopenhauer's universal Will, he feels responsible for all the energy being expended throughout the world, for every knock on a door or table, for all toasts, and for lovers everywhere, in beds, on scaffolding, against walls in dark alleys, or on the ottomans of brothels. On stepping into his private room, however, the man becomes pensive for no identifiable reason.

It does not help to throw open the window and to hear music (the symbol, incidentally, of the never-resting universal Will in Schopenhauer's thought) still being played in a garden somewhere. A socially successful life, it appears, can seem satisfactory for as long as the individual keeps on the move, imagining himself to be in step with the world, but as soon as he is alone and at a standstill, the mood changes abruptly from enthusiasm to melancholy. The public world that "tore" the protagonist of "Window onto the Street" out of his isolation and toward imagined "human harmony" proves ultimately to disappoint even someone who has achieved success in social and commercial life. Neither in lonely stasis nor in social progress, it seems, can the characters of *Betrachtung* find rest. The final flinging-open of the window suggests an agitation of the spirit that can as little find an adequate outlet in the competitive business of normal life as it can derive consolation from music as the aesthetic apotheosis and overcoming of movement.[11]

In another story with a similar theme, entitled "Der Kaufmann" (KAF, 1:22–24) ("The Shopkeeper"), where the narrator-protagonist is denied even temporary success in the world of commerce, this kind of inner restlessness breaks out much more powerfully. The man's business is small and brings him nothing but worry, but as he shuts up shop to go home, his troublesome work suddenly appears in a new light, as an activity that has at least kept at bay for a few hours the inner *Aufregung* ("agitation") that had been trying to claim his attention since the morning:

> Wenn nun am Abend eines Werktages das Geschäft gesperrt wird und ich plötzlich Stunden vor mir sehe, in denen ich für die ununterbrochenen Bedürfnisse meines Geschäftes nichts werde arbeiten können, dann wirft sich meine am Morgen weit vorausgeschickte Aufregung in mich, wie eine zurückkehrende Flut, hält es aber in mir nicht aus und ohne Ziel reißt sie mich mit. (KAF, 1:22)

> (Now, as my business is locked up at the end of the working day and I suddenly see before me hours in which I shall not be able to work for the unceasing needs of my business, the agitation that I had sent out far ahead of me in the morning hurls itself back into me like a returning tide, but will not be contained within me and, although lacking a goal, tears me away with it.)

As he is unable or unwilling to make use of the impulse, the protagonist's barely suppressed agitation has to express itself in other ways during his return home so that he walks "wie auf Wellen" ("as if on waves"),[12] his fingers shake, and he runs his hand over the hair of the children he meets coming toward him. When he is eventually alone and motionless in the elevator that will carry him up to his flat (or, more likely, room within a flat), he looks into the mirror and his agitation finds a new outlet as he begins to speak to some unidentified figures whom he sends out into the world on invisible wings, telling them at least to enjoy the constantly changing spectacle of movement the world provides, the feelings aroused by such sights, and the opportunities for adventure:

> Doch genießet die Aussicht des Fensters, wenn die Prozessionen aus allen drei Straßen kommen, einander nicht ausweichen, durcheinandergehn und zwischen ihren letzten Reihen den freien Platz wieder entstehen lassen. Winket mit den Tüchern, seid entsetzt, seid gerührt, lobet die schöne Dame, die vorüberfährt. (KAF, 1:23)

> (But enjoy the view from the window as all the processions coming out of all three streets refuse to give way to one another, weave through one another, and then allow the empty square to re-appear in the gaps between the last rows. Wave with your handkerchiefs, be horrified, be touched, praise the fair lady riding past.)

The pleasurable movements and actions welling up in the imagination of the shopkeeper as he stands alone in the elevator are as anarchic as the agitation that feeds them, and they contrast strongly with the desperate, goal-directed haste of the man determined to escape the "confidence trickster" in order to join the party on the upper story of the "well-to-do house." As soon as the lift stops on his floor, however, the little shopkeeper's excited visions give way once more to quotidian routine (and the stasis awaiting him at home) as he rings the door-bell and says good evening to the maid who opens the door for him.

Considered in relation to other stories in *Betrachtung,* the impulse experienced as agitation or excitement by the shopkeeper appears to intimate his subjection to a desire for some utterly free and undirected form of movement that may be the source of, but could never find adequate expression in, the patterns of movement that pervade everyday life, whether in the diurnal cycle of activity and rest, the pursuit of particular goals, the desire to progress up the social hierarchy, or the general concept of life as a predictable journey from birth to death. Constrained within a rationally understood and ordered life, the desire felt—and feared—by the little shopkeeper can only be experienced as disruptive agitation. That impulse finds its most unconstrained expression in one of the shortest texts of *Betrachtung,* entitled "Wunsch, Indianer zu werden" (KAF, 1:30) ("Wish to Become a Red Indian"). It runs like this:

> Wenn man doch ein Indianer wäre, gleich bereit, und auf dem rennenden Pferde, schief in der Luft, immer wieder kurz erzitterte über dem zitternden Boden, bis man die Sporen ließ, denn es gab keine Sporen, bis man die Zügel wegwarf, denn es gab keine Zügel, und kaum das Land vor sich als glattgemähte Heide sah, schon ohne Pferdehals und Pferdekopf. (KAF, 1:30)

> (If only one were a Red Indian, ready straight away, and on the galloping horse, leaning forward in the air, trembling briefly and repeatedly above the trembling ground, until one let go the spurs, for there were no spurs, until one threw away the reins, for there were no reins, and hardly saw the land ahead any more as a smooth-mown heath, already without the neck and head of the horse.)

As the narrator articulates this wish, he transforms himself verbally into something that approximates to an image of pure movement, more like an arrow flying through the air than like an Indian on horseback, as all the elements of riding disappear one after the other—spurs, reins, the neck and head of the horse, and even the land ahead of him. The story breaks off without telling us what would happen if that transformation were to be completed and self and movement were to become one. But perhaps then nothing more would happen. Perhaps being able to wish that wish would mean the end of all wishing to reach any goal. Perhaps, in other words, the rider would have achieved that paradoxical condition of rest in movement once identified by Zeno and jotted down by Kafka in one of his later notebooks: "Der fliegende Pfeil ruht" (KAF, 9:104) ("The flying arrow is at rest").[13] In comparison with such oneness of movement and rest, the alternation of agitation and stasis, or the sense of moving and getting nowhere that is experienced in everyday life, could only ever represent a poor copy of an ideal *coincidentia oppositorum.* But the story leaves us in doubt about whether the wish can even be wished. The notion of riding without reins or horse or the ground below negates everything we understand about riding. The images drawn from life and the use to which the narrative imagination wants to put them are fundamentally dissonant; the verbal vehicle cannot support the tenor. If such a thing as pure movement (that is simultaneously pure rest) exists, it cannot be narrated, since words are saturated with the things of this world, and the things of this world do not behave like that. As it breaks off in mid-sentence, the little wish-cum-story leaves the reader hovering, as it were, in mid-air. We cannot decide whether to see or feel in the conundrum of the horseless, groundless ride an intuited mode of extraordinary movement that demands to be communicated via the negation of the verbal images that allow us to share the intuition or whether the paradoxes implicitly concede the absurdity and hence the failure of any wish for another, "higher" mode of experience. In another context, Kafka concluded that a similar wish (to conceive of the world as both weighty and weightless at one and the same time) could not be wished, since it proved, on reflection, not to be a wish but rather a "Verteidigung, eine Verbürgerlichung des Nichts" (KAF, 11:180) ("a defense, an attempt to populate and domesticate nothingness") with the help of images created from the words with which we attempt to master the world. The single, breathless, unfinished sentence of the "Wish to Become a Red Indian," by contrast, at least leaves two possibilities open: either that the wish does indeed adumbrate the presence of some transcendent energy in the person making the wish, an energy that defies all attempts at verbal containment or logical comprehension, or that the story expresses a deluded attempt to escape the constraints on all forms of movement, physical or mental, imposed by life in this world and the language by which we organize our lives.

One of Kafka's chief problems as a story-teller was to devise means of expressing and doing justice to these contrary views or experiences of life, each related to a different form of movement: the familiar, earth-bound life that is subject to social norms and the laws of nature and verbal order on the one hand, and, on the other, a sudden, extraordinary eruption of energy that is imagined to be capable of raising the self out of and beyond the confines of such controlled and regular patterns of activity and thought. Most of the stories in *Betrachtung* fail to achieve a balance between these conflicting experiences because they tend to reduce the sense of unconstrained movement, such as that envisaged in "Wish to Become a Red Indian," to the status of a brief fantasy of escape from the routines of normality to which the protagonist must return and submit in the end. What Kafka was feeling his way toward from the outset was a form of narration in which the abnormal emerged as a form of experienced reality in its own right, a reality that asserts a claim to validity that contradicts but cannot simply be relativized by the claims of rationality and order. A few of these early stories do point to Kafka's later narrative method by asserting more boldly the extraordinary dimension of experience as precisely that, as something that escapes the control of all norms of understanding and behavior. One might say that in these more daring experiments Kafka allows the centrifugal force of an intuited, ungovernable dimension of reality to challenge successfully the centripetal, controlling force exerted by reason. There may therefore have been programmatic intent in his decision to open and close the collection with two of these radical experiments.

In "Kinder auf der Landstraße" (KAF, 1:13–16) ("Children on the Country Road") with which *Betrachtung* opens, the narrator-protagonist, a child at the time of the events, is introduced seated and at rest after an afternoon spent playing on a swing that hangs between two trees in his parents' garden. He is listening to the wagons passing along the road outside the garden fence and sometimes glimpsing them through gaps in the foliage as it is moves weakly, presumably blown by the wind. The swing (*Schaukel*) brings into focus a form of movement (hovering or oscillating) that will recur not just in this little story but again and again throughout Kafka's oeuvre.[14] The child's experiences represent the meeting place of a sense of orderly routine governed by parental authority and a generalized, disorienting dynamism to which he succumbs by stages:

> Dann flogen Vögel wie sprühend auf, ich folgte ihnen mit den Blicken, sah, wie sie in einem Atemzug stiegen, bis ich nicht mehr glaubte, daß sie stiegen, sondern, daß ich falle, und fest mich an den Seilen haltend, aus Schwäche ein wenig zu schaukeln anfing. Bald schaukelte ich stärker, als die Luft schon kühler wehte und statt der fliegenden Vögel zitternde Sterne erschienen. (KAF, 1:13)

> (Then birds flew up as if in a spray, I followed them with my gaze, saw how they rose in an intake of breath until I no longer believed that they were climbing but rather that I was falling, and, out of weakness, holding on firmly to the ropes, I began to swing a little. Soon I was swinging more strongly, as the breeze turned cooler and trembling stars appeared in place of the flying birds.)

The precarious balance between the opposing tendencies of order and disruption, rest and movement, is undone progressively as the tired child sits over an evening meal: the curtains are swelled like sails by the warm wind, passers-by speak to him through the open window, and finally someone jumps over the window ledge to report that "the others" are waiting outside, at which point the child gets up with a sigh and runs out of the house. Once he has joined the others, a group of children apparently outside the laws not just of bed-time but of rationally graspable experience, he feels liberated:

> Wir durchstießen den Abend mit dem Kopf. Es gab keine Tages- und keine Nachtzeit. Bald rieben sich unsere Westenknöpfe aneinander wie Zähne, bald liefen wir in gleichbleibender Entfernung, Feuer im Mund, wie Tiere in den Tropen. Wie Kürassiere in alten Kriegen, stampfend und hoch in der Luft, trieben wir einander die kurze Gasse hinunter und mit diesem Anlauf in den Beinen die Landstraße weiter hinauf. . . .
>
> Einer schrie einen indianischen Kriegsruf heraus, wir bekamen in die Beine einen Galopp wie niemals, bei den Sprüngen hob uns in den Hüften der Wind. Nichts hätte uns aufhalten können; wir waren so im Laufe, daß wir selbst beim Überholen die Arme verschränken und ruhig uns umsehen konnten. (KAF, 1:14)

> (We broke through the evening with our heads. There was no day-time and night-time. Sometimes our waistcoat buttons rubbed against each other like teeth, at others we ran at a steady distance from one another, fire in our mouths, like animals in the tropics. Like cavalry in old wars, stamping and high in the air, we drove each other down the short lane and with this run-up in our legs chased each other farther up the country road. . . .
>
> One of us shouted out an Indian war-cry, we felt a gallop in our legs like never before, as we jumped the wind lifted us by the hips. Nothing could have stopped us, we were so at one with our running that even as we overtook one another we could fold our arms and look around calmly.)

Such moments of elated and elevating dynamism (recalling the state of oneness with sheer movement imagined in "Wish to Become a Red Indian") are interspersed with others where the child is so overcome with tiredness that he has to lie down in a ditch to sleep, a bodily reminder of the sphere of rational, social, and natural order from which he has not yet quite escaped. Indeed, toward the end of the story the child seems about to return home to bed, for he leaves the other children and heads back toward the village before suddenly striking off alone at the next crossroads, across the fields and into the woods, with the aim of reaching the town in the south where no one sleeps, as all who live there are "fools."

Such a place would be one of unending movement but also one where movement is indistinguishable from rest, since the "fools" who live there never become tired.

The closing story of the collection, entitled "Unglücklichsein" (KAF, 1:31–36) ("Being Unhappy") offers no such utopian prospect of perpetual motion in perpetual rest, although it too uses the intrusion of an unusual form of movement to create a robust challenge to the conventional order of things. Here again, it is the figure of a child who, by trespassing across the threshold between the familiar and the abnormal, points to a way out of the confines of the conventional order maintained by rational consensus. In this case, however, the narrator-protagonist is not himself a child but an adult who receives an unexpected visit from a strange child that he immediately takes to be a ghost. At the beginning of the story the protagonist is in that condition of static agitation to which other figures in the collection have been subject. He runs around his room as if on an endless race-track, repulsed as much by the world beyond his window as by the image of himself reflected back from a mirror on the opposite wall of the room. As neither the outside world nor the self present an acceptable goal for his restless energy, the narrator seeks relief from the pent-up frustration within him by at least emitting a scream, the acoustic equivalent of the pure movement envisaged in "Wish to Become a Red Indian":

> . . . und aufschrie, um nur den Schrei zu hören, dem nichts antwortet und dem auch nichts die Kraft des Schreiens nimmt, der also aufsteigt, ohne Gegengewicht, und nicht aufhören kann, selbst wenn er verstummt. (KAF, 1:31)

> (. . . and screamed, just so that I could hear the scream to which nothing responds and from which nothing takes away the force of the screaming, and so just rises, without a counterweight, and cannot stop, even when it falls silent.)

At that point, as if in response, an abnormal form of movement occurs as a door suddenly opens in the wall separating the protagonist's private room from the dark communal corridor beyond:

> . . . da öffnete sich aus der Wand heraus die Tür, so eilig, weil doch Eile nötig war und selbst die Wagenpferde unten auf dem Pflaster, wie wildgewordene Pferde in der Schlacht, die Gurgeln preisgegeben, sich erhoben. (KAF, 1:31)

> (. . . then the door opened out of the wall so quickly, because after all speed was needed and even the carriage horses down on the street reared up, exposing their throats, like horses that had gone wild during a battle.)

This portentous moment, echoing the transformation of the protagonist of "A Sudden Walk" as he rises (*sich erheben*) to assume his "true form," or the rearing cavalry imitated by the children charging along the country road, heralds the appearance of the ghost-child who darts *(fuhr)* out of the dark corridor and comes to rest standing on his toes "auf einem unmerklich schaukelnden Fußbodenbalken" ("on a floorboard that was rocking almost imperceptibly"), in an echo, perhaps, of the child rocking on its *Schaukel* in the opening story of the collection.[15] As the child stands there, it "ließ den Luftzug von draußen um die Gelenke der Füße streichen, auch den Hals, auch die Schläfen entlang" (KAF, 1:31) ("let the draught from outside play around his ankles, and over his neck and his temples"), thereby foreshadowing a motif from a later story, namely the motif of the *Luftzug* ("draught or movement of air") that will forever cool the ankles of the tamed ape Rotpeter as it blows through the tiny gap in the horizon that separates his new, socialized, and self-aware life from the pre-conscious existence with "Freiheit nach allen Seiten" ("freedom on all sides") (KSS, 79) that he had once known as a wild young ape. As the protagonist prepares to greet this unexpected visitor, he tries to expel his pent-up agitation ("my eyelashes trembled in my face"), but the child recognizes his lack of calm (*Ruhe*) unerringly. That no proper meeting between the host and his guest can take place (they address each other throughout with the formal *Sie*, although one of them is a child) is pre-determined by the man's designation of the child from the outset as a ghost. On the one hand, although he claims not to believe in ghosts, this is the only category to which he can assign the intruding figure; on the other hand, he claims to have been waiting for the visit from the child for a long time: "Ich bin ja so froh, daß Sie endlich hier sind. Ich sage 'endlich,' weil es schon so spät ist. Es ist mir unbegreiflich, warum Sie so spät gekommen sind" (KAF, 1:33) ("I'm glad you're here at last. I say 'at last,' because it is already so late. It is incomprehensible to me that you have come so late"). He recognizes that he and the child share a common identity: "Ihre Natur ist meine" ("Your nature is mine"), but it is the child who points out how limited is their ability to draw close to one another: "So nah, als Ihnen ein fremder Mensch entgegenkommen kann, bin ich Ihnen schon von Natur aus" (KAF, 1:33–34) ("By nature I am as close to you as any stranger can get to you"). The encounter of these mutually alienated beings is marked by irritation and ends with the protagonist's departure from the room. When he returns to the empty room, however, he feels *verlassen* ("lonely, abandoned," like the protagonist of "Window onto the Street"). Finally he seeks refuge in sleep, presumably because, like so many of these early protagonists, he is exhausted by the conflict he has just experienced between the world of familiar routine and the dark world beyond his room that he glimpsed beyond the door created by the entry of the child-ghost, a figure he both fears and wishes to call his own. Thus, the story that closes *Betrachtung* appears to create a pessimistic counterpoint to the optimistic story with which the collection opened. Whereas the first protagonist, still a child, leaves the highway and sets out across open country to find the city in the south where "fools" never sleep, the last protagonist, too little of a "fool" to be able to communicate with the child "ghost" who comes to visit him in a dark hour of agitation, is left feeling *verlassen* ("lonely, abandoned"), with only sleep to provide perhaps some respite from the conflict brought to a head by the visit.

In these early stories, Kafka had already moved into what he was later to call a *Grenzland* ("borderland") between contrasting areas or modes of experience, and he had begun to practice a method of narration that relied to an unusual degree on images of movement to characterize the relationship between these spheres.[16] The descriptions of the process of writing in his diaries and letters are also pervaded by the same dynamic imagery, and there too its function is to capture and communicate a very similar structure of experience. Writing, he stated repeatedly, was the "direction" taken by his whole being, the only form in which he could feel truly alive and hence connected with the life of the world:

> Mein ganzes Wesen ist auf Literatur gerichtet, die Richtung habe ich bis zu meinem 30(s)ten Jahr genau festgehalten; wenn ich sie einmal verlasse, lebe ich eben nicht mehr. Alles was ich bin und nicht bin, folgert daraus. (F, 456)

> (My whole being is directed toward literature; I have followed this direction unswervingly until my 30th year and the moment I abandon it I cease to live. Everything I am and am not is a result of this.) (KLF, 313)

Recognizing his essential "direction" was one thing, maintaining momentum proved to be quite another. Writing to Felice Bauer about the intermittent process of composing his first novel, for example, Kafka compared it to loading and driving a wagon:

> Arme, arme Liebste, möchtest Du Dich doch nie gezwungen fühlen, diesen elenden Roman zu lesen, den ich da stumpf zusammenschreibe. Schrecklich ist es, wie er sein Aussehn ändern kann; liegt die Last auf (mit welchem Schwung ich schreibe! Wie die Kleckse fliegen!) dem Wagen oben, dann ist mir wohl, ich entzücke mich am Peitschenknallen und bin ein großer Herr; fällt sie mir aber vom Wagen herunter (und das ist nicht vorauszusehn, nicht zu verhindern, nicht zu verschweigen) wie gestern und heute, scheint sie unmäßig schwer für meine kläglichen Schultern, dann möchte ich am liebsten alles lassen und mir an Ort und Stelle ein Grab graben. (F, 231)
>
> (Poor, poor dearest, may you never feel compelled to read this miserable novel that I am writing away at so dismally. It is terrible how it can change its appearance; once the load (the ardor I write with! How the ink-spots fly!), is on the cart, I am all right; I delight in cracking the whip and am a man of importance; but once it falls off the cart (which cannot be foreseen, prevented, or concealed) as it did yesterday and today, then it feels excessively heavy for my pitiful shoulders; all I want to do then is abandon everything and dig my grave on the spot.) (KLF, 142)

For Kafka, the progress of narration meant following the path taken by his innermost being; conversely, when writing came to a stop he experienced the cessation as a form of death. As long as a story and its characters, which he had to follow wherever they led, were in motion, the dynamism of the narrative also animated the hand of the author: "once the load is up on the wagon (with what verve I write! how the splashes of ink fly!), all is well." To fail to tell a story to its conclusion, by contrast, was to leave the characters to die and to wish that he himself could fall into the grave, as Kafka went on to explain to Felice:

> Schließlich kann es keinen schönern, der vollkommenen Verzweiflung würdigern Ort für das Sterben geben als einen eigenen Roman. Gerade unterhalten sich zwei seit Gestern recht matt gewordene Personen auf zwei benachbarten Balkonen im 8ten Stockwerk um 3 Uhr in der Nacht. Wie wäre es, wenn ich ihnen von der Gasse aus ein "Adieu" zuriefe und sie gänzlich verließe. Sie würden dort auf ihren Balkonen zusammensinken und mit Leichengesichtern durch die Geländerstangen einander ansehn. (F, 231)
>
> (After all, there can be no more beautiful spot to die in, no spot more

> worthy of total despair, than one's own novel. At this moment two people—grown somewhat dim since yesterday—are talking to each other on two adjacent balconies on the eighth floor at 3 in the morning. How would it be if I called out "goodbye" to them from the street, and abandoned them completely? They would collapse there on their balconies and with corpselike expressions stare at each other through the railings.) (KLF, 142)

In another passage, Kafka likened writing to traversing space by means of a telescope in order to bring into view the inner self that he felt to be separated by a great distance from the everyday, non-writing part of his self:

> Aber jeden Tag soll zumindest eine Zeile gegen mich gerichtet werden wie man die Fernrohre jetzt gegen den Kometen richtet. Und wenn ich dann einmal vor jenem Satze erscheinen würde, hergelockt von jenem Satze, so wie ich z. B. letzte Weihnachten gewesen bin und wo ich so weit war, daß ich mich nur noch gerade fassen konnte und wo ich wirklich auf der letzten Stufe meiner Leiter schien, die aber ruhig auf dem Boden stand und an der Wand. Aber was für ein Boden! was für eine Wand! Und doch fiel jene Leiter nicht, so drückten sie meine Füße an den Boden, so hoben sie meine Füße an die Wand. (KAF, 9:15)

> (But every day at least one line should be trained on me, as they now train telescopes on comets. And if I then should appear before that sentence once, lured by that sentence, just as, for instance, I was last Christmas, when I was so far gone that I was barely able to control myself and when I seemed really to be on the last rung of my ladder, which, however, rested quietly on the ground and against a wall. But what ground, what a wall! And yet that ladder did not fall, so strongly did my feet press it against the ground, so strongly did my feet raise it against the wall.) (KD, 3–14)

Alternatively, the journey to the inner self could be experienced as a descent into the depths or plunging down into a stream (*Strom*) or river (*Fluß*) of creativity: "Es ist notwendig, förmlich unterzutauchen und schneller zu sinken als das vor einem Versinkende" (KAF, 11:76) ("You have to dive down, as it were, and sink more rapidly than that which sinks in advance of you" [KD, 330]). Although Kafka wanted to reach out to others once a piece of writing was complete, he was convinced that he could only gain access to the depths of inspiration by separating himself from the "surface" or social dimension of life and by making the descent (or ascent) in complete isolation:

> Was von dieser Oberfläche ins Schreiben hinübergenommen wird—wenn es nicht anders geht und die tiefern Quellen schweigen—ist nichts und fällt in dem Augenblick zusammen, in dem ein wahreres Gefühl diesen obern Boden zum Schwanken bringt. Deshalb kann man nicht genug allein sein, wenn man schreibt, deshalb kann es nicht genug still um einen sein, wenn man schreibt, die Nacht ist noch zu wenig Nacht. Deshalb kann nicht genug Zeit einem zur Verfügung stehn, denn die Wege sind lang, und man irrt leicht ab, man bekommt sogar manchmal Angst und hat schon ohne Zwang und Lockung Lust zurückzulaufen. . . . Oft dachte ich schon daran, dass es die beste Lebensweise für mich wäre, mit Schreibzeug und einer Lampe im innersten Raume eines ausgedehnten, abgesperrten Kellers zu sein. . . . Was ich dann schreiben würde! Aus welchen Tiefen ich es hervorreißen würde! (F, 250)

> (Writing that springs from the surface of existence—when there is no other way and the deeper wells have dried up—is nothing, and collapses the moment a truer emotion makes that surface shake. That is why one can never be alone enough when one writes, why there can never be enough silence around one when one writes, why even night is not night enough. That is why there is never enough time at one's disposal, for the roads are long, and it is easy to go astray, there are even times when one becomes afraid sometimes and has the desire—even without any constraint or enticement—to run back. . . . I have often thought that the best mode of life for me would be to sit in the innermost room of a spacious locked cellar with my writing things and a lamp. . . . And how I would write! From what depths I would drag it up!) (KLF, 156)

The self that Kafka was bent on sighting revealed itself, he believed, precisely through the imagery and dynamic patterns of the writing itself:

> Wer weiß denn aus sich selbst heraus, wie es um einen steht. Dieses stürmische oder sich wälzende oder sumpfige Innere sind ja wir selbst, aber auf dem im geheimen sich vollziehenden Weg, auf dem die Worte aus uns hervorgetrieben werden, wird die Selbsterkenntnis an den Tag gebracht, und wenn sie auch noch immer verhüllt ist, so ist sie doch vor uns und ein herrlicher oder schrecklicher Anblick. Nimm mich also, Liebste, in

> Schutz vor diesen widerlichen Worten, die ich da in der letzten Zeit aus mir herausbefördert habe. (F, 306)
>
> (After all, who knows within himself how things really are with him? This tempestuous or floundering or morass-like inner self is what we really are, but on the secret, self-creating path along which words get driven out of us, self-knowledge is brought to the surface, and though it may still be veiled, yet it is there before us, wonderful or terrible to behold. So protect me, dearest, from these horrible words that I have mined out of myself recently.) (KLF, 198; translation modified)

The references here to the "im geheimen sich vollziehenden Weg" (the "secret, self-creating path," literally, "the way which completes itself in secret") and to the sense that the words "get driven" out of the writer express Kafka's belief that, when writing, he was to an extent the passive instrument of a dynamic impulse that operated independently of his conscious will. As his ill body became ever thinner, he even joked blackly that his body had clearly fashioned itself into a writing implement for the use of whatever higher power (if such a thing existed) might wish to use him, via his own hand and pen, to tell its self-revealing and self-concealing stories:

> Und tatsächlich, so mager wie ich bin und ich bin der magerste Mensch, den ich kenne (was etwas sagen will, da ich schon viel in Sanatorien herumgekommen bin) ebenso ist auch sonst nichts an mir, was man in Rücksicht auf das Schreiben Überflüssiges und Überflüssiges im guten Sinne nennen könnte. Gibt es also eine höhere Macht, die mich benützen will oder benützt, dann liege ich als ein zumindest deutlich ausgearbeitetes Instrument in ihrer Hand; wenn nicht, dann bin ich gar nichts und werde plötzlich in einer fürchterlichen Leere übrig bleiben. (F, 65–66)
>
> (As thin as I am, and I am the thinnest person I know (and that's saying something, for I'm no stranger to sanatoria), there is nothing to me that one which, in relation to writing, one could call superfluous, superfluous in the sense of overflowing. If there is a higher power that wishes to use me, or does use me, I am at its mercy, if no more than as a well-prepared instrument; if not, I am nothing and will suddenly be abandoned in a dreadful void.) (KLF, 21)

Kafka's dependence on the dynamic impulse supplied by the "higher power," or whatever it was that released the unfolding of his imaginative world, meant that narration was an extremely uncertain undertaking. As he observed in a letter to Grete Bloch, "Ich habe meine Fähigkeit des Schreibens gar nicht in der Hand. Sie kommt und geht wie ein Gespenst. Seit einem Jahr habe ich nichts geschrieben, kann auch nichts, so viel ich weiß" (F, 555–56) ("I have no control over my capacity for writing. It comes and goes like a phantom. I haven't written anything for a year, nor can I, as far as I know" [KLF, 390]). Again and again Kafka was made to feel that the strength needed for the "Darstellung meines traumhaften inneren Lebens" (representation of my dream-like inner life) was "completely unpredictable" although he never quite gave up the hope that "vielleicht kommt sie doch noch einmal über mich" (KAF, 10:167) ("perhaps it will come upon me again" [KD, 302]). Equally frustrating, however, were those moments when he could glimpse the jostling life in the depths of his imagination but could not gain access to it because of some inner barrier or grille: "Gestern unfähig auch nur ein Wort zu schreiben. Heute nicht besser. Wer erlöst mich? Und in mir das Gedränge, in der Tiefe, kaum zu sehn. Ich bin wie ein lebendiges Gitterwerk, ein Gitter, das feststeht und fallen will" (KAF, 10:142) ("Yesterday incapable of writing even one word. Today no better. Who will save me? And the turmoil in me, deep down, scarcely visible. I am like a living latticework, a lattice that is solidly planted and would like to tumble down" [KD, 267]). At other times he would succeed in reaching down into the "stream" of a story, only to discover that the dynamism through which the sense of pulsing life in the imagined experience became manifest then got lost in the attempt to capture that vital energy in words:

> Sicher ist, daß ich alles, was ich im voraus selbst im guten Gefühl Wort für Wort oder sogar nur beiläufig aber in ausdrücklichen Worten erfunden habe, auf dem Schreibtisch beim Versuch des Niederschreibens, trocken, verkehrt, unbeweglich, der ganzen Umgebung hinderlich, ängstlich, vor allem aber lückenhaft erscheint, trotzdem von der ursprünglichen Erfindung nichts vergessen worden ist. Es liegt natürlich zum großen Teil daran, daß ich frei vom Papier nur in der Zeit der Erhebung, die ich mehr fürchte als ersehne, wie sehr ich sie auch ersehne, Gutes erfinde, daß dann aber die Fülle so groß ist, daß ich verzichten muß, blindlings also nehme nur dem Zufall nach, aus der Strömung heraus, griffweise, so daß diese Erwerbung beim überlegten Niederschreiben nichts ist im Vergleich zur Fülle, in der sie lebte, unfähig ist, diese Fülle herbeizubringen und daher schlecht und störend ist, weil sie nutzlos lockt. (KAF, 9:195)

(It is certain that everything I have conceived in advance, even when I had the good feeling of having done so word by word or even just fleetingly, but in specific words, appears dry, wrong, immobile, an obstacle to everything and everyone around, timid, but above all full of gaps, when I try to write it down at my desk, although I have forgotten nothing of the original conception. This is naturally related in large part to the fact that I only conceive something good away from paper at times of exaltation, which I fear more than I long for, much as I do long for them, but then the fullness is so great that I have to let things go past untouched. Blindly and arbitrarily I snatch handfuls out of the stream, so that when I write it down consciously and deliberately, my acquisition is nothing in comparison with the fullness in which it lived, is incapable of summoning up that fullness, and thus is bad and disturbing because it tempts to no purpose.) (KD, 118; translation modified)

On another occasion Kafka lamented the fact that when inspiration did finally come, he was still unable to write because the idea or *Einfall* (literally, "falling in") of a story tended to occur somewhere in the middle rather than at the point where the narrative movement originated:

Alle Dinge nämlich die mir einfallen, fallen mir nicht von der Wurzel aus ein, sondern erst irgendwo gegen ihre Mitte. Versuche sie dann jemand zu halten, versuche jemand ein Gras und sich an ihm zu halten das erst in der Mitte des Stengels zu wachsen anfängt. (KAF, 9:15)

(All those things, that is to say, those things that come into my mind don't come from the root up, but rather only somewhere about their middle. Let someone then attempt to seize them, let someone attempt to seize a blade of grass and hold himself up by it when it begins to grow only from the middle.) (KD, 12; translation modified)

If the flow of writing was interrupted, as inevitably happened when he dared to attempt a longer narrative, Kafka would feel "thrown out" (*ausgeworfen*) by the story or excluded ("heute verschließt sie sich völlig" [F, 204]) (today it is completely closed up [KLF, 121]) and tormented by the switch from creative dynamism to uncreative stasis: "Vollständige Stockung. Endlose Quälereien" (KAF, 11:76) (Complete standstill. Unending torments [KD, 330]).

Kafka's despair at the interruptions of the writing process or at being subjected to the *Einfälle* of stories without a beginning related above all to his failure to achieve the wholeness and continuity (*Zusammenhang*) that he considered to be the essential criterion of writing as he felt compelled to practice it: "Das Unglück, das man ertragen muß, wenn man in einer Arbeit, die immer nur in ganzem Zug gelingen kann, sich unterbricht" (KAF, 10:51) ("The unhappiness one must suffer when one interrupts oneself in a task that can only succeed if done in a single, complete movement" [KD, 192; translation modified]). By *Zusammenhang* Kafka understood two distinct but interrelated things. One was the internal connectedness of a narrative. The other was the connection between the writing self and what it wrote. The ideal for which Kafka strove was a "Darstellung, die von Wort zu Wort mit meinem Leben verbunden wäre, die ich an meine Brust ziehen und die mich von meinem Platz hinreißen sollte" (KAF, 9:115) ("description in which every word would be linked to my life, which I would draw to my heart and which would transport me out of myself" [KD, 36]). His ideal was to "pour out" his deepest self into a story ("mich in sie auszugießen"), so that he could feel *fortgerissen* ("torn away"), "im Fluß der Arbeit . . . und von ihr getragen" (F, 300) ("in the flow of work . . . and borne along by it" [KLF, 194]). The objective of such writing, he realized, was existential exploration rather than artistic perfection:

> Ich habe jetzt und hatte schon Nachmittag ein großes Verlangen, meinen ganzen bangen Zustand ganz aus mir herauszuschreiben und ebenso wie er aus der Tiefe kommt in die Tiefe des Papiers hinein oder es so niederzuschreiben daß ich das Geschriebene vollständig in mich einbeziehen könnte. Das ist kein künstlerisches Verlangen. (KAF, 9:223)

> (I have now, and have had since this afternoon, a great yearning to write all my anxiety entirely out of me, write it into the depths of the paper just as it comes out of the depths of me, or write it down in such a way that I could draw what had been written into me completely. This is no artistic yearning.) (KD, 134)

The complete work, then, ought to flow directly from the self and reveal through its evolving, self-creating dynamic patterns the character and direction of the impulses it embodied. Where the desired flow could not be sustained, as in his first novel, *Der Verschollene* (*The Man Who Disappeared*), the work had to be "in kleinen Stücken mehr aneinander als ineinander gearbeitet" (KKAB1, 163) ("worked in small pieces, joined to one another rather than integrated one with the other"). As a consequence Kafka regarded the composition as a forced, artificial construction rather than as the trace of a dynamic, organic whole.

Given all these difficulties, it was extremely rare for Kafka to feel that he had succeeded in capturing the dynamism of his inner life and its moments of "Erhebung" satisfactorily in his narratives. His repeated failures in this respect resemble the conflicts experienced by the characters in *Betrachtung* between the empty stasis of a life spent tracing the routine patterns of social existence (to which Kafka too remained committed, to the detriment of his continuous concentration on his writing) and the pull of a quite different kind of movement that the majority of the figures refuse to follow. The one instance where Kafka felt certain that he had achieved something like complete abandonment to a unique kind of movement (such as he had envisaged in "Wish to Become a Red Indian") was his "breakthrough" story "Das Urteil" ("The Judgment"). The story, written at a single, night-long sitting in September 1912, fulfilled the double criterion of *Zusammenhang*—that is, complete internal connectedness and immediate connection with the writer's inner self (and, so he hoped, with any reader able to recognize and respond to such "inner truth" as it might possess). The diary entries recording this extraordinary creative event describe it as one in which the author experienced the flow of writing as a paradoxical combination of activity and passivity, as if Kafka were both a mother giving birth to a child and the child that was being brought into the world:

> Diese Geschichte "das Urteil" habe ich in der Nacht vom 22 zum 23 von 10 Uhr abends bis 6 Uhr früh in einem Zug geschrieben. . . . Die fürchterliche Anstrengung und Freude, wie sich die Geschichte vor mir entwickelte wie ich in einem Gewässer vorwärtskam. Mehrmals in dieser Nacht trug ich mein Gewicht auf dem Rücken. Wie alles gewagt werden kann, wie für alle, für die fremdesten Einfälle ein großes Feuer bereitet ist, in dem sie vergehn und auferstehn. . . . Nur so kann geschrieben werden, nur in einem solchen Zusammenhang, mit solcher vollständigen Öffnung des Leibes und der Seele. (KAF, 10:101)

> (This story, "The Judgment," I wrote at one sitting during the night of the 22nd to the 23rd from ten o'clock at night until 6 o'clock in the morning. . . . The fearful strain and joy, how the story developed before me, as if I were advancing through water. Several times during this night I heaved my own weight on my back. How everything can be dared, how for everything that comes into one's mind, even the strangest things,

> there waits a great fire in which they disappear and rise up again. . . . Only in this way can writing be done, only with such coherence, with such a complete opening out of the body and the soul.) (KD, 212–13)

> . . . die Geschichte ist wie eine regelrechte Geburt mit Schmutz und Schleim bedeckt aus mir herausgekommen und nur ich habe die Hand, die bis zum Körper dringen kann und Lust dazu hat. (KAF, 10:125)

> (. . . the story came out of me like a real birth, covered with filth and slime, and only I have the hand that can reach to the body itself and the strength of desire to do so.) (KD, 214)

The dynamism experienced by Kafka during the process of writing "The Judgment" is reflected in the story itself, imbuing it with such inner coherence that Kafka even dared speak of the "music" that had emerged along with the fear (*Angst*) he felt while composing it.[17] This is not the place for an extensive analysis of the dynamics of the whole work, but some brief remarks about the beginning and ending may help to clarify how closely the unfolding of the narrative itself is related to movement as it affects the figures who are first summoned into being and then disposed of on the "self-creating path" of narration.

The opening paragraph of the story reads as follows:

> Es war an einem Sonntagvormittag im schönsten Frühjahr. Georg Bendemann, ein junger Kaufmann, saß in seinem Privatzimmer im ersten Stock eines der niedrigen, leichtgebauten Häuser, die entlang des Flusses in einer langen Reihe, fast nur in der Höhe und Färbung unterschieden, sich hinzogen. Er hatte gerade einen Brief an einen sich im Ausland befindenden Jugendfreund beendet, verschloß ihn in spielerischer Langsamkeit und sah dann, den Ellbogen auf den Schreibtisch gestützt, aus dem Fenster auf den Fluß, die Brücke und die Anhöhen am anderen Ufer mit ihrem schwachen Grün. (KAF, 1:39)

> (It was on a Sunday morning when spring was at its most beautiful. George Bendemann, a young businessman, sat in his private room on the second floor of one of the low, lightly built houses that ran alongside the river, stretched out in a long row, hardly distinguishable from one another except in height and color. He had just finished a letter to a boyhood friend who was living abroad, closed it with playful slowness and then, with his elbow propped on the desk, looked out of the window at the

river, the bridge and the slopes on the opposite bank with their faint green.) (KSS, 3; translation modified)

The sentence with which "The Judgment" begins contains, but crucially *is not simply* a description of the day of the week and the time of year: "It was on a Sunday morning." Although the verb "was" (*war*) would normally be classed as stative (as in: "It was Sunday morning"), its use here in combination with the preposition "on" (*an*) has a destabilizing and dynamic effect, making the sentence seem curiously incomplete. One would expect the sentence to continue with a "that" or "when" clause of some kind, such as "It was on a Sunday morning at the height of spring that Georg Bendemann decided to sit down and write a letter to an old friend now living abroad." The absence from the opening sentence of any information about *what* precisely "it was" that happened on that morning impels the reader on to the next sentence in the expectation of completing the sense that is implied but partly withheld. This tiny grammatical oddity is the first, unremarkable manifestation of a restlessness at work in the story that seems to want to pull the reader forward to its conclusion, a dynamic force that will become ever more powerful, unmistakable and at the same time indecipherable as it creates the path of its own unfolding.

The element of instability is also at work in what the sentence describes and, although as yet unrecognizable to any first-time reader, in the ironic quality of the description. The first thing the story draws our attention to is time, specifically a Sunday morning at the height of spring. Presented like this, time seems, if anything, a beneficent force, in that Sunday morning connotes a period of rest and recuperation after the exertions of the working week, while the reference to "spring at its most beautiful" invites contemplation of the new life it brings. By the time the reader has reached the end of the story and looks back at its beginning (as certain analeptic elements will prompt him to do), time will present an utterly other, deadly, and indifferent aspect. A complicated narrative movement will have been generated thereby, one that is both circular (compelling the perplexed reader to go back to the beginning in the hope of grasping why the ending is as it is) and final (in the sense of providing a full release of the energy that has been pulsing through the story from the outset).

In the remainder of the opening paragraph, the creative restlessness that was present but barely detectable in the first sentence gradually grows more apparent as it becomes embodied in a figure's actions and thoughts.

On the one hand, the description of Georg Bendemann as a young businessman seated in his private room develops the positive aspects of the first sentence, for he is a young man with the rest of his life to look forward to and already a man of property. On the other hand, although physically at rest, Georg Bendemann is not entirely at ease. His gaze out of the window falls on the river and the line of houses that *sich hinzogen* ("ran along") beside it. The river picks up, inconspicuously, the theme of transience hinted at in the mention of spring, while the fact that Georg perceives the "lightly built" houses as if, like the river, they too were in motion, suggests that the narrative is creating in him a figure whose consciousness is filled with the same sense of instability that gave rise to the tensions in the story's deceptively promising first sentence. The third, and last, sentence of the opening paragraph both varies these tensions and introduces some new elements that promise some information about Georg Bendemann's past life (such as his relation to the friend abroad and his reasons for writing the letter) while also prompting questions about what he will do next. The positive possibilities in the situation then seem to come to the fore increasingly, as Georg is shown leaning on his desk and closing the letter to his friend with "playful slowness," while his gaze travels across the river, up the slopes, and comes to rest on the "faint green" of the new shoots of spring. Yet not one of these details is unambiguously positive: the gaze across the river may hint at a restlessness that is at odds with Georg's seemingly comfortable static situation, while the slowness with which he closes the letter may be a sign that he is hesitating, for some reason, to complete this act of communication.

In summary, the opening paragraph of "The Judgment" is impregnated with a sense of movement that issues in the unfolding of the sentences and prepares the reader for the leap across to the next and subsequent paragraphs. The instability that is most readily apparent at a thematic level, particularly in the mentality of the protagonist, is already present, as I have tried to show, *before* Georg is called into being by a narrating consciousness which is itself charged with a restlessness that seeks an outlet in such things as sentence structure, ambivalence and irony. From this beginning, the narration will unfold through a sequence of events that will move through conflict to resolution, or at least to an ending. On its way to that ending, the story will enact a conflict between the forward-driving impulse that generated the instability in the very first sentence and the numerous forms of resistance and retardation that first took shape in Georg Bendemann's remaining seated at his desk long after he had finished the letter to his friend. It is not possible here to elaborate the whole, intricate interplay between the dynamics of narration itself and the thematic and figural manifestations of movement throughout the story. Nevertheless, it is worth looking briefly at the way the story comes to an end, in order to make it clear just how unusual, possibly even unique, the part played by movement in Kafka's mode of narration actually is.

The end of the story is notoriously catastrophic. The unfolding continuum of movement in which Georg Bendemann is caught up from the outset eventually leads him not across the river and up the slopes towards the first green shoots of spring he was contemplating at the beginning but downward to the river in which he drowns. As he drops into the water, the final direction of the movement that has seized hold of Georg's life cuts diametrically across the trajectory of an omnibus and the rest of the "geradezu unendlicher Verkehr" (KAF, 1:52) ("virtually endless traffic") crossing the bridge at that very moment. More radically than anything attempted in *Betrachtung,* what "The Judgment" narrates is thus the imagined intersection of a strange, new, disruptive form of movement with the familiar movements of natural and social existence, cyclical in the one case and goal-directed in the other. As Jim Phelan points out quite correctly, however, the path from the beginning of the story to its end leads across an "interpretive gap," since it is never made explicit why Georg, initially introduced as a young man with good prospects, submits so rapidly to his father's annihilating judgment.[18] Yet the effect of that "gap" is precisely to highlight the peculiar character and integrative role of movement in Kafka's mode of narration.

The moral crux and the interpretive gap arise from the fact that Georg accepts his father's judgment of his conduct and carries out his lethal verdict without there being any evident, adequate justification for him to do so. Georg certainly has reason to feel guilty about having neglected his old father, but the death sentence is a wholly disproportionate punishment for such a failing. The father, himself a deceiver (*Komödiant,* or play-actor, as Georg calls him) and someone who clearly relishes the recovery of his former dictatorial powers, gives no sign of having the moral authority to pronounce any kind of verdict, far less one as severe as this. Psychological explanations, although rather more persuasive, also lack conviction ultimately. The father assumes the appearance of a giant Oedipal patriarch only intermittently, behaving at other times like a deranged, malicious, infantile old fool for whom Georg feels no respect. One can suggest other reasons for Georg's submission to the death sentence, such as seeing in his father's fate an image of the pointlessness of the notions of progress on which he intended to base his own life, or realizing that he does not possess enough strength of feeling for his fiancée simply to sweep aside his father's mockery of their relationship. The movement out of his own room, with its window facing across to the greening hills of springtime, and into his father's room, darkened by the wall that looms outside the window, has certainly confronted Georg with the inescapable stasis in his life that he has been trying to keep hidden from himself with his plans for marriage and the expansion of the business. But none of this quite suffices to make Georg's self-execution understandable within the limits of psychological plausibility. Faced with this problem, an early reviewer even felt compelled to argue that the story showed the sudden collapse of a mind into insanity, a view that only needs to be stated for it to become clear that the events simply cannot be contained within any psychological or even pathological framework.[19]

By this point in the story, the narration has passed out of the realm of social, moral, and psychological constraints and into one where other forces hold sway, principally the force of narrative dynamism itself, whatever its obscure source may be. What has happened on the social, moral, and psychological levels of the narrative is the progressive destruction of all the flimsy defenses that the narrator, with a mixture of sympathy and malice, has let Georg Bendemann erect around a lonely and static existence that does not fundamentally believe in itself. Once that superstructure has been destroyed in the interaction with other characters so that Georg is left with nothing to contemplate but the ruins of all the illusions on which he has based his bourgeois identity in recent years, there is nothing left to block the final unfolding of the story's self-creating path. The dynamic force that was evident, from the beginning of the narrative, both in the world as Georg perceived it and in his own growing unease, as he closed the letter to his friend slowly and "playfully," can now be released in full. At the very moment when the father pronounces his judgment, Georg is seized by an impersonal force (defined simply as *es*) and is "driven" out of the house and down to his death in the river:

> Georg fühlte sich aus dem Zimmer gejagt, den Schlag, mit dem der Vater hinter ihm aufs Bett stürzte, trug er noch in den Ohren davon. Auf der Treppe, über deren Stufen er wie über eine schiefe Fläche eilte, überrumpelte er seine Bedienerin . . . Aus dem Tor sprang er, über die Fahrbahn zum Wasser trieb es ihn. Schon hielt er das Geländer fest, wie ein Hungriger die Nahrung. (KAF, 1:52)

> (Georg felt himself driven from the room, the crash with which his father

> collapsed behind him on to the bed went on ringing in his ears. On the stairs, down whose steps he raced as if down a sloping surface, he nearly bowled over his cleaning woman . . . He leapt out of the house door, across the road it drove him. He was already clutching the railing, like a hungry man clutching food.) (KSS, 12; translation modified)

As he disappears in the river below, one might say that Georg is being returned by the act of narration to the element from which the story as a whole emerged, the restless energy that formed the opening paragraph in which Georg Bendemann was brought into existence and which will continue to flow after his death in the figurations of the river and the endless flow of traffic (*Verkehr*) on the bridge. The opening "*Es* war an einem Sonntagmorgen" is answered by the "trieb *es* ihn" which carries the action to a close, thereby confirming the dynamic nature of that deceptively unassuming impersonal pronoun. It may well be the same little pronoun (*Es* rather than *Er*), incidentally, that Kafka allowed to assume universal proportions in one of his best-known aphorisms: "Das Wort 'sein' bedeutet im Deutschen beides: Da-sein und Ihm-gehören" (KAF, 6:235) ("The word '*sein*' means both things in German: to exist and to belong to it").[20]

Nowadays, we tend to feel uncomfortable about things that defy rational explanation. Kafka too was tempted to devise explanations for the strange inner experiences of movement to which he was subject during those all too rare periods of *Erhebung* when he felt the pulse of creativity within him. In his aphorisms, for example, on which so many readings of his work rely, Kafka interpreted the biblical story of the Fall in such a way as to construct an account of all human existence as a state of permanent *Vertreibung* (i.e., a condition not simply of *having been* driven out of Paradise once and for all but of *being* driven out of Paradise unceasingly, for all time).[21] His own, private experience of some extraordinary form of dynamism while writing could thereby be regarded as a particular, perhaps privileged, symbolic concretization of the general human condition *post lapsum,* as a mode of being that is both driven in perpetual motion and yet static, a "stehender Sturmlauf" or charging on the spot. Yet so many of Kafka's stories embody movement in such a wide variety of ways that it is questionable whether they can all be reduced to just so many illustrations of a single overarching myth of origin and destination (like the above) or of any other single principle that his commentators might construct, such as the oft varied view that movement in Kafka's writing is a self-referential allegory of writing itself. In the stories examined in this essay, for example, movement also serves as a vehicle to achieve other ends, such as exploring the complexities of psychological and social existence, and it serves these purposes outstandingly well. At the same time, these stories repeatedly show the movements of social existence being intersected or interrupted by some other mode of movement for which they offer no explanation. Kafka himself felt that an extraordinary experience of movement was somehow part and parcel of his writing, although he could have no certainty about its nature, origin, or purpose, far less any control over its appearance or disappearance. At times he hoped that it was a revelatory, elevating experience of general significance. At others he felt that writing involved going down into forbidden depths, doing service to the devil and unleashing forces that, by their nature, ought to remain bound up forever.[22] On yet another occasion, he felt that the movement of writing was merely a form of vanity, as the mind of the writer circled, moth-like, around its own reflection (MB, 2:384). In conversation with Max Brod, Kafka is reported to have said that when he wrote the last sentence of "The Judgment" ("At this moment a virtually endless [flow of] traffic went across the bridge") he was thinking of "eine starke Ejakulation" ("a powerful ejaculation"),[23] which suggests that the source of the energy pulsing through the story could be understood as intensely physical rather than metaphysical or transcendent. One could also argue that the movement of Kafka's narratives is part of a "psycho-poetics,"[24] serving, for example, as a means of exercising power, in imagination at least, over particular kinds of figure (sons, fathers, women), or indeed the world in general, calling them into being and disposing of them more or less capriciously in order to create an outlet for private psychological impulsions. Whatever the source and nature of the creative restlessness that took over his life periodically, Kafka's narratives could only convince him of their "inner truth" for as long as he sensed that strange, dynamic impulse carrying him forward from word to word, sentence to sentence. That, at all costs, had to be "brought to the surface." The interpretations of that impulse may multiply, but, to paraphrase Kafka's version of the Prometheus myth: "There remains the inexplicable movement."[25]

Notes

1. The secondary literature listed below identifies and interprets a range of different manifestations of movement in Kafka's fiction, from the "failure to arrive" stressed by Beißner (1958) to the "stehender Sturmlauf" ("charging on the spot") discussed by Allemann (1998), Corngold (1988), Ramm (1971, 1979), and others,

the patterns of reversal and deviation identified by Neumann (1973), the "temporal space" discussed by Rolleston (1978), the link between movement and the search for knowledge discussed by Thiher (1987), the attempts to escape or find the self considered by Zilcosky (2003), and multifarious approaches taken by the contributors to the volume edited by Scheuer and others. While most commentaries focus on the limitations of movement, this chapter seeks to identify the exceptional conditions under which movement, both narrative and narrated, is achieved successfully.

2. Although *Contemplation* is available in English translation (published by Twisted Spoon Press, Prague), I have chosen to use my own translations throughout so as to follow as closely as possible the German original, regardless of whether the result makes for attractive English. In other cases (such as Kafka's diaries or letters) I have generally used published translations where available, supplying my own where they are not.

3. See Kurz (1994) and Rolleston (1984).

4. "Die ungeheuere Welt, die ich im Kopfe habe. Aber wie mich befreien und sie befreien ohne zu zerreißen. Und tausendmal lieber zerreißen, als sie in mir zurückhalten oder begraben. Dazu bin ich ja hier, das ist mir ganz klar" (KAF, 10:179) ("The monstrous world I have in my head. But how to free myself and free it without being torn to pieces. And a thousand times rather be torn apart rather than retain it in me or bury it. That indeed is why I am here, that is quite clear to me" [KD, 222]).

5. *Der Verschollene,* more commonly known as *Amerika,* the title given to the fragmentary novel by its first editor, Max Brod.

6. "Doch sah ich letzthin auf der Freitreppe selbst einen ganz einfältigen Gerichtsdiener mit dem Fachblick des kleinen Stammgastes der Wettrennen den Advokaten bestaunen, als dieser, hoch die Schenkel hebend, mit auf dem Marmor aufklingendem Schritt von Stufe zu Stufe stieg" (KAF, 1:199) ("Yet recently I saw a quite simple court usher with the knowing eye of a racetrack regular staring in astonishment at the lawyer as the latter, raising his flanks high in the air, mounted step by step with a stride that made the marble clang" [KSS, 60]).

7. Kafka's notebooks contain numerous passages that cast doubt on humans' capacity for free will. One of the most vivid describes an animal seizing its master's whip and whipping itself in order to become master, while unaware that this is simply an illusion created by a new knot in the master's whip; see KAF (6:232).

8. See, for example, Kafka's despairing remarks in a letter to Felice from 1913: "Wo bin ich denn? Wer kann mich nachprüfen? Ich wünschte mir eine kräftige Hand nur zu dem Zweck, um in diese unzusammenhängende Konstruktion, die ich bin, ordentlich hineinzufahren" (F, 306) ("For where am I? Who can examine me? I wish for a strong hand for the sole purpose of thrusting it into this incoherent construction that I am" [KLF, 198]).

9. "Gesellschaft" can either mean a small gathering, such as a party, or society at large; Kafka is probably playing on both senses of the word.

10. The best known instance is the closing words of *The Trial:* "es war, als sollte die Scham ihn überleben" (KAF, 3:241) ("It was as if the shame were destined to survive him").

11. There is a marked contrast here between the figure's response to music and Schopenhauer's claim that music could bring solace and release from the turmoil

of life, since it was an aesthetically distanced and disinterested symbol of the Will; see Schopenhauer (1938, 2:516). If, as seems quite likely, Kafka was well acquainted with Schopenhauer's world-view, he appears to offer only partial assent. Schopenhauer's conception of the blind Will could only be acceptable to the later Kafka at any rate as a diagnosis of the post-lapsarian condition of human life, not as an account of the essence of the world; equally, Schopenhauer's view that the spirit could escape domination by the Will through aesthetic experience and philosophical reflection was at odds with Kafka's own speculations about the hopeless severance of human beings from the oneness of spiritual existence ("die geistige Welt") as a result of the expulsion from Paradise, which allowed no escape, whether aesthetic or philosophical, for the spirit within the "sinnliche Welt" ("world apprehended by the senses").

12. Josef K. experiences a similar kind of movement in the corridor outside the offices of the court officials in *The Trial:* "Er war wie seekrank. Er glaubte auf einem Schiff zu sein, das sich in schwerem Seegang befand. Es war ihm als stürze das Wasser gegen die Holzwände, als komme aus der Tiefe des Ganges ein Brausen her, wie von überschlagendem Seewasser, als schaukle der Gang in der Quere und als würden die wartenden Parteien zu beiden Seiten gesenkt und gehoben." (KAF, 3:84) ("It was as if he were sea-sick. He believed he was on a ship that was in the midst of a heavy swell. He felt as if the water were flinging itself against the wooden walls, as if a roar were coming from the depths of the corridor, like that of water breaking, as if the corridor were rocking sideways, and the plaintiffs waiting on each side were being made to rise and fall"). Here again there is a striking resemblance to Schopenhauer's image of individual existence as a frail craft afloat on a stormy sea; see Schopenhauer (1938, *1*:416).

13. For a discussion of the place of this allusion in Kafka's work, see Gerhard Neumann, "Umkehrung und Ablenkung: Franz Kafkas 'Gleitendes Paradox.'"

14. See, for example, the story of the Hunter Gracchus (KAF, 6:43) who repeatedly believes he is climbing some great staircase, only to find himself, on awakening, stuck on board ship in the same earthly waters he has been traversing for centuries since falling to his death.

15. This gentle, but nonetheless disturbing rocking may be a relative of the much more violent "Schaukeln" experienced by Josef K. in *The Trial*; see note 10 above.

16. See the introduction of this volume.

17. "Each sentence in this story, each word, each—if I may say so—music is connected with 'fear.' On this occasion the wound broke open for the first time in one long night" (KLM, 191).

18. See James Phelan's discussion in chapter 1.

19. See Born (1979, 89).

20. In German "sein" is a homonym. As a verb it means "to be." It is also a possessive adjective or pronoun, meaning "his" or "its." Kafka detects in this ambiguity the possibility that "being" entails "belonging to something or someone." The lack of autonomy implied by this idea may relate to the numerous involuntary forms of movement analyzed in this essay.

21. "Die Vertreibung aus dem Paradies ist in ihrem Hauptteil ewig" (KAF, 6:239) ("The expulsion from paradise is in its principal aspect eternal").

22. See the introduction of this volume.

23. See Brod (1966, 114).
24. See, for example, Bernheimer (1984, 154–83).
25. Cf. KAF (6:193).

Works Cited

Allemann, Beda. 1998. Stehender Sturmlauf: Zeit und Geschichte im Werke Kafkas. In *Zeit und Geschichte im Werke Kafkas, 15–36.* Göttingen: Wallstein Verlag.

Beißner, Friedrich. 1958. *Kafka der Dichter.* Stuttgart: Kohlhammer Verlag.

Bernheimer, Charles. 1984. Psychopoetik: Flaubert und Kafkas *Hochzeitsvorbereitungen auf dem Lande.* In *Der junge Kafka,* ed. G. Kurz, 154–83. Frankfurt am Main: Suhrkamp Verlag.

Born, J., ed. 1979. *Franz Kafka: Kritik und Rezeption, 1912–1924.* Frankfurt am Main: Fischer.

Brod, Max. 1966. *Über Franz Kafka.* Frankfurt am Main: Fischer Bücherei.

Corngold, Stanley. 1988. *Franz Kafka: The necessity of form.* Ithaca, NY: Cornell Univ. Press.

Kurz, Gerhard. 1994. Lichtblicke in eine unendliche Verwirrung: Zu Kafkas *Betrachtung.* In *TEXT + KRITIK Sonderband: Franz Kafka,* ed. H. L. Arnold, 49–65. Munich: Edition TEXT + KRITIK.

Neumann, Gerhard. 1973. Umkehrung und Ablenkung: Franz Kafkas "Gleitendes Paradox." In *Franz Kafka,* ed. H. Politzer, 459–515. Darmstadt: Wissenschaftliche Buchgesellschaft.

Ramm, Klaus. 1971. *Reduktion als Erzählprinzip bei Kafka.* Frankfurt am Main: Athenäum Verlag.

———. 1979. Handlungsführung und Gedankenführung. In *Kafka-Handbuch,* ed. Hartmut Binder. Vol. 2, 93–107. Stuttgart: Alfred Kröner Verlag.

Rolleston, James. 1978. Temporal space: A reading of Kafka's *Betrachtung. Special Franz Kafka Issue, Modern Austrian Literature* 11, nos. 3–4:123–38.

———. 1979. Die Erzählungen. In *Kafka-Handbuch,* ed. Hartmut Binder. Vol. 2, 249–59. Stuttgart: Alfred Kröner Verlag.

———. 1984. *Betrachtung:* Landschaften der Doppelgänger. In *Der junge Kafka,* ed. G. Kurz, 184–99. Frankfurt am Main: Suhrkamp Verlag.

Scheuer, Hans Jürgen, Justus von Hartlieb, Christina Salmen, Georg Höfner, eds. 2003. *Kafkas Betrachtung: Lektüren.* Frankfurt am Main: Peter Lang Verlag.

Schopenhauer, Arthur. 1938. *Sämtliche Werke. Dritter Band. (Die Welt als Wille und Vorstellung. Zweiter Band).* Leipzig: Brockhaus.

Sterne, Laurence. 1893. *The Life and Opinions of Tristram Shandy, Gent.* London: George Routledge and Sons.

Thiher, Allen. 1987. The *Nachlass:* Metaphors of *Gehen* and ways towards science. In *Kafka and the contemporary critical performance,* ed. A. Udoff. Bloomington: Indiana Univ. Press.

Walser, Martin. 1961. *Beschreibung einer Form.* Munich: Carl Hanser Verlag.

Zilcosky, John. 2003. *Kafka's travels.* New York: Palgrave Macmillan.

Contributors

STANLEY CORNGOLD is professor emeritus of German and comparative literature at Princeton University. Among his major publications are *The Commentators' Despair: The Interpretation of Kafka's "Metamorphosis"* (Port Washington, NY: National Univ. Press, 1973), *The Fate of the Self: German Writers and French Theory* (New York: Columbia Univ. Press, 1986), *Franz Kafka: The Necessity of Form* (Ithaca, NY: Cornell Univ. Press, 1988), *Complex Pleasure: Forms of Feeling in German Literature* (Stanford Univ. Press, 1998), and *Lambent Traces: Franz Kafka* (Princeton Univ. Press, 2004). He has translated and edited Norton Critical Editions of Kafka's *The Metamorphosis* (Norton, 1996) and *Selected Stories* (Norton, 2007). A new book, *Franz Kafka: The Ghosts in the Machine,* co-written with Benno Wagner, is due out in 2011 (Evanston, IL: Northwestern Univ. Press).

ANNIKEN GREVE is associate professor of comparative literature at the University of Tromsø, Norway. She obtained her doctorate in philosophy in 1998 for the dissertation "Her: Et bidrag til stedets filosofi" ("Here: A Contribution to the Philosophy of Place"). She obtained in 2009 her second doctorate with the dissertation "Litteraturens meddelelse: En litteraturvitenskapelig tolkningsmetodikk i teoretisk, praktisk og skeptisk lys" ("The Communicative Effect of Literature: A Theoretical, Practical and Skeptical Discussion of a Methodical Approach to the Interpretation of Literature"). She has published articles in Norwegian books and academic journals on issues ranging from Wittgenstein's philosophy, philosophy of language and philosophical anthropology to modern Norwegian, Irish and English poetry, narrative theory, and especially methodological issues.

GERHARD KURZ is professor emeritus of German literature, the University of Giessen. His books include *Traum Schrecken: Kafkas literarische Existenzanalyse*

(Stuttgart: Metzler, 1980), *Metapher, Allegorie, Symbol* (Göttingen: Vandenhoeck & Ruprecht, 1982), and *Macharten: Über Rhythmus, Reim, Stil und Vieldeutigkeit* (Göttingen: Vandenhoeck & Ruprecht, 1999). He is the author of numerous essays on Kafka, Hölderlin, and other German authors, as well as on literary theory and literary history.

JAKOB LOTHE is professor of English Literature at the University of Oslo. His books include *Conrad's Narrative Method* (Oxford Univ. Press, 1989) and *Narrative in Fiction and Film* (Oxford Univ. Press, 2000). The author of numerous essays, he has edited or co-edited several volumes, including *Franz Kafka: Zur ethischen und aesthetischen Rechtfertigung* (Freiburg: Rombach Verlag, 2002; with Beatrice Sandberg), *The Art of Brevity* (Univ. of South Carolina Press, 2004), *Literary Landscapes* (Basingstoke: Palgrave, 2008), *Joseph Conrad: Voice, Sequence, History, Genre* (Columbus: Ohio State Univ. Press, 2008; with Jeremy Hawthorn and James Phelan), and the forthcoming *After Testimony* (Columbus: Ohio State Univ. Press; with Susan R. Suleiman and James Phelan). During the 2005–2006 academic year he was the leader of the research project Narrative Theory and Analysis at the Centre for Advanced Study, Oslo.

J. HILLIS MILLER taught for many years at the Johns Hopkins University and then at Yale University, before going to the University of California at Irvine in 1986, where is he now UCI Distinguished Research Professor. He is the author of many books and essays on nineteenth and twentieth-century English, European, and American literature, and on literary theory. His recent books include *Zero Plus One* (València: Biblioteca Javier Coy d'estudis nord-americans, Universitat de València, 2003), and *Literature as Conduct: Speech Acts in Henry James* (New York: Fordham Univ. Press, 2005). A *J. Hillis Miller Reader* appeared in 2005 from Edinburgh University Press and Stanford University Press. His *For Derrida* appeared from Fordham in 2009, and *The Medium is the Maker: Browning, Freud, Derrida and the New Telepathic Technologies* appeared with Sussex Academic Press, also in 2009. A new book, *The Conflagration of Community: Fiction before and after Auschwitz*, will be published by The University of Chicago Press in 2011. A longer and differently oriented version of his essay will appear in *The Conflagration of Community.* Miller is a fellow of the American Academy of Arts and Sciences and a member of the American Philosophical Society. He received the MLA Lifetime Scholarly Achievement Award in 2005.

GERHARD NEUMANN is professor emeritus of Ludwig-Maximilian-Universität München. His main publications include *Konfiguration: Studien zu Goethes "Torquato Tasso"* (Munich: Wilhelm Fink, 1965) and "*Ideenparadise*"*: Untersuchungen zur Aphoristik von Lichtenberg, Novalis, Friedrich Schlegel und Goethe* (Munich: Wilhelm Fink, 1976). The author of many essays on various aspects of German literature, he has written extensively on Kafka and was one of the principal editors of the major new edition of Kafka's works based on the manuscripts.

JAMES PHELAN is Distinguished University Professor of English at The Ohio State University. He is a founding member of Project Narrative at OSU, the editor of the journal *Narrative* and co-editor (with Peter J. Rabinowitz) of the Theory and Interpretation of Narrative series. He has also edited or co-edited several collections in the field, including *Joseph Conrad* (Columbus: Ohio State Univ. Press, 2008; with Jakob Lothe and Jeremy Hawthorn), *Teaching Narrative Theory* (New York: MLA, 2010; with David Herman and Brian McHale), and the forthcoming *After Testimony* (Columbus: Ohio State Univ. Press; with Jakob Lothe and Susan R. Suleiman). Phelan has written extensively about the rhetorical theory of narrative, especially in *Worlds from Words* (Chicago: Univ. of Chicago Press, 1981); *Reading People, Reading Plots* (Chicago: Univ. of Chicago Press, 1989); *Narrative as Rhetoric* (Columbus: Ohio State Univ. Press, 1996); *Living to Tell about It* (Ithaca: Cornell Univ. Press, 2005); and *Experiencing Fiction* (Columbus: Ohio State Univ. Press, 2007).

BEATRICE SANDBERG is professor in German literature at the German Department, University of Bergen, Norway. She has published widely on Swiss literature, Franz Kafka, the twentieth-century novel, and national and cultural identity. Co-author (with Ronald Speirs) of *Franz Kafka* (Basingstoke: Macmillan, 1998), she has edited or co-edited a number of volumes, including *Fascism and European Literature* (Bern: Lang, 1991), *Franz Kafka: Zur ethischen und aesthetischen Rechtfertigung* (Freiburg: Rombach Verlag, 2002; with Jakob Lothe), *Autobiographisches Schreiben: Grenzen der Identität und der Fiktionalität* (Munich: Iudicium 2006), *Meldungen aus Norwegen 1940–45* (Munich: Oldenbourg, 2008), and *Familienbilder als Zeitbilder: Erzählte Zeitgeschichte bei Schweizer Autoren vom 18. Jahrhundert bis zur Gegenwart* (Berlin: Frank & Timme, 2010).

RONALD SPEIRS is emeritus professor of German at the University of Birmingham, England. He is an editor of the journal *German Life and Letters* and the author of *Brecht's Early Plays* (Basingstoke: Macmillan, 1982), *Bertolt Brecht* (Basingstoke: Macmillan, 1987), *Thomas Mann: Mario und der Zauberer* (London: Grant & Cutler, 1990), and *Franz Kafka* (Basingstoke: Macmillan, 1998; with Beatrice Sandberg), and of a number of essays on German literature. He has also translated and edited Max Weber's *Political Writings* (Cambridge Univ. Press, 1994; with P. Lassmann) and Nietzsche's *The Birth of Tragedy and other Writings* (Cambridge Univ. Press, 1999; with R. Geuss), and is the editor or co-editor of several volumes of essays, including *Fascism and European Literature* (Bern: Lang, 1991; with B. Sandberg and S. Larsen), *Brecht's Poetry of Political Exile* (Cambridge Univ. Press, 2000), *H. G. Adler und Hermann Broch: Zwei Schriftsteller im Exil. Briefwechsel* (Göttingen: Wallstein, 2004; with J. White), and *Germany's Two Unifications: Anticipations, Experiences, Responses* (Basingstoke: Palgrave, 2005; with J. Breuilly).

BENNO WAGNER is associate professor of Literary Theory and German Literature at the University of Giessen. His main publications include *Im Dickicht der politischen Kultur* (Munich: Wilhelm Fink, 1991). He is co-editor of the S. Fischer Critical Edition of Kafka's "Amtliche Schriften" ("Office Writings") and has published widely on various aspects of Kafka's work. A new book, *Franz Kafka: The Ghosts in the Machine,* co-written with Stanley Corngold, is due out in 2011 (Evanston, IL: Northwestern Univ. Press).

Index